By KATIE HAFNER

A ROMANCE ON THREE LEGS:
Glenn Gould's Obsessive Quest
for the Perfect Piano

WHERE WIZARDS STAY UP LATE:
The Origins of the Internet (with Matthew Lyon)

CYBERPUNK:
Outlaws and Hackers on the
Computer Frontier (with John Markoff)

THE HOUSE AT THE BRIDGE:
A Story of Modern Germany

THE WELL:
A Story of Love, Death & Real Life in the
Seminal Online Community

MOTHER DAUGHTER ME:
A Memoir

Random House Trade Paperbacks
New York

PRAISE FOR

MOTHER DAUGHTER ME

"Resolutely upbeat and hopeful, plus beautifully observed."

—James Fallows, *The Atlantic*

"Brilliant . . . *Mother Daughter Me* is a beautifully written, intimately provocative, and courageous unpeeling of the deep rhythms of love, hate, fear, and redemption in three generations of females. I love this book!"

—Louann Brizendine, author of *The Female Brain*

"Witnessing the dynamics among women with such a complicated history is moving."

—Hope Reese, *The Boston Globe*

"Katie Hafner's *Mother Daughter Me* delivers an unusually graceful story, one that balances honesty and tact. . . . Hafner narrates the events so adeptly that they feel enlightening rather than enervating."

—Jane Smiley, *Harper's*

"An emotional whodunit that uses brilliant journalistic acumen to crack the code of old family secrets."

—Madeleine Blais, Pulitzer Prize–winning author of *Uphill Walkers*

"In a narrative that skillfully moves between her present predicament and her difficult childhood, Hafner offers a compelling portrait of her remarkable mother and their troubled relationship. . . . Heartbreakingly honest, yet not without hope and flashes of wry humor."

—*Kirkus Reviews*

"Hafner's midlife juggling act, presented here warts-and-all, will appeal to an army of readers whose major difficulty will be finding time in their day to read the book." —Therese Nielsen, *Library Journal*

"Scrap any romantic ideas about what goes on when a forty-something woman invites her mother to live with her and her teenage daughter for a year. As Hafner hilariously and touchingly tells it, being the center of a family sandwich is, well, complicated." —*Parade*

"Hafner writes with compassion and wit about the often uneasy alliance between mothers and daughters and the surprising ways in which relationships can be redeemed even late in life." —*Booklist*

"[An] emotionally raw memoir examining the delicate, inevitable life shift from dependence to independence and back again."
—*O: The Oprah Magazine* (Ten Titles to Pick Up Now)

"It's a wonder that Katie Hafner is still in one piece, to say nothing of enough in possession of her faculties and enough perspective to write such a poignant, honest, and complex account of such difficult, too often tragic family matters." —Daniel Menaker, author of *My Mistake*

"This brilliant, funny, poignant, and wrenching story is quite unlike anything I have ever read. I love Hafner's prose, her humor, the images she conjures, her choices of what to tell and when, the weaving together of family threads to produce this luminous and lasting tapestry. The story lingered with me long after I read the last page."
—Abraham Verghese, author of *Cutting for Stone*

"Weaving past with present, anecdote with analysis, Hafner's riveting account of multigenerational living and mother-daughter frictions, of love and forgiveness, is devoid of self-pity and unafraid of self-blame. . . . [Hafner is] a bright—and appealing—heroine."
—Cathi Hanauer, *Elle*

"[A] frank and searching account . . . Currents of grief, guilt, longing and forgiveness flow through the compelling narrative."

—Steven Winn, *San Francisco Chronicle*

"Marked by emotional upheaval, painful insights and moments of wry humor, [Hafner's] experience is documented with clear-eyed honesty."

—*San Jose Mercury News*

"Hafner may not have worked out the issues she wanted to in her own private Biosphere 2, but she has produced an ultimately very loving account of the episode—one in which, ironically, she works out a great deal indeed."

—*AARP Blog*

"A touching saga that shines. We see how years-old unresolved emotions manifest."

—Lindsay Deutsch, *USA Today*

"[Hafner's] memoir shines a light on nurturing deficits repeated through generations and will lead many readers to relive their own struggles with forgiveness."

—Erica Jong, *People*

"*Mother Daughter Me* is not a story of redemption so much as it is the unraveling of a long, slow process of coming to terms with what happened and absorbing it. Hafner describes some ugly events. The book must have been painful to write. . . . There's beauty here too, as Hafner movingly describes building a life of custom and ceremony. *Mother Daughter Me* is a story of growing up, of loss and love, and it's beautifully told. I couldn't put this book down. Mothers and daughters will love reading it; and those who love them should read it too."

—*The Brooklyn Bugle*

"*Mother Daughter Me* might very well go on to be a classic of the genre. . . . That Hafner was able to overcome emotional, often tragic, circumstances to at all succeed at professional and personal life is a marvel, and she proves it further with a book that, in its quiet way, shows just how she did it."

—Liz Baudler, *Newcity Lit*

MOTHER
DAUGHTER
ME

Mother Daughter Me

A Memoir

Katie Hafner

Mother Daughter Me is a work of nonfiction. Some names and identifying details, along with some chronology, have been changed. Any resulting resemblance to persons living or dead is entirely coincidental and unintentional.

2014 Random House Trade Paperback Edition

Published in the United States by Random House Trade Paperbacks, an imprint of Random House, a division of Random House LLC, New York, a Penguin Random House Company.

Random House and the House colophon are registered trademarks of Random House LLC.

Random House Reader's Circle & Design is a registered trademark of Random House LLC.

Originally published in hardcover in the United States by Random House, an imprint and division of Random House LLC, in 2013.

Portions of Chapter 21, "Culling a Life," originally appeared in the March 2010 issue of *O: The Oprah Magazine* as "On Grief: A Widow Finally Confronts the Boxes Her Husband Left Behind" in slightly different form.

Permissions credits appear on page 267.

LIBRARY OF CONGRESS CATALOGING-IN-PUBLICATION DATA

Hafner, Katie.

Mother daughter me / Katie Hafner.

p.cm.

ISBN 978-0-8129-8169-8 — ISBN 978-0-8129-8459-0 (eBook)

1. Hafner, Katie—Family. 2 Journalists—United States—Biography. 3. Authors, American—21st century—Family relationships. 4. Mothers and daughters—United States. I. Title.

PN4847.H213A3 2013

070.92—dc23

[B]

2012033758

Printed in the United States of America on acid-free paper

www.randomhousereaderscircle.com

2 4 6 8 9 7 5 3

Book design by Barbara M. Bachman

To Bob and Zoë

Prologue

DEL MAR, CALIFORNIA, 1967

MY LONGING FOR HER WAS ALWAYS THERE. WHAT I WANTED MORE than anything was my mother's attention. I plotted and I campaigned. I hatched plans. I pleaded. Then, just when I thought I had her, she would slip from my grasp. As the disappointments piled up, I learned to focus on pinpoints of hope: The less demanding the request, I figured, the greater my chances of success.

By fifth grade, I had pared my expectations back to a single meal. I invited my mother to have lunch with me, a tradition at the elementary school in our little beach town. Once or twice a week a parent could be seen in the lunchroom, seated at one of the short tables, knees high to the chest, gamely eating a Sloppy Joe or a hamburger or a grilled cheese sandwich, washing it down with the standard-issue carton of milk.

I wanted my mother to be one of those lunchtime parents. I would make it easy for her. I would get Mr. Cook's permission to leave class early and wait for her out front. She would drive up in the Buick station wagon, and as she walked toward me she'd beam one of her megawatt smiles that told me no one and nothing else in her life mattered. I would beam back. Though barely clearing five foot three (and only with the help of a profusion of thick, wavy hair), she was huge in my mind's eye and would grow still taller as she approached me. I would take the hand of this giant among mothers and guide her to the lunchroom.

We would sit down at the spot I had picked out for us. She would gush about the delicious food and the fresh milk ("Divine," she would say). In deference to my sweet tooth and her own caloric vigilance, she would offer me her dessert. By the time she left, all the other kids' doubts about my mysterious home life would be put to rest once and for all, as this mother–daughter breaking of bread would signal to them an epoxy-like bond. For thirty precious minutes my schoolmates would see that I, too, had a mother—and not just any mother but one to beat the band, beautiful and glamorous and shiny with life.

For months, I begged her to do this one thing. Her excuses were many and resolute, if not always convincing. (Even a nine-year-old can sift the linguistic chaff from the grain.) But I persisted with my entreaties until, finally, one day she came.

It was Taco Day, my favorite. The visit lasted one lunch period, but my memory stretches it to become an epic. Our beige Buick, a mighty vessel of a car, glided into the parking lot with regal ease. As my mother opened the car door and touched her high heels onto the ground, the pavement glistened in the Southern California sunlight. I was waiting for her, of course, and, true to my fantasy, when she caught sight of me her look was one of unalloyed delight. In the lunchroom, we sat with a few of my classmates, whom she greeted with one of those radiant smiles. I could tell that they were bewitched. She placed her small paper napkin in her lap and lingered over the two beef tacos on her plate as if they were foie gras, pronouncing them—yes—divine. I ate my own small square of white cake with chocolate icing and my mother's too.

After lunch, I took her to my classroom. Mr. Cook was seated at his desk, grading papers. As we entered the room, he looked over his reading glasses and raised his eyebrows ever so slightly. Tipsy with pride, I introduced him to my heavenly mother. No doubt he had been expecting a dowdy bluestocking, for his gaze was fixed on her. "This is the mother who sends Katie to school with math puzzlers to share with the class?" he must have asked himself. Then I showed her my desk, which was in the middle of the room, "equidistant" to the walls, I pointed out, casually tossing off my new vocabulary word. There at the front of the desk stood my golden spelling-bee trophy.

When it was time for her to go, I accompanied her back to the car, past my regular four-square group out on the playground, past the courtyard where a papier-mâché version of Quetzalcoatl was under construction, past the girls' room and the principal's office and into the parking lot.

She put her hand inside her purse and I heard the jangle of keys. Instead of stiff with fear at the sound, I was calm and happy. I hugged her and held on. "I'm so proud of you, sweetie pie," she said. When she reached the car, she turned to look at me, rounded her lips, and sent a loud smooch into the air. And then she was gone.

Part One

Summer

1.

August 2009: North on I-5

We the globe can compass soon,
Swifter than the wandering moon.

—Oberon in William Shakespeare,
A MIDSUMMER NIGHT'S DREAM

WHENEVER I ARRIVE IN SAN DIEGO, THE FIRST THING I WANT TO do is leave. It's the sun, which shines without mercy. At the airport, I'm surrounded by happy travelers streaming in from sun-deprived cities, their compasses set for the beach and SeaWorld. I want to stop them and ask if they'll take me home with them—to Minneapolis or Des Moines, Seattle or Detroit. San Diego is stingy with its shade, and the ever-present sun makes me feel not lifted but low, unsure of my footing.

The summer sun, of course, is the worst, and today, in late August, it's already relentlessly bright at 9:30 A.M. To my relief, I've arrived with plans to stay no more than a few hours. I'm on a mission. I've flown to San Diego to help my mother carry out her plan to leave after nearly forty-five years.

A seasoned mover (some would say a compulsive one), I've spent weeks helping my mother with the logistics, even recruited my favorite moving man—a burly and jocular Irishman named Kieran, who specializes in transporting pianos but hauls around entire households, too—to drive his truck down from Northern California and collect my mother's possessions. And now it's time for us to get on the road and start the drive to San Francisco.

I take a taxi from the airport to my mother's house, and when I arrive, Kieran and his crew are already there, loading the truck with the possessions my mother has chosen to bring with her. Among them are two pianos—one Steinway grand and one Yamaha upright. I pull up just as Kieran and two of his guys are rolling out the stunning Steinway, my idea of perfection embodied in a single musical instrument.

Cheryl, the professional downsizer my mother hired a month ago, is directing the movers and making a few last-minute additions to the contents of my mother's Honda sedan, which Cheryl has packed expertly with several boxes of legal files, a Waterpik, various driving pillows, a couple of large exercise cushions held together with duct tape, paper bags filled with a month's worth of various vitamins, medications, and Metamucil, and at least a dozen rolls of paper towels. I notice right away that my delicate, birdlike mother, for years reluctant to venture much beyond a ten-mile radius from her house, is surprisingly calm, and I guess that Cheryl is the reason.

A large woman in her early sixties who towers over my mother, Cheryl gives the car a final inspection. Then something happens that's completely out of character—not for Cheryl, I gather, but for my often skittish and always hyper-cerebral mother. Cheryl folds my mother into a lingering hug, then stands back, sets her large hands on my mother's shoulders, looks deep into her chestnut eyes, holds her gaze, and takes several deep inhalations. "Remember to breathe," she says, like a football coach sending a nervous freshman onto the field. My mother nods obediently.

I climb in behind the wheel. We wave goodbye to Cheryl and the movers and pull away from the house. Pretty soon, we're zooming north on Interstate 5. With nearly five hundred miles to travel, I hope to reach San Francisco in nine hours, a calculation trickier than your average Google Maps reckoning, as I've had to figure in frequent restroom breaks for my mother. Once we're out of L.A. and heading inland, we hit the southern Central Valley and long, monotonous stretches of I-5. But the miles aren't boring to my mother, who sits in wide-eyed wonderment at towns with names like Buttonwillow and Lost Hills.

For the past thirty-five years she has been living with a bland accountant named Norm, their routines carved with exacting precision into every hour of every day. Over time my mother became not merely unadventurous, her world became smaller and smaller. She seldom left her house except to go somewhere she'd already been—hundreds of times. Yet I'd always known that a worldly, interested person lurked in there somewhere, waiting for a chance to break out. Now she seems to delight in everything she sees. For here we are, a seventy-seven-year-old woman, her adult daughter, and a dozen rolls of Scott one-ply Choose-a-Size paper towels, sailing toward a new life. With each mile we clock, I see her body relax, her face soften.

In the car, my mother talks. She talks a lot about the urgency with which she felt she needed to leave San Diego after so many years. She talks about what happened with Norm, whose confusion "presented," as a doctor would say, in the usual small ways at first, then escalated. But it was Norm's sudden and intense allegiance to his fifty-six-year-old daughter that ultimately drove my mother away. Of course, she's rehashing a drama I lived through right alongside her—all within the past few months. I'm familiar with every twist and turn of the tale, yet I understand that talking about it for the umpteenth time is something she needs to do. So I nod a lot and punctuate the ends of her sentences with sympathetic sounds and the occasional "Yes, it's unbelievable" or "I know. Crazy."

During a bathroom break at the halfway point—break number five, I'm guessing—I receive a text from Zoë, my only child and for the past sixteen years my main reason for getting out of bed every morning. Where are you? (Somewhere in the Central Valley, I respond.) Will you be home in time for dinner? (No.) Is it okay if I use your Visa card to buy flowers for Grandma Helen? (Of course!)

As I drive, my attention toggling between my mother's Norm recap and my own freeway-induced series of free associations—mostly about Zoë, who is soon to be a junior in high school—my mother suddenly changes the subject.

"I'm going to take driving lessons," she says.

"But you know how to drive."

My mother explains that she is in fact scared of driving, particularly on freeways. She confesses that she never learned how to parallel park. "I never needed to learn," she explains. "No one in San Diego parallel parks." Besides, when Norm was still in possession of his faculties—and even after he began to fall apart—he did all the driving. I tell my mother I'm impressed by her pluck. Driving lessons sound so enterprising, so independent.

It's nearly 9:00 P.M. when we approach San Francisco from the East Bay, and as we pass Oakland's baseball stadium, we see fireworks. My mother is spellbound by the show.

"Stop so we can watch!" she insists.

Stopping isn't an option. We're not ambling down a country road on horseback, taking in a full moon. We're in the farthest left lane of a six-lane freeway in Northern California, 1.2 tons of metal traveling at 75 miles an hour. But I do slow down a little, just in time for the finale.

"Mom!" I say. "They knew you were coming!" I look over and she's smiling. For a second, I think she believes it.

An hour later, we're in my neighborhood of Lower Pacific Heights, and I turn each corner slowly so that my mother can take in the lovely old houses. My mother has been to San Francisco only once in her life, and although it's dark I hope she can see how beautiful it is here—the silhouettes of the mansions against the night sky; the Golden Gate Bridge shimmering just beyond the hill's crest.

We pull in to the garage and I unload the car. We'll be spending a couple of weeks in my apartment before we can move in to the house I've found for my mother, Zoë, and me, an experiment in multigenerational living that I'm embarking on filled with high hopes. As I walk through the back door, I see to my amazement that my soon-to-be-sixteen-year-old daughter, who has never tidied so much as a square inch of her own room, has cleaned the entire 950-square-foot apartment. The place sparkles. Not only has she decluttered, dusted, and scrubbed (how did she even know where I keep the cleaning supplies?) but, knowing that I was intending to give my mother my own room until we move, she has made up my bed on the living room couch, complete with slippers set out on the floor. At the center of the dining room table, Zoë has placed an extravagant bouquet of roses, lilies, and peonies from a nearby flower shop I seldom dare enter for fear of its prices. Propped against the vase is a handmade card: "Welcome Home, Grandma Helen." My mother is overcome. And so am I.

I'm disappointed that Zoë's door is shut, with no light showing underneath. But within a few minutes, having heard us come in, she emerges from her room, rubbing her eyes. She greets my mother with a long hug.

"Hi, Grandma Helen. How was the drive?"

My mother squeezes her granddaughter hard. "Hi, sweetie! The flowers are beautiful. And I love my card!"

I'm thrilled. I thank Zoë for the superlative cleanup. She acts as if it were nothing and excuses herself to go back to bed. After showing my mother to my bedroom, I settle into my makeshift bed and drift off. I don't know how long I've been asleep when I'm awakened by the sound of someone's tread against the hardwood floor in the kitchen. I open my eyes and, with a clear line of sight to the refrigerator, I see a brief burst of light with the opening and closing of the door, followed by the uncorking of a wine bottle. It's my mother. I hear her pour herself some wine, then pad away. I've known for many years that she still drinks at night, to help her sleep, but I don't know when, exactly, or how much—and I've never asked her. My senses are on full alert; a whorl of emotions—fear, helplessness, panic—streaks through me. *Stop it,* I tell myself. *You're not ten. Those years are long past. Everyone's safe. It's all fine.* I will myself back to sleep.

The next morning my mother and I are in the car and, as I have learned to do when broaching a delicate topic with my teenage daughter, I stare straight ahead as I speak. "There's one thing that's nonnegotiable for me," I say to the steering wheel. "Excessive drinking."

I see out of the corner of my eye that she has turned to look at me. Her response is immediate. "It's nonnegotiable for me too."

2.

Our Year in Provence

One does not discover new lands without first, and for a long time, losing sight of the shore.

—André Gide, SI LE GRAIN NE MEURT

MY MOTHER AND NORM HAD NEVER MARRIED, FOR WHAT MY MOTHER explained were "tax reasons." They owned a large and comfortable tract house in a drowsy middle-class neighborhood near UC San Diego. They had few friends, but they had each other, and their dogs. For years they had been slavishly devoted to a series of large German shepherds—usually two at a time—which they took for hikes every day at a nearby dog park. And they had Costco, which, near as I could figure, was the only place they shopped.

In their odd and insular world, my mother and Norm weren't merely glued at the proverbial hip. My mother micromanaged Norm's every move. When he went to the bathroom, she all but paced outside the door until he was back in her hovering presence. His health was basically sound, but she monitored his mild cardiac condition so closely you'd think he'd had a heart transplant. She planted timers strategically throughout the house, set to chime or beep or ring when it was time for Norm's blood thinner, or cholesterol medicine, or whatever other drug he happened to be on at the time. As suffocating as such a relationship appeared from the outside, it clearly worked for my mother, and Norm seemed to putter through his days happily enough. He had the love and undivided attention of an intelligent, lively woman who brought *New Yorker* cartoons and balsamic vinegar into his life.

As the two of them grew older, doctors' visits occurred at least twice a week, knees got replaced, teeth crowned, skin cancers lasered away. The dogs became too much to handle, and my mother resignedly placed the last remaining dog in a new home. Then one day Norm strained a muscle in his back while lifting a flat of plants. He was in terrible pain and from then on grew increasingly anxious about being left alone. Whenever my mother tried to leave the house, Norm panicked and asked her to stay. There were innumerable other small red flags that popped up along the way, along with a few doozies, like the time he accused my mother of getting his socks "all wet" when he had in fact opened his bureau drawer and sent a stream of pee straight into it. Overwhelmed, my mother called me several times a day for support and advice. The support was easy, but having never been the life partner of an eighty-four-year-old man who was unraveling, I could offer little advice.

These are the stories you hear about the elderly. One thing happens and it triggers a cascade of other debilitating incidents, the seriousness of each new event compounded by whatever preceded it. And now my mother and Norm were living a textbook case of this downward spiral.

One afternoon a few weeks after Norm's back sprain, my mother called me with surprising news. Norm's daughter, Paula, a penniless classical pianist and dancer, had just moved to San Diego from New York and had driven Norm to the doctor that morning. On the way back she called my mother to say her dad wanted to go home—not to his own house but to the house Paula was now sharing with her mother, Norm's ex-wife. My mother's voice was subdued, as if she couldn't quite lend credence to the words she was speaking. I told her I was sure everything would soon settle down, that Norm would get better and go home. In my own mind I had never considered any scenario other than one in which Norm and my mother would navigate advanced old age together.

Sure enough, after playing caregiver to her father for a few days, Paula called my mother to say that Norm was too heavy a burden for her. But this was an egg that couldn't be unscrambled. Just a few Norm-free days were enough to give my mother some perspective. With Norm in constant pain and his mental state growing worse, my mother understood that she wasn't up to the task of caring for him either. And now she didn't know what to do.

I had landed a role in the *Aging in America* script as we have come to know it, part of the sandwich generation of middle-aged adults caught between teenage kids and aging parents. I enlisted a friend to stay with Zoë and flew to San Diego. In the absence of Norm or any large canines, the house felt empty when I arrived. My mother, thin and frail, was doing all she could to appear chipper. Still, within thirty seconds I could tell she was in no position to take care of Norm, even if he was to decide to return. She was still hobbling from knee-replacement surgery a few months earlier. On top of that, she had developed severe carpal tunnel syndrome, making her right hand numb and weak, and would need wrist surgery for that sometime soon.

We needed a different arrangement not only for Norm but for my mother as well. For several months, my mother and I had been discussing the possibility of having both of them move to San Francisco. While my mother had resisted the idea at first, her attitude toward her progressive disabilities was shifting on the Kübler-Ross scale, from denial to acceptance. But Norm was opposed to the idea of such a big change and had grown even more reluctant since the arrival of his daughter. Now, within hours of my walking through my mother's front door, she told me she had made up her mind: She would be moving to San Francisco, Norm or no Norm. She had made a bold decision, and I was relieved that she would be so close to me, eliminating the need for frequent trips to San Diego.

Shortly after hearing this news from my mother, Paula made plans to install her father in an assisted-living place called the Cloisters, where she was now occasionally performing her "therapeutic healing dances."

Norm himself had nothing whatever to do with determining his own fate. Paula was in charge. And my mother was so determined to get out of Dodge that she was willing to cede control of her partner's life to his daughter.

Within a few months, my mother's quiet life of carefully prescribed routine had become a clanging mess. Impressively, she kept her head high. She called Norm at the Cloisters frequently, but she could tell he wasn't always in possession of his faculties. My stalwart mother even paid regular visits. But whenever she went, Paula was in Norm's room, protecting her father as if my mother—the man's constant companion for thirty-five years—were a mortal enemy. To top it off, soon after Norm entered the Cloisters, Paula went to court for conservatorship of Norm's estate, which was worth a surprisingly hefty sum. Since my mother and Norm had never married, she had no claim to his estate.

My mother decided to sell the house, which Norm had deeded to her several years earlier for one of their unfathomable tax reasons. She hired Cheryl the downsizer to help her sort through four decades' worth of accumulation. The house hadn't reached a level of pathological clutter, but there was certainly no shortage of stuff, all of it relatively well organized and much of it a testament to hundreds of hours spent at Costco: roll after roll of paper towels, dozens of flashlights, reams of paper and file folders, and countless tools and canned goods.

A dozen steel file cabinets were spread around the house, jam-packed with pay stubs, credit-card bills, receipts, work documents, and health-plan descriptions. Norm wasn't merely bland, but also creepy, and this side of him was revealed when my mother found in the cabinets black-and-white snapshots from the 1960s of young women wearing nothing but high heels. She also found a rich collection of skin magazines, *Playboy* mostly, going back decades.

A couple of weeks later, a meeting was held to divide the possessions in the house. As my mother recounted the scene to me, Norm, now wheelchair-bound, was rolled into the house by Paula, followed by her lawyer. The court-appointed conservator arrived soon after. They all seated themselves on one side of the dining room table. My mother, her lawyer, and Cheryl the downsizer, who by now was more friend to my mother than employee, sat on the other.

"I have an announcement to make," Norm said in a feeble voice, amid the general chatter. My mother, still tuned in to Norm as no one else in that room could ever be, was the only person who heard him. She asked everyone to quiet down and listen to what Norm had to say.

"I have an announcement to make," he repeated, a bit more loudly.

"I don't want—I don't want—" he stammered. Had his mind suddenly snapped into focus? Would he tell the assembled group that he didn't want to be in San Diego after all? That he had made a terrible mistake and indeed wanted to accompany his partner of nearly four decades in her move north? The room was hushed as all eyes rested on Norm. Finally he got the words out. "I don't want any of the old *Playboys*."

MY MOTHER THOUGHT SHE might be content in an independent-living place of some kind. That made sense, but it also reminded me that my elderly mother was now heading down that one-way road we all dread: first independent living, then assisted living, followed by planetary exit.

Finding a suitable independent-living arrangement was problematic. The San Francisco Bay Area is expensive to begin with, and growing old in comfortable fashion is even more so, as I was about to discover. A few weeks before I brought my mother to San Francisco, I consulted Anne Ellerbee, a woman who owns a business that places seniors in independent- and assisted-living communities. Anne and I discussed a few possibilities, and thick brochures from places with names like The Sequoias, Sterling Court, and Drake Terrace began to arrive in the mail. But they were all "buy-ins," which means that you pay several hundred thousand dollars up front; in return, you get a "membership" of sorts. On top of that, you pay rent for your apartment, which can run as high as $6,000 every month. Who could afford this? Moms and dads of the Silicon Valley crowd, no doubt, but not my own fixed-income parent. Or me. As the search progressed, my mother began to get cold feet. Even if she found an affordable place, she said, she wasn't sure she was ready to join a retirement community.

Next we explored the idea of finding her an apartment close to Zoë and me. Preferring not to get on a plane and come to San Francisco to go apartment hunting herself, my mother entrusted me with the job. She requested a building with a doorman—a rarity in San Francisco. Nonetheless, I scored almost immediately, with a one-bedroom apartment in a building a mile from my own. The distance felt just right. The apartment itself was small but otherwise perfect. Pleased with myself, I sent my mother iPhone photos, including one of Abdel, the doorman. She didn't like it; it was too close to the street. Nor did she like any of the other apartments I looked at over the next week.

With each day, her desire became clearer: She wanted to live not merely near me but *with* me. She didn't say this outright, but I could tell it was where she was headed. While it wasn't my initial choice, I began to warm to the idea. If I went out of town, she'd be there to stay with Zoë, a luxury for a single parent, to be sure. And I wouldn't have to travel—even a mile—to see her. We'd need a bigger place, which would cost more, but she could help pay for it. These pragmatic advantages were nice, but there was something deeper: This was finally my chance to have a real family home—with my mother in it—making up for many years of lost time.

I decided that having her live with us was the solution. One afternoon, I called her to suggest it, and she was thrilled. For my part, I was guided by a combination of love, protectiveness, and, as I would eventually come to see, magical thinking. I believed we were as close to the mother–daughter ideal as two women could be. We often spoke several times a day. I confided everything to her. I told myself I had long since put any lingering anger about my childhood behind me, that I had taken the ultimate high road. And I had little tolerance for those who harbored bitterness toward their own mothers for transgressions far less serious than those my sister, Sarah, and I had had to endure. With a transcendent eye, I now see that it's far easier to imagine a future we can invent than to reckon honestly with a painful past.

ONE NIGHT SHORTLY AFTER inviting my mother to live with us, I found Zoë at the dining room table, flipping through homemade flash cards of famous paintings she had memorized for an art history class the previous year.

"Wow, I can't believe how much work I put into this," my daughter said. "I wonder how many I still know."

"Want me to quiz you?"

"Sure. No, wait. I'll quiz *you*."

She held up a card: four goldfish in a glass cylinder. That was easy—I'd owned the poster for years.

"Matisse."

The next one—a famous fifteenth-century masterpiece that gives the mistaken impression of a shotgun wedding—was easy too.

"Van Eyck. *The Arnolfini Portrait*."

Zoë smiled. "Which Van Eyck?"

"Jan," I answered.

"Yeah!" said Zoë. I was eating up her praise.

Next came a sculpture of two figures in a sinewy embrace.

"Henry Moore?"

"Nope. Rodin. *The Kiss*."

"Uh-oh. I'm an idiot."

"No, you're *good*!"

With Zoë in such a cordial mood, this seemed as opportune a moment as any to ask her how she felt about having her grandmother live with us.

"Sweetie, Grandma Helen might move in with us. How would you feel about that? We can live in a bigger place, because she'll help with the rent."

Zoë had been present during many of my phone conversations with my mother and didn't look surprised. She nodded. "And we'll have a grandparent right here with us," she said.

She was quiet and fanned out the index cards in her hand. Then she said, "I think she *should* come live with us. That would be nice."

I was relieved.

At that moment, encouraged by my daughter's easy acquiescence, I chose to disregard the risks. I knew my mother was free with her opinions, that she took up a lot of psychological space in a room, and that she and Zoë hadn't exactly bonded over the years. I also knew that Zoë was a teenager living the full complement of her age group's psychodramas. And then there was the fact that I was working hard to make a living, and this new arrangement could be a distraction. But I wasn't aspiring to turn us into the Huxtables. I was just trying to take these remnants of a family and weave them together as best I could.

After a few more minutes, Zoë asked, "So if Grandma Helen lives with us, what will happen to *us*?" I knew exactly what she meant. For the past eight years—since the day Matt, her father, died suddenly of a heart attack at age forty-five—Zoë and I have been tiptoeing together through life. We have grown remarkably close. Zoë doesn't simply tell me everything, she entrusts me with her fragile heart, much as her father did. Other mothers say they envy me, but I wouldn't wish on anyone the circumstances that bound my daughter to me this tightly. Since Matt's death, Zoë has worried that I, too, will die, leaving her an orphan. More than once, I have awakened in the middle of the night to see my daughter's eyes large in the dark, inches from my head, checking to make sure I'm breathing.

So the "us" she was referring to was the us that had managed to get her through the past eight years without her father—the us that saw her through the grief of losing him; the us that struggled through my disastrous remarriage to a man who first embraced, then rejected, his stepdaughter with breathtaking completeness. It was the us that emerged on the other side of all that, a unit as close as two wounded people can be.

But she also meant the everyday us—the us that flips through her old art cards; the us that goes to In-N-Out Burger on a whim when nothing else will do; the us that watches *Desperate Housewives* every single Sunday night, no matter what; the us that loves to listen to Christmas music in the car year-round, especially Eartha Kitt singing "Santa Baby." How would my mother fit into that us?

My answer to her was that we wouldn't be any less us than we ever were. Zoë and I knew how to be a family. Now we would have a chance to show my mother what we knew, to show her the true meaning of family, to show what I had to learn on my own, without her.

—

I FOUND THE PERFECT house for our little threesome, a tall Victorian from the late 1800s, yellow with white and gold-leaf trim on a rare flat stretch of Pacific Heights—an important requirement for an older woman unaccustomed to steep hills. The fanciest neighborhood in San Francisco, Pacific Heights embodies every tourist's vision of the city: block upon block of mansions built in a hodgepodge of dazzling architectural styles—an Arts and Crafts cheek by jowl with a Dutch Colonial; a Queen Anne confection next door to a Georgian fortress—many with postcard-worthy vistas of the San Francisco Bay and Golden Gate Bridge. Pacific Heights has the signs of contented wealth stamped all over it. It's long on boutiques and short on gas stations. You'll trip over day spas and specialty pet shops, but don't go looking for Walmart.

The neighborhood runs along a series of hills so steep that the population remained sparse until the late nineteenth century, when the construction of a new cable-car line finally made the area accessible. After the 1906 earthquake—then fire—that destroyed the grand homes on Nob Hill, many of the city's wealthy families migrated to Pacific Heights and built new mansions. Many of those old families—the Hellmans of Wells Fargo, the Haases of Levi Strauss, and the descendants of oil tycoon J. Paul Getty—are still there. But there are plenty of ten-thousand-square-foot estates to go around, and since the 1960s, when the computer industry started churning out millionaires, a steady stream of new wealth has arrived in Pacific Heights. The neighborhood also has an abundance of apartment buildings, as well as apartments carved from single-family homes, which brings a measure of economic—if not racial—diversity to the neighborhood. It was Zoë's choice of high schools that had first brought us to Pacific Heights, and we were living in a cozy and quiet two-bedroom apartment close to Zoë's school when I started searching for a place with room for the three of us.

Stately and commanding, the house I found on Sacramento Street, in Lower Pacific Heights, was an architectural jewel; tour buses drove down the street several times a day and the guides pointed out our Victorian "painted lady" not just for its curb appeal but also for its lucky survival of the earthquake. Meticulously renovated, the house had a layout that I was sure would work perfectly: a three-room suite on the lower level with a bathroom and laundry room for my mother, living space on the next level, and, on the top floor, bedrooms for Zoë and me. The master bedroom was large enough to double as my office. Moreover, it seemed symbolic that we should find a three-story nineteenth-century Victorian, whose original intention was to house multiple generations. Set back slightly from the street, the house had the additional, and much desired, perk of a spacious two-car garage. When Zoë saw the house, she begged me to rent it. We could never have afforded to buy it, but, thanks to the recession, the rent had already been reduced twice, and with my mother paying half, we could swing a year's lease. My mother couldn't have been more pleased. She started calling our experiment "our year in Provence."

Bringing my mother to San Francisco made perfect sense to me, if not to others. "Isn't this all happening kind of quickly?" asked Candace, my best friend, who knows me better than I know myself. I explained to her just why it would work. I described the house I had found, with kitchen, living room, and dining room on the middle level, serving as the buffer floor between my mother's domain and Zoë's and mine. I emphasized the word "buffer," as if I could use it to erase any lingering doubts Candace might have about my moving in with a woman whose behavior three decades earlier—on a night when Candace had witnessed my mother in a flat-out vicious alcohol-fueled rant against me—had horrified her. Candace remained unconvinced that a buffer floor was enough, but she stopped questioning it. She saw that I had made up my mind.

In the face of naysayers, I chose instead to embrace the reaction of another friend, who was living in Beijing: "How Chinese of you!" she said upon hearing the news. When I told my mother, she was delighted. "What have the Chinese got on us?" she declared. And I agreed. The Chinese revere their elderly. If they could live happily with multiple generations under one roof, so could we. And then almost instantly, it seemed, my mother's house in San Diego was in escrow and I was behind the wheel of her white Honda, bound for our new life.

3.

Intonation

Alas! All music jars when the soul's out of tune.

—Miguel de Cervantes, DON QUIXOTE

ALL THREE OF US ARE IN ONE WAY OR ANOTHER FEELING DISPLACED. With my mother now in my bedroom, my domain is the couch; Zoë's life has gone slightly sideways; and my mother is living out of a half dozen or so paper bags. Despite her altered routine, my mother is overjoyed at being with us. She tells me she has fallen in love with San Francisco, the city's beauty, its friendly people, its convenience. She says that being able to walk across the street to buy a container of orange juice is a miracle. She says she never wants to live anywhere else. In fact, she has a lot to say. Has she always talked so much, I wonder?

For the first couple of days, Zoë seems happy to have her grandmother around. While I pack up the apartment, Zoë tends to my mother's every request. And those requests are many: My mother needs things from the hardware store; she needs a mailbox with late pickup times; she needs a smaller towel, a larger pair of rubber gloves.

"Mom," Zoë says, "it's like babysitting a little kid." Her tone is good-natured, but I can tell that the novelty and excitement are quickly wearing off. I remind Zoë that her grandmother is going through a difficult transition and that in a few days she'll have fewer needs. "Just hang in there," I tell her.

My more-skeptical friends had from the beginning expressed concern about how my mother's presence would affect Zoë. But between my mother's stated intention that she'd like to have a good relationship with her only grandchild and Zoë's warm embrace of her grandmother upon her arrival, my optimism ran high. Deep down, though, I knew this wasn't going to be easy. Zoë was a mommy-oriented child from the start. Even as a toddler, she disliked it when I paid attention to anyone other than her and was particularly sensitive when my focus turned to my mother. In retrospect, I realize that she didn't react that way to my interactions with my father, my mother-in-law, friends, or strangers. It's possible that Zoë was tuned in to something of which I was unaware: the almost umbilical hold my mother had on me, the emotional energy of unfinished business. She acted out. When she was two and my mother was visiting, as the three of us lay on the big bed in the master bedroom, watching *Sesame Street*, Zoë sat up abruptly and hit her grandmother on the arm, something I had never seen her do to anyone. My mother shrieked.

As for my mother, she has never really known how to be with Zoë. It's a problem I've always written off as part of her general awkwardness around children. But perhaps she sensed the unusually strong bond between Zoë and me. Instead of delighting in it, as many grandparents do, she let it grate on her.

For a while, I chose to see the problem through the narrowest possible lens: My mother just needed a little coaching on the basics of interacting with young children, I told myself. "Try asking her questions," I'd say to her on the phone before a visit to San Diego. "Sometimes that can help kick-start a conversation. Before you know it, you'll have a chatterbox on your hands."

"A question? Like what?"

"Well, try something easy, like 'How's school?' or 'What's your favorite class?' "

So when we visited, my mother would lob Zoë a question, and Zoë would answer. Silence would follow, my mother unable to think of a follow-up query that might keep the conversation alive. And my heart would sink.

Then there was my mother's reluctance to travel, which caused her to miss important events in her granddaughter's life. The most notable milestone she missed was Zoë's bat mitzvah. Her reasons for not attending: Religion wasn't her thing; Norm couldn't be left alone; Norm couldn't be left alone with the dogs. In the end, who really knew? Grandparents Day at Zoë's school was a topic I never mentioned, though each year when the day arrived I felt a vague sadness. The fact is, Zoë and my mother hardly know each other.

There was one area in which my mother did show great interest in her granddaughter's life: her cello-playing.

From the time Zoë started to play the cello, at age six, Matt and I bought her progressively larger instruments until, finally, we found an exquisite eighteenth-century cello of unknown provenance, as dark and mysterious as some of the music Zoë was growing into. For years, we sent Zoë to music schools around the Bay Area. It wasn't easy getting her to go. With few exceptions, kids hate to practice a musical instrument—it's just no fun, and progress is excruciatingly slow. Our fights over practicing were epic. But whereas many parents decide the battle isn't worth it, for some reason her father and I didn't give up. And after Matt died, I kept pushing. I knew it was worth something, though I wasn't sure what. She has no desire to become a professional musician. At the age of five she grew fascinated with the Discovery Health Channel and hasn't budged since from a desire to become a physician. But I'm convinced that music saved her, perhaps not literally but by giving her focus and resilience she wouldn't otherwise have had. Music was always the outlet for something she couldn't express in words. Zoë must know this, too, because after a decade of scraping that bow across the strings, one day out of the blue Zoë told me how much she appreciated my perseverance. "That was a real gift you gave me, Mom," she said. "Thanks."

But Zoë is a self-conscious musician who dislikes practicing around people she isn't comfortable with, and there's no telling how the presence of my mother might inhibit her. A week into our new life, I go out to dinner with a friend, and as I leave the house I remind my daughter to practice while I'm out. She has an important audition the next day for the chamber-music program at the San Francisco Conservatory. Until she moved in with us, my mother had never heard Zoë play so much as a scale. I can tell Zoë is queasy and tentative about practicing around my mother, but she promises she'll do it.

I return home at around 10:00 P.M. to find both mother and daughter already in bed. The house is calm and peaceful; I settle under the covers on the couch and fall into a deep sleep. I'm awakened by a tap on my back. It's Zoë. She's crying and asks me to come into her room.

I climb into her bed. "Sweetie, what's wrong?"

"Grandma Helen said I suck at the cello."

"What?!"

"She said I have good technique but my intonation sucks. She said I should take up the piano."

"But she has no ear!" I say into the dark. "How can she know if you're playing in tune? Ignore her."

I should have seen this coming. My mother had cornered me the day before to make the same pronouncement. "Zoë has excellent technique," she said when she caught me alone, after hearing Zoë practice. "But I think the piano might be the better instrument for her. On the piano you don't have to worry about getting the intonation just right."

Clearly, she had been thinking about this and considered it her solemn duty, after a week of living with us, to influence the course of Zoë's musical future.

My antennae had gone straight up. This was a topic my mother was going to sink her teeth into, and I knew I needed to say something before she inflicted real damage.

"Mom," I said. "Zoë's music is Zoë's and my thing." I thought I was being clear and that she had heard me. But she hadn't. Or she had chosen not to. Either way, she waited until I had gone out to dinner before raising the subject with her granddaughter. And now here is my child, distraught and unable to sleep—on the eve of an audition.

"Don't listen to her, sweetie," I tell her again. "You're a wonderful cellist."

But it's too late. My kid is spooked. I'd like to think this is an isolated incident, but I know it isn't, for it has reminded me that my mother is incapable of keeping her opinions to herself. I am enraged, and for an instant, in a disturbing surge of emotion, I hate my mother with every fiber of my being. I recall in a flash that many years ago, while still married to my father, my mother took cello lessons but quit after getting up from her practice chair one day, cello in hand, to answer a ringing phone. According to family legend, as my mother rushed through the narrow doorway, the instrument broke into some number of pieces. With that, the lessons ceased. As I remember this now, I wish my mother had tripped and been impaled by the instrument's long, sharp endpin.

THE NEXT MORNING, MY mother is making her breakfast drink, an awful-looking concoction of instant coffee, hot water, nonfat Lactaid, and four or five packets of Splenda, mixed together in a tall drinking glass (a facsimile of a Starbucks drink, she tells me).

Struggling to find a calm voice, I ask my mother what she said to Zoë.

She's shocked by my insinuation that she might have given Zoë anything but the highest of compliments. "What? I told her she plays beautifully, that she's a marvelous technician!"

She insists her intentions were only the very best. She omits the part about telling Zoë she found her ability to play in tune wanting, along with her suggestion that Zoë switch instruments after having labored for so many years on this one. Not wanting to argue with her, I leave the kitchen and go tap on Zoë's door to get her up. When she tells me she doesn't want to go to the audition, I summon every ounce of parenting wile I can and finally talk her into it. A few days later, Zoë gets a call from the conservatory telling her she hasn't been selected.

4.

Boxes

The house a woman creates is a Utopia. She can't help it—can't help trying to interest her nearest and dearest not in happiness itself but in the search for it.

—Marguerite Duras, PRACTICALITIES

KIERAN AND CREW HAVE DELIVERED MY MOTHER'S FURNITURE TO the new house. The most ungainly of the objects to move, of course, was the Steinway. My mother has always loved piano music and hungered to play. When she was in her early sixties, she retired from her job as a computer programmer so that she could devote herself more fully to the piano. As she had done with her dog obsession, she took her piano education to an extreme. She bought not one, not two, but three pianos. One was the beautiful Steinway B, a small grand piano she purchased with a modest inheritance left by a friend of her parents'. She photocopied all her music in a larger size so she could see it better and mounted it on manila folders. She practiced for several hours every day. When she wasn't practicing the piano she was talking about the piano. When we spoke on the phone, I heard about the difficulty she had keeping time to a metronome; about Erika, her German piano teacher; and about her shortcomings as a duet partner. I had to hand it to her: She had finally found a passion that moved her beyond the world of Norm and the dogs.

I love pianos, too, and wrote an entire book about the life of one piano, a Steinway owned by the renowned pianist Glenn Gould. And I shared my mother's love for her piano. During phone conversations, I listened raptly as she told me about the instrument's cross-country adventures. The action—the keyboard and its associated works—had been removed and sent to the East Coast for a full overhaul. When I visited her in San Diego after the piano's return, I was struck by how buttery the action felt under my hands.

I once mentioned quietly to my mother that I hoped the Steinway would stay in the family and someday pass on to Zoë. Shortly thereafter she told me she would add a codicil to her will specifying that upon her death the Steinway was to go to me. I was touched by her gesture, even after she added that she was doing it in part to keep the piano out of the greedy clutches of Norm's daughter. A gifted pianist, Paula was withering about my mother's playing.

Before bringing the Steinway north, my mother had mentioned that she was considering selling it. I was surprised, but instead of reminding her that, last I knew, she was setting it aside for me, I said nothing, unable to utter the simple words, "But, Mom, don't you remember your promise?" If I did, it would be a way of asking for something, and asking my mother for something was always dangerous because of the risk of disappointment.

Once I see it installed in my living room, I'm reminded how much I like it and I choose to dismiss the earlier talk of a sale as idle chatter. I'm comforted by the thought that the piano will someday be mine, then Zoë's.

Now we've been in the house for two weeks, but we're not really *in* it yet. Boxes are everywhere. Part of the problem is that for eight years and through multiple moves I've been carrying around my late husband's possessions, thinking that Zoë will eventually cherish them as much as I do. But now Matt's boxes are feeling like a burden. Each is filled with things I know I should sort through, but I can't bring myself to start.

Late one afternoon, as I'm considering just how brutal the move-in process is going to be, my cellphone rings. It's my friend Candace, calling to check in. Sometimes you don't know what's missing from your life until it falls into your lap. That's what happened in 1977, when I met Candace. Although we've both made close friendships with others over the years, we view our best-friend status as sacred. This is how it often works with best friends: Something happens to cement the friendship, and after that you're inseparable. In our case, Germany happened. We were both there for our junior year in college, and we met soon after arriving, on a bus during a field trip. I was knitting a sweater, racing to get it done and mailed off to my sister in time for her birthday. Candace, also a knitter, sat down next to me. Her mother owned a yarn shop near San Francisco, she told me. And she began to chat. By the end of the bus ride, we knew we had something special.

Our bond remained strong, even during years when we lived thousands of miles apart. As adults we saw each other through romantic reversals and breakups, Candace's reassessment of her sexuality, the births of our children, the death of my husband. Candace knows how to call my bluff, as only a best friend can. She also protects me, as only a best friend will.

It's hard to get Candace down. She must have been born with endorphins coursing through her veins. She inherited her good spirits from both her parents: her persistently jovial father and Ramona, her calm, good-hearted mother, who is now eighty-three. When Candace's father died, she moved Ramona closer to her and Julie, her partner of many years. I love watching Candace and Ramona together and envy the calm waters on which their relationship has glided for the three decades I've known them. They've always done things together. They both bleed orange and black for the San Francisco Giants, and they travel as a pair to spring training in Arizona. Ten years ago, when Ramona was seventy-three, she and Candace ran a 5K together.

"How's it going?" Candace asks, referring to my newest housemate.

"It's been a little bumpy," I reply. I tell her about the cello incident.

One of Candace's two sons, a serious violist who is Zoë's age, is, like Zoë, still reckoning with the tricky business of performing, or even practicing, where others can hear. Candace knows only too well how fragile young egos can be, and she's appalled.

"Oh, Katie, what a sucky thing to do," she says. "Did you tell your mother to back off?"

"I tried," I say. "I'm not sure she got it."

"How's Zoë doing?"

"Miserable," I say.

"I can imagine."

Candace has to run, but before hanging up she says, "Your mother doesn't understand the effect she has on other people."

I'm mulling Candace's perceptive words when I hear my mother climbing her stairs. As she enters the kitchen, she acknowledges something that has gone unspoken all day.

"It's Sarah's birthday," she says, as if simple verbal recognition might lessen the unhappiness we both feel.

"I know."

We say nothing more about my sister or the feelings either of us may be having about her absence from our lives. My mother hasn't spoken to Sarah in years, and my own contact with her has been sporadic, long spells of silence punctuated by brief periods of sisterly closeness. Sarah didn't become a mother but has always had an easy, relaxed way with Zoë. Her self-absorbed eccentricities can be endearing and funny. She makes the FedEx guy wait while she tries on shoes purchased from Zappos.com, in case she decides to send them back on the spot. She's an extreme hypochondriac: At one point while in her twenties, she was going to the emergency room so often she would call ahead to ask how long the wait was. She inherited my father's dry humor and can make me laugh like no one else. Yet our periods of closeness invariably end with flare-ups—the catalyst for which can be something as trivial as my failure to return her phone calls promptly enough—leading in turn to extended intervals of estrangement that can last months or years. This most recent period of mutual silence has lasted more than a year, and, as always, I feel like a traitor to our bond, especially now that our mother has moved in with me, a fact I have yet to reveal to Sarah.

Instead of dwelling on Sarah, my mother and I choose to distract ourselves with what surrounds us in the here and now—several dozen boxes filled with kitchenware. I usually enjoy setting up a new kitchen, but this has become a joyless and highly charged task. My mother and I each have our own set of kitchen boxes, which means that if there are two cheese graters between us, only one will make it into a cupboard. The other will be put back in a box or given to Goodwill. Each such little decision has the weight of a Middle East negotiation.

At first, it was fine enough. As we put away bowls and plates, salad servers and toast tongs, my mother turned to me and said, undiluted joy in her voice, "We're co-mingling!"

I shuddered, perhaps even panicked, which is why I've now turned churlish.

While her kitchenware is serviceable, I'm a sucker for the high end: All-Clad saucepans and Emile Henry pie dishes. Before long, I'm shaking my head at pretty much everything my mother removes from her San Diego boxes. She takes each rejected item as a personal slight—which in fact it is. I begrudge her even her lightweight bowls, which she can lift easily with her injured hand.

I'm determined to stake my claim as the expert at equipping and running a kitchen, which is, after all, the focal point of domestic life. But there's something else at work too. Here she is, a fragile old woman barely able to bend down as she peers into a low cupboard, looking for a place where she can share life with her grown daughter. At such a sight my heart should be big, but it's small, so small that when I see her start stuffing her serving spoons into the same drawer as my own sturdy pieces, lovingly accumulated over the years, it makes me crazy. Suddenly I'm acting out decades of unvoiced anger about my mother's parenting, which seems to be materializing in the form of her makeshift collection of kitchenware being unpacked into the drawers.

When I became a mother myself, I developed a self-righteous sense of superiority to my mother: I was better than my mother, for having successfully picked myself up and dusted myself off, for never having lain in bed for days on end, too blotto to get my child off to school or even to know if it was a school day. By sheer force of will and strength of character, I believed, I had risen above all that she succumbed to and skirted all that I might have inherited. This, of course, is too obnoxiously smug to say in words. So I say it with flatware.

5.

Oranges

Oh life, clear cup, suddenly you fill up
with dirty water.

—Pablo Neruda, "Ode to Life"

IN 1952, WHEN SHE WAS TWENTY, MY BRILLIANT MOTHER, WHO HAD been studying physics at Radcliffe College, dropped out in her junior year to marry my father, who was thirty. Eleven years later, when I was five and Sarah seven, my mother went on a trip. She was gone from our home in Rochester, New York, for several days. But she was often gone—not always from the house but missing from our lives nonetheless. Then one day Sarah and I returned from school to find her standing at the door, a piñata in her hand, smiling her spellbinding, I-am-overjoyed-at-the-sight-of-you smile. Now when I imagine that scene, my mind's eye puts a sombrero on her head, but I doubt she was wearing one. She had just come home from a trip to Juarez, Mexico, where she had obtained a quickie divorce. She told my sister and me that she was taking us to live in Florida. We had no idea where—or what—Florida was.

"There will be oranges there," she said. "They're everywhere. You can reach up and pull them off trees."

None of this was supposed to happen. My childhood in the house on

Chelmsford Road in Rochester was much like any other suburban kid's. I was in first grade at Council Rock Elementary School, mischievous and addicted to candy. Sarah and I rode tricycles up and down our long driveway. My father, whom we both adored, had augmented the pedals with wooden blocks so our stubby legs could reach them. We dug our way to China in the backyard. We made pot holders out of yarn loops. We had a cat named Penelope and a dog named Dido. The dog died and we got another cat. And this, I thought, was as my life would remain—uncomplicated, with two parents, a big sister, always a pet or two, snowy winters that made going outdoors a complicated production, and a bedroom to myself on the second floor of a big stucco house set back from a quiet leafy street.

A month or so before my mother's trip to Mexico, or maybe it was six months, or maybe a week, I had heard about this thing called divorce. It had happened to kids down the street—the same kids who had taken a kitchen knife to their cat's tail. I had come home that day and asked my mother what divorce meant, and when I heard her explanation, it sounded like the worst fate that could possibly befall a family. I decided that it must have been punishment for what those kids did to the cat. This dark assumption made me feel safer, since I had never committed such an act and never would. Still, as added insurance, I made my mother promise to never ever get divorced. And she promised. Now the same horrific thing that had happened to those other kids was happening to me. We were to be taken away from our school, our friends, our father. Yet everything was going to be all right because we would have all the oranges we could eat? That was her consolation? All I could think, for years to come, was *You broke a promise.* But why?

At the time I had no words for it, but I remember being stunned by what felt like the sheer arbitrariness of what was happening. Now I think of my search for a cause as a five-year-old's crude version of the famous butterfly effect: Did a random butterfly clinging to a vine somewhere in the Australian outback flutter its wings at some moment in 1953, so that ten years later two little girls in Rochester, New York, were sent down a path of no return?

In fact, there was nothing arbitrary about what occurred that day in 1963. The foundation had been built long before we entered the scene.

In her memoir, *The Architect of Desire,* the writer Suzannah Lessard suggests that family history can be seen as similar to architecture in certain ways. "Like architecture, it is quiet. It encompasses, but does not necessarily demand attention," she writes. "Like architecture, too, family history can suddenly loom into consciousness. . . . One can go about one's life with no thought of the past, and then, as if waking from a dream, be astonished to see that you are living within its enclosure."

Such was the case with our family and the thread of behavior that had remained consistent through generations, reverberating powerfully down into my brief life. I can document this only as far back as my maternal grandparents, but it almost certainly began long before they showed up. My mother's parents were both scientists, she a biologist and he a physicist. They had lived their lives for themselves, not their two children, modeling a form of narcissistic behavior that my mother would in turn emulate. When I was in my twenties, I once asked my aunt, who is eleven years younger than my mother, whether her father had encouraged her in her studies or, later, her profession. "My dear," replied my quick-witted aunt, "he hardly encouraged me to draw breath."

My grandfather's ancestors had first come to the United States from Germany in the middle of the nineteenth century, part of a tide of Jewish immigrants escaping the laws in post-Napoleonic Europe that severely limited the occupations in which Jews were allowed to engage. They settled among some two hundred other Jewish families in Jacksonville, Florida. By the time my grandfather was born, the family was well-to-do and packed with musicians. My grandfather himself gravitated first to engineering, then to physics. He went to Columbia, where in his junior year he met my grandmother, a sophomore at Barnard who was already a serious biologist.

They married in 1927, when he was twenty-two and she twenty. My mother was born four years later. By 1937, both of my grandparents possessed PhDs and not a shred of self-doubt. As my grandfather once recounted to a biographer, for one job interview at Princeton early in his career, he stood at a blackboard, drawing diagrams and formulas, then turned, looked the great Albert Einstein straight in the eye, and asked, "Is that clear?"

My grandfather would later go on to develop advances in radar that were used during World War II, then to Los Alamos to work on the Manhattan Project, where he headed a division that engineered precursors to the atomic bomb. My grandmother stayed behind with her two daughters. While separated, they each had conspicuous affairs, my grandfather with a secretary at Los Alamos, my grandmother with a Russian physicist named Sergei Feitelberg. My grandmother was a domineering woman, an emotional tyrant who gave free rein to her opinions, most of them biting and belittling. She was especially judgmental of her older daughter, my mother. But my mother's childhood in a large apartment on the Upper West Side of Manhattan was a happy one, she has told me many times, because she was raised not by her cold mother but by a kindly black woman in my grandparents' employ, named Anna. And she liked Sergei, whose presence softened her hard-hearted mother and who promised to take my mother dogsledding in Alaska. (The adventure never materialized, but Sergei's promise alone was enough to win my mother's lasting affection.)

When she was twelve, my mother started ballet. She was late to it but dedicated, practicing several hours a day. And she was talented enough to catch the eye of George Balanchine himself. My mother was crushed when, in 1946, just three years into her dancing career, my grandfather returned from Los Alamos to reclaim his wife and daughters and move them to Boston, where he had been recruited into the physics department at MIT. The move put an end to my mother's dancing. While at MIT, my grandfather built the first atomic clock (a more stable and precise tool for measuring time than any that preceded it), served as a science adviser to President Eisenhower, and helped transform the teaching of physics to American high school students. My grandmother worked as a research biologist at Harvard Medical School, and with her limited free time she built a rich social life for herself and her husband. But when it came to their child-rearing instincts, neither appeared to possess one nurturing or attentive bone.

My grandfather started a company, then sold it for a substantial sum. My grandparents became discerning collectors of books and art, buying rare first editions and original works by Marc Chagall and M. C. Escher. Their Steinway, a majestic ebony grand, occupied a corner of its own in the living room of their large, stately house in Belmont, just outside Cambridge.

In the 1950s they expanded their domestic domain with the purchase of a mansion on Tobey Island in Cape Cod's Buzzards Bay. Theirs was one of four homes—compounds, really—on the small private island. The other families, the Jacksons and the Emmonses, had been there for generations, and my grandparents weren't merely the only newcomers, they were also the only Jews. I was a small child when we made regular visits there, and one of my clearest memories is of my grandmother as the island's resident bully. Tobey Island was joined to Monument Beach, the adjacent town on the mainland, by a small bridge followed by a saddle of road, with a marsh on one side and the bay on the other. If my grandmother spotted someone she didn't recognize walking even a hundred feet along the unpaved road on the Tobey Island side of the bridge, she chased the interloper in her car, rolled down the window, and said in a withering voice, "May I help you?" Invariably, it turned out that the trespasser had set out on an innocent stroll from Monument Beach, but this made no difference to my grandmother, whose stinginess of spirit always managed to find its full expression in the presence of someone she considered beneath her—which was just about everyone. She would turn off the car's engine and wait until the hapless stranger had made an about-face and was headed back over the bridge.

My grandmother ruled over both her houses with absolute power. She was rigid about rules: Bathtubs must be scrubbed clean after each use; utensils must be removed from the dishwasher by the handle. One day when I was about eight, during a summer visit to Tobey Island, something I did or said incited my grandmother's wrath. She stopped me in the dark downstairs hallway, placed both hands firmly on my shoulders, and scolded me. Her words were razor-sharp, intended not to instruct me on how to be better but to make me feel ashamed of who I was. Her message: I was a bad child, hardly worthy of her lecture. There were other people in the house, but they must have known to give this scene a wide berth, because it felt to me as if she were the only person for miles around. For the several minutes that she held me by the shoulders—her fingers pressing so hard against my bones I would be left with small bruises—I didn't look in her eyes and focused instead on a prominent blue vein snaking up her left temple. I remember thinking that I had never noticed that vein before. When the ordeal was over, I went to look for my grandfather in his study. He was at the other end of the house but must have known what had happened, because he suggested we go sailing out on the bay in the smaller of their two boats, just the two of us. He invited me to take the tiller, and as we skimmed along the gentle water, watching the sail's luff, I asked him the only question I could find the words for.

"Why did she do that to me?"

He kept his gaze sailward. "I don't know, Katie."

And that was all he said. At the time, his answer struck me as a cop-out. I wanted his sympathy. But sympathizing with me would have been more of an acknowledgment of his wife's cruelty—and his own imprisonment—than my grandfather was willing to express. It would be years before I was able to imagine how horrendous being raised by such a woman must have been for my mother.

WITH PERFECT ENTRANCE EXAMS, my mother was accepted at Radcliffe, declaring herself a physics major, in the hopes, she told me years later, of getting her father's attention. But that was not to be—until she took up with my father, a brilliant and shy young physicist from the Flatbush section of Brooklyn.

The same way some women are addicted to shoes, the women in my family were addicted to male attention. Going through life alone wasn't considered a sign of strength but of failure. From an early age, my mother instilled in me the belief that life wasn't worth living—at least not with any pride—unless you were the object of a man's attention. She picked this up from her own mother, and, of course, from society's ceaseless cues about the importance of beauty in the pursuit of men.

Looks mattered. A lot. While her own mother was a natural knockout, my mother worked hard at her looks. She struggled to keep her hair free of frizz. For decades, in pursuit of a slimmer waist, my mother monitored what she ate. She was a saccharin trailblazer in the 1960s, when the artificial sweetener became popular among dieters. Throughout our early years, Sarah and I witnessed our mother's pursuit of physical perfection as we accompanied her to get her hair frosted, watched her exercise along with Jack LaLanne on television, and spent hours with her at Merle Norman cosmetics stores.

I have a clear childhood memory of one outing we took while visiting my grandparents in Boston. My grandmother drove and my mother sat beside her in the front. My aunt and my sister were in the back with me. At some point, the conversation turned to everyone's figure. Once the three adults had exhausted the topic of their own shapes, they focused on the two little girls. My grandmother remarked that Sarah, age nine, had a lovely figure. As for me, she said, she was skeptical. She commented on our bodies as if those bodies would determine our futures. I still remember the feeling of inadequacy that washed over me. I was seven and already thinking, *I'll never get married.*

When my mother was a teenager, her breasts blossomed into wondrous lobes—freakishly large against her small frame. Men loved them. Although my mother cursed her breasts for giving her bad posture and for generally getting in the way, she also knew they added to her allure. Even as small children, Sarah and I were aware of the effect our mother's looks could have on those around her. Years later, Sarah put it well when she said that our mother's beauty was so radiant that looking at her was like staring straight at the sun. When we lived in Rochester, my mother took up the can-can with a dozen or so other faculty wives. When the local newspaper photographed the dance troupe in action, even with a dozen women lined up and my mother far from the camera, the lens might as well have been trained on her alone, so completely did her slender legs and perfect face dominate the frame.

As soon as my mother opened her mouth, this brunette bombshell with the doe eyes became the object of resistless fascination. She wasn't merely smart—she was smart about *science,* and gifted in mathematics. For men of a certain type, the beauty–brilliance combination was an attraction like no other.

My mother and father met in the summer of 1950, when both were working at Brookhaven National Laboratory. My mother was almost nineteen, my father thirty. She has told me that her friend Mariette von Neumann (the first wife of John von Neumann, the famous mathematician) had warned her that this Everett Hafner fellow was quite the ladies' man. My mother was intrigued. She met the handsome playboy in question one day while out sailing with friends. My father had started out with one woman as his designated date, and by the end of the excursion, he was climbing off the boat with another—my triumphant mother.

Both of my grandparents disliked their daughter's choice, considering my Brooklyn-born-and-bred father inferior in social rank to her (or, rather, to them) and a bit of a dilettante. Horrified at the thought of such a union, they did their best to torpedo it. But their tactics backfired. My father traveled to Cambridge and stayed at the Sheraton Commander, where he and my mother carried out their trysts. Then they eloped.

Such are the makings of wrongheaded marriages. My mother once told me that she had married my father only to defy her parents. My grandparents, for their part, redoubled their efforts to shun my father. When my parents, newly married, went to Tobey Island to visit, my grandmother locked the sails away to keep my father from using the boats.

My father, kind, warm, and charming, but also emotionally stunted, had lived in his head most of his life and was no doubt at a loss when it came to dealing with my beautiful mother. She was restive from the start. My father was equally ill-suited to marriage—at least to a woman like my mother. He was in love with my mother but didn't know how to love her. She could bring a room to life merely by entering it, but my father failed to make her feel special. He was a master at telling jokes and stories. Sarah and I always found the jokes hilarious, and Sarah inherited his gift for pacing, for reading an audience, for perfect delivery of a punch line. But my mother resented my father's jokes. For years after the divorce, my mother told me that she used to feel like just one more member of the audience. Individual attention was something she craved, perhaps because it was denied her as a child. My father reacted to her unhappiness by retreating into work, which only angered her more. It wasn't long before my mother began to find the attention she longed for by taking lovers among the Rochester faculty.

When Sarah and I were little, one of my mother's favorite novels, *Zuleika Dobson*, told the tale of a femme fatale in Oxford, England, whose beauty cast a spell on the entire student body. My mother became the Zuleika Dobson of Rochester, attracting not undergraduates but faculty members. Her tastes were interdisciplinary: a physicist, a mathematician, and an economist. But, unlike Miss Dobson, my mother was married. As such, she followed her parents' example. Even more than the narcissism, and no doubt connected to it, the penchant for affairs was handed down from one generation to the next. My mother's parents modeled infidelity for her, and she in turn modeled it for us. The way my mother handled her affairs was bizarre. In Rochester, she had an affair with the husband of one of her best friends, and when we got a cat, we named it after her lover. We named a parakeet Malcolm, after another. And about the unsuspecting wife of a professor named Edgar Falk, who was in love with my mother, I remember chanting over and over, "Regina Falk is a bum bum." What to others might seem like a hideous violation of the trust between parent and child was our version of normal. For all we knew, the neighbors across the street and our teachers at Council Rock Elementary had similar extramarital pairing habits—and pets whose names bore witness to them.

After my mother's return from Mexico and before the dreaded move to Florida, my father moved out. For a while he stayed on a friend's couch, and we went to visit him. I remember how out of place he seemed away from our house. Still, I was sure that wherever Florida might be, it couldn't be far from him, because life for this five-year-old by definition had my father in it.

Although my grandparents had openly detested my father, when my mother finally announced that she was divorcing him, they were appalled. People of their ilk held their heads high and carried on, no matter what. Lesser people divorced. But my grandfather did reach back to friends from his home state to help my mother find a job in Florida teaching high school math and physics. (She'd finished her undergraduate physics degree while living in Rochester.)

In late fall 1963, I said goodbye to my classmates in Rochester. The next day, my mother put Sarah and me and the two cats into the black Nash Rambler station wagon and set out for the land of sun and oranges. I can still see her small frame elevated by a cushion as she drove headlong into years of tumult and torment. My sister and I were just along for the ride.

—

I DO NOT RECALL having eaten a single orange while living in Florida. And while I must have seen many groves of trees bearing the fruit, I have no memory of them. What I do remember is the bungalow my mother rented in a grimy neighborhood in Melbourne, a city on east central Florida's Space Coast. The house was dark and cramped. A family named the Browns lived across the street, in a slightly larger but equally run-down rattrap. Because she had to leave the house earlier than we did, my mother started sending us over to the Browns' every morning before school. The father regularly beat his children with a belt. I was spared, but Sarah wasn't. What my sister's transgression was, I have forgotten (if I ever knew). It could have been as minor as a public belch or a refusal to eat the vile creamed eggs on toast Mrs. Brown made for us. Whatever it was, I remember watching as Mr. Brown took Sarah to a front room, removed his belt, and delivered what must have been stinging pelts to my sister's behind. Luckily for Sarah, it happened only once.

I was grateful that I had escaped Mr. Brown's brutality, but that fact made little sense to me at the time, for in my mind my sister and I were one and the same. Throughout my early childhood, I possessed no viewpoints of my own. I took in the world through the prism of my older sister. Her desires and preferences instantly became my desires and preferences—so much so that it would be years before I was able to distinguish between Sarah's perceptions of the world and my own.

On our first day of school, I cried inconsolably after my mother dropped us off, and I refused to let anyone near me except my sister. Someone took me to Sarah's third-grade classroom, where I sat in the back until class let out. Every morning thereafter, I cried until someone took me to Sarah's classroom. My mother pulled us both out after a week or two and put us in a different school. I cried less at the new school yet still demanded to be taken to my sister.

It was in Florida where Sarah and I first identified alcohol as a culprit.

In Rochester we had been mystified by my mother's occasional absences, mostly because we were protected from their cause—by my father, by my parents' friends, by various babysitters. But once we'd been in Florida for a few months, we knew there was a link between the bottles and the smell of her breath—we came to associate the combination with her bouts in bed.

She began to ricochet between involvements with various men. There was a dentist whose first name I forget but whose last name was Cain; he had a dog named Nova, which Sarah and I thought was a laugh riot. Next came Joe, who seemed nice enough and might have lasted a few months, or maybe even a year. Then there was a fellow science teacher with an exotic name that might have been Ivar, who owned a nine-foot Indian python definitely named Sheila. The snake once disappeared (my memory gives her the run of the house, but she must have lived in a cage), and we eventually found her, safe and warm behind the refrigerator. The men didn't live with us, but, for the duration of their relationship with my mother, they were fixtures. Each breakup brought a succession of sodden days, my mother in bed. With each new man, Sarah and I grew warier. We stopped greeting them as potential new fathers and started keeping our distance, bracing ourselves for what would happen when the affair ended.

We didn't stay long in the Melbourne house. As my mother told the story years later, my grandparents came from Boston to visit and, horrified by the neighborhood we were living in, demanded we move to a nicer area—without, of course, offering financial help. My mother found an apartment in a complex in a nearby town called Satellite Beach, close to Cape Canaveral. In Satellite Beach, Sarah and I were liberated from the Browns, and my mother found a woman to look after us for a few hours in the afternoons until she returned from work. But much of the time it was Sarah who took care of me. She prepared meals for us, or at least an eight-year-old's idea of meals. Breakfast was usually a Hershey's bar, Jordan almonds, or licorice twists. Sarah got me ready for school, and we walked there and back together. We became the closest thing I can imagine to urchins. We seldom wore shoes when not in school, and we spent so much time outdoors we turned a golden brown.

My sister and I were allied not so much against our mother (we both loved her desperately and craved her attention above all else) but against the alcohol that kept her from us. During the periods when alcohol was her central organizing principle, our needs went unmet and often unseen. On the good days, my mother came home from work and prepared dinner. On the bad days, we came home to find her still in bed, just as we had left her, and we fended for ourselves. Often we turned the stove's electric burner on until it glowed a bright red, and we roasted marshmallows.

Neither Sarah nor I enjoyed returning to our small, sandy apartment after school. While we waited for our afternoon babysitter to arrive, we watched TV and kept ourselves busy with our stovetop marshmallow roasts. And we ate prodigious amounts of candy, which we purchased at a convenience store across the parking lot from our complex. In our way, we were content. After all, we had each other. When my mother went out and stayed out until very late, we knew there would be the same pungent smell as when the bottles were around. And we knew the next day would be bad. On those nights, I got into bed with Sarah and hoped she had some nickels. With enough nickels, we could stock up on candy until things got better. Sarah always had the nickels. She never let me down.

Ability in a longer book to do more setup + hinting before revealing the full story.

6.

Lia

"Oh, I know all about my mother and me," you may say.
"All that business with my mother was over years ago."
You don't and it wasn't.

—Nancy Friday, MY MOTHER/MY SELF

MY MOTHER HAS NO INTEREST IN RELIGION. SHE CONSIDERS HERself "a cultural Jew," if anything. I doubt she has ever set foot in a synagogue, and tonight will be no different, though it is Yom Kippur and Zoë and I are going to the synagogue for evening services. However, my mother joins us for our pre-sundown meal, at a Mexican restaurant a few blocks from the house. We set out on foot, my mother moving slowly. She tells us to walk ahead of her, but I don't want to leave her behind. Zoë is clearly impatient, but she slows to our deliberate pace.

At the restaurant, I order a steak salad, and my mother says she'd like the same. Zoë points out to my mother that she might not want that particular salad, as the beef is coated in a very spicy marinade. So my mother chooses a different salad. Mine arrives in a bowl filled with luscious, chlorophyll-infused field greens. My mother's bowl is filled with pale romaine.

"Why is your lettuce so much greener than mine?" she asks, eyeing my bowl. I understand that this is her indirect way of saying that she wishes she had my food. Under different circumstances I'd have offered to swap, but, knowing the meat would be too spicy for her, I hold back.

I'm mulling how to answer her, when Zoë gets there first.

"Because they're different kinds of lettuce?" Zoë says, ending her sentence in grating teenage up-speak. Since my mother's remark about the cello, I've noticed a shift in Zoë's attitude toward her—from fondness and protectiveness to occasional short-tempered annoyance.

My mother's face grows taut. "I know they're different kinds of lettuce," she says. She mumbles something about asking for field greens next time, then she's quiet.

After we leave my mother to go to the synagogue, Zoë is still irritated.

"What was that all about?" she asks.

"Well, Grandma Helen doesn't always express herself directly," I say. "And sometimes she even speaks in code, especially when she hopes to be given something that she doesn't want to have to ask for outright."

"What?" Zoë, one of the most direct people I know, isn't familiar with my mother's linguistic cryptograms.

"She wanted my lettuce, not hers. But she couldn't bring herself to say that. I've gotten pretty good at deciphering her code, but I guess it's just confusing to you."

"Yeah, I guess."

We drop it. I hope everything will be fine once we get home from services and watch the season premiere of *Desperate Housewives*, which we've been looking forward to for months. I ask Zoë if she shouldn't have recorded the show, in case services run long. She likes to watch it as it happens, she says, and even enjoys the commercials. It's all part of the ritual.

When we return home after services, the house is cold and dark. As winter approaches, it's becoming evident that the house may be beautiful but, when the wind picks up off the ocean and roars down our street, the single-pane windows on the house rattle, and there's little in the way of insulation to keep the heat in. Our first utility bill was more than we could afford, so now Zoë and I keep the heat off altogether on our floor, while my mother tries to regulate hers by climbing her stairs multiple times a day to fiddle with the thermostat. I've bought fingerless gloves for my mother and me and a down vest for Zoë. Still, the cold air seems to follow us around the house.

I decide to spring for a little heat for *Desperate Housewives* and go to turn up the thermostat while Zoë races upstairs to change out of her good clothes. My mother intercepts me in the hallway. She's swaying from side to side, shifting her weight from one leg to the other, and wringing her hands, habits she's probably had for years but I've never noticed. While she stands there, clearly agitated, I find myself examining the top of her head. Where her head was once covered with thick, wavy hair, I see swaths of white scalp, and reflexively I touch my hand to my own thinning hair. There's so much about my mother that has escaped my notice until now.

She's brooding about the lettuce incident, mainly about how Zoë treated her. "Isn't this holiday you're celebrating all about religion?" she asks rhetorically. "And if it is, then shouldn't it be about trying to be nice?"

"Mom, you're against religion," I reply. "You can't just pull it out of your hat when it's convenient. That's like never praying except in emergencies."

"My point is that she isn't nice."

"Yes, I know that's your point. But let's forget about it."

I leave her in the hallway, and, before long, Zoë and I are on the couch, happily immersed.

My mother comes into the room and seats herself in a stiff chair in the corner. She knows nothing about *Desperate Housewives*, and I hope she won't start asking us to explain what's going on. Luckily, she doesn't. Instead, when a commercial comes on, she asks, "Why didn't you record the show? Then you could skip all this crap."

Zoë starts to explain for the second time that night, but my mother interrupts her. "But you could have recorded it. I don't even remember the last time I sat through a commercial."

A Sprint commercial has ended and we're back on Wisteria Lane, but I'm having trouble focusing on the action on the screen. I'm watching Zoë. My daughter, who has been waiting months for this one television moment, is quiet for a few seconds, then does something that astounds me.

"I don't have to put up with this," she says, and she gets up and leaves the room.

MY MOTHER AND I decide to seek help. We're only six weeks into this and things are already difficult and tense. There are some basic ground rules we have yet to establish. We live in the same house, but does that mean we should be eating dinner together every night? When I make dinner for friends, is she automatically invited as well? And what about the difference in demands on our time? I have to earn a living, while my mother has nothing but free time and wants my attention. This is problematic because I work from home, where my mother has access to me anytime she feels like chatting—which is often. Money is getting tricky too. My mother has suggested splitting all household expenses down the middle, but I can tell she's feeling shortchanged with her living quarters, which are dark and a little oppressive.

We make an appointment to see Lia Manor, a family therapist in Berkeley who specializes in helping people and their aging parents cope with new living arrangements. We've been referred to Lia through a friend of mine, who, like Candace, had voiced reservations about my rescue operation. My hope is that Lia will help us establish a framework for the future, something that will help get us through this cohabitation experiment we've rushed into. I imagine us walking out of Lia's office with a brochure containing intergenerational do's and don'ts. I imagine us taping it on the refrigerator, next to our list of San Francisco composting guidelines. And I imagine everything fixed, those initial signs of trouble nipped in the bud.

Lia looks like she's in her late fifties, hair so gray it's luminescent, her face open and kind. Her office is nestlike and warm, with an area rug under her chair and family photos. I imagine all the people who have sat in this very pair of seats, trying to navigate their way through similar situations.

"So," Lia says. "You haven't lived together in a very long time."

My mother and I both nod.

"Not since I was ten," I say, and I meet my mother's eyes. I turn back to Lia. "Mom was an alcoholic and I was taken away from her." It's the first time in my life I have said anything resembling these words in the presence of my mother.

"Yes," my mother says matter-of-factly. "That's right."

That's all we say, but it's all Lia needs. Once she has heard this two-sentence version of our history, she declares that she is "leery" of our succeeding at the adventure we have embarked upon.

"Whenever a parent moves in with an adult child, it is a crisis," Lia says.

At this moment, the word "crisis" sounds a little over the top to me (I'll change my mind later), but I let it go. No matter what we might think, she continues, we cannot simply act like housemates. Everything that we say and do will be charged with subtext and emotions that are a legacy of the past. Lia clearly knows her stuff. After all, working with elderly people and their adult children is her specialty; she has been doing it for more than two decades.

I'm nodding in affirmation, but my mother decides she's offended by Lia's words and tells her so. Offended? She's taking it personally? Hasn't Lia explained how difficult this is for everyone, even parents and children who have enjoyed a completely peaceful and harmonious relationship with each other? Even when the change involves just a parent moving from another city to an apartment or independent-living facility near the child? And here we are, three generations—my mother, my teenage daughter, and me—sharing one refrigerator. I look over and see that my mother's mouth is pinched. This isn't going the way I had imagined, not at all. In fact, nothing in the experiment my mother and I have set in motion is going the way I had imagined.

Usually, Lia tells us, she's helping a family adjust to having an elderly parent move closer, not in. It's very rare, she explains, for parents and children to move in together, as we are doing, which is why Lia pronounces our situation "a crisis." Having established that as our frame of reference, she tells us there are some basic issues we will need to focus on, issues that affect nearly every family she sees: time, space, and money. She adds that much of our success will hinge on our ability to define clear boundaries—both physical and psychological—when it comes to these things. All of this rings true. It's a lot to absorb in one session, and the hour seems to stretch out much longer than that, though I note as we leave that it was the usual fifty-minute therapy hour.

Walking down the sidewalk toward the car, my mother a few steps ahead of me, I look at her and see not a tiny elderly woman but someone else. There's something about her posture and gait that put me in mind of a cowboy traversing a swamp filled with water moccasins—all on a dare. The very fact that Lia said this won't be easy has hardened my mother's resolve. As soon as we're in the car and the door is shut—as if she wants to be absolutely sure Lia won't hear us—my mother says, "She was so patronizing to me. She kept saying, 'You're so smart.'"

"But you are smart."

"It was still patronizing."

Then she's quiet. We're on our way to a nearby Trader Joe's, and I savor the silence, wondering if she's going over her mental grocery list: Lactaid, frozen vegetables, and salmon, which she'll fret about the entire time it's in the cart as it gathers warm-air "contamination." When we get there, she suggests we take a single cart to avoid redundancies but divide our groceries—my items on one side, hers on the other. Then she says, "We'll make it work." At first I think she's referring to the divided grocery cart, but then I realize she means something else, and I'm not so sure I agree with her. If she's not going to give therapy an honest try—and she seems to distrust Lia already—that's surely going to make things harder. In no mood to be agreeable, I watch her struggle with her good hand to retrieve a half gallon of Lactaid from a high shelf. Pretending I haven't noticed, I turn my back and, cruelly, offer no help.

When we get home, my mother pulls from her bag a receipt for something I had asked her to buy for me a few days earlier.

"You owe me ten dollars," she says.

You owe me a childhood.

And with that I realize that perhaps I should have sought help before creating this situation. For years, whenever I told people about my childhood but assured them that my mother and I were now close, that

I held no anger, they would ask, "How can you be so forgiving?" I always responded with this: You can spend your life carrying hurt and anger toward a parent, or you can get over it and move on. All that time I had thought I resided safely in the latter category, but now I'm seeing that I'm still in the former.

I'm not over it. Not one little bit.

7.

Escape

Don't wait to be hunted to hide.

—Samuel Beckett, MOLLOY

CHERYL THE DOWNSIZER IS ONE OF THOSE PEOPLE WHO PARACHUTE into your life just when it's spinning out of control and perform miracles. Nearly a month after my mother and I started unpacking, we're still surrounded by boxes, and my mother flies Cheryl up from San Diego to help.

Before becoming a professional winnower, Cheryl spent twenty-five years working as a psychiatric nurse. Helping people sort through mountains of accumulated junk requires some psychological hand-holding, a skill Cheryl possesses in abundance, and her presence changes our overall dynamic. If my mother needs something, Cheryl is there to take care of it. If a decision needs to be made, Cheryl is ready to weigh in with an opinion or simply make the decision on her own. I'm in awe of Cheryl's patient tolerance.

My mother's particular and overriding concern is with her car, which is parked on one side of our two-car garage, with stacks of boxes on the other. Since most of the boxes belong to me, I have volunteered to keep my car on the street. Although early evidence appears to indicate that my mother's trips in and out of the garage with her car will be infrequent, she is consumed with worry that the driveway will be blocked—by my car, my friends' cars, strangers' cars, a garbage truck, a presidential motorcade. And she worries that the dozens of boxes stacked on my side of the garage will inch their way over like characters in a Pixar film, preventing her from maneuvering into her spot. She voices this concern to both Cheryl and me. We try to reassure her that even were someone to park a car in a way that hampered her ability to get in or out of the garage, chances are good that we'd be able to track down the owner quickly and get the offending vehicle moved. But what's at stake feels bigger than that. She is asserting a right to her space; half the garage is rightfully hers. If she doesn't keep reminding us of her right to this domain, the boxes are certain to creep over, it is guaranteed someone will block her car. I understand that this need for control is part of what happens when people grow old: They begin to feel diminished or, worse, invisible. But I'm finding it a struggle to be patient in the face of her constant anxiety over small things.

A few days into this, Cheryl lets me know that my mother's attempts at exerting control are not lost on her.

"How do you handle it?" she asks me quietly one day, while in the kitchen helping me organize a cupboard. We're sharing a rare moment without my mother present.

I struggle to find an answer to Cheryl's question, then give up. "I have no idea," I say.

By late that afternoon, I'm feeling frayed, overwhelmed by the mountain of boxes in the house and on guard against the growing tension between my mother and my daughter. So I've retreated to the garage. I'm surveying the collection of boxes out there when my phone rings. It's Bob, a man I've been seeing for the last couple of months. He's in the neighborhood and wants to know if I'd like to meet for a drink. I'm free until 7:15 P.M., when I'm meant to give Zoë and four of her friends a ride to an 8:00 comedy show she told me about two weeks earlier. It's nearly 6:00 P.M., but I figure there's plenty of time.

I walk inside and shout up the stairs to Zoë, "Sweetie, I'm going out. But I'll be home in time to drive you downtown."

"Where are you going?" she shouts back.

I haven't clued Zoë in to Bob's existence, so my response is vague. "Just out. I'll be back."

Next I go to the top of my mother's stairs. She's downstairs with Cheryl.

"Mom, I'm going out," I call down. She, too, knows nothing about Bob.

"When do you think you'll be back?" Then she does something that has begun to annoy me, as it has gradually dawned on me that I am now living my whole life in front of my mother. Without waiting for a reply, she offers her own estimate. "In about an hour?"

"Something like that," I answer, and set out on the ten-minute walk to meet Bob.

Bob and I met through mutual friends. An academic physician, Bob is teddy-bearish, and his looks reflect his easygoing personality. Our first date, dinner at one of Bob's favorite places, was a small disaster. I liked him instantly, but I'm not accustomed to dating. When it comes to relationships, I'm binary: married or not married. In fact, I've never done much traditional dating, which is guided by many unspoken rules. One of those rules, I gathered after my first date with Bob, is that on an initial encounter people usually steer clear of intimate or painful topics. Bob hewed closely to the first-date protocol, offering a brief, polite, and well-rehearsed description of his twenty-year marriage, a union that sounded singularly joyless.

But in the first fifteen minutes of our dinner, even before the wine had been poured, I gave Bob an entire data dump of my convoluted life so far—divorced parents, alcoholic mother, waiflike childhood, dead husband, disastrous marriage on the rebound. Reporting the facts felt like the right thing to do. But partway through my soliloquy, I noticed that Bob looked uncomfortable. Still, I plowed ahead. He told me later that he wasn't merely uncomfortable but was seeking a polite excuse to leave. At the same time, he was taken with my lack of guile, and apparently the latter reaction won out over the former, because since then we've gone out several times.

We're growing on each other. We know people in common beyond the couple who set us up on that first blind date. Bob was a medical resident with Carolyn, one of my closest friends. He's devoted to his two sons (one in college, the other Zoë's age), and he's funny. He's also pragmatic—even programmatic—in his approach to life. When we established the connection to Carolyn on our first date, he suggested, in all earnestness, that I call her for a "reference," which I found endearingly businesslike. Also that evening, he told me that in the two years since his separation he had gone out with thirty-two women and kept a spreadsheet containing each woman's name and age, children's names and ages, and other pertinent information, mainly to ensure that he didn't repeat himself on subsequent dates. I was at once appalled and impressed and made a mental note to myself: *Should Bob and I ever grow close, ask to see that spreadsheet—not just my own entry but those of the thirty-two others.*

Bob travels a lot, mostly to give talks on preventing medical mistakes and on hospital medicine (he helped create the "hospitalist" specialty, which refers to internists who see only hospitalized patients). Dating someone who's out of town a lot is fine with me. Having recently climbed my way out of a swamp of pain, I'm more than content to be seeing someone whose frequent absences will make a deep romantic entanglement a challenge.

Unaware of my shuttle-service obligation, Bob has decided we should scrap the drinks and go for a full meal. I say nothing to him about the tight timing. I love the idea of a meal with Bob, and things are so new between us that I'm not ready to confess I'm a slave to my child. We go to a neighborhood Italian restaurant known for its homemade pastas. But the math isn't adding up. By the time our food arrives, it's already 6:45. When Bob orders a second glass of wine, I know I'm sunk. So I carry out a small rebellion—against the tether of Zoë's constant stream of needs and requests, their intensity compounded by her separation anxiety. I ignore both the time and my phone, vibrating from somewhere deep inside my bag.

By 7:20, Zoë is placing her fourth or fifth call to me. I see this only by accident, when I reach into my bag for something else. I answer the call.

"Where are you??" she yells.

"I'm in a restaurant."

"What? I told you we had to leave by 7:15!"

My jailbreak isn't going well. How I expected to get away with this I am currently at a loss to explain, even to myself.

Bob has yet to meet Zoë, and until this moment she hasn't been much more to him than an entry under "Children Y/N" in his dating spreadsheet. But he's going to meet her now, because I tell her to walk down to the restaurant.

Bob's seat faces the door, and ten minutes later he looks up to see a sudden squall in the form of an enraged teenager sweeping into the quiet restaurant. Zoë doesn't say hello to Bob, since he, at this moment, is merely a prop in the drama, at least to her. Perhaps I should introduce them—my potential new boyfriend and my crazed teenager—but even in my delusional state of mind I can see that events are overtaking any possible attempt at normal etiquette. And it has just now occurred to me that telling Zoë to come to the restaurant made no sense, because I left my car at home. It also made no sense because, in general, if one is going to have a scene with a fuming child, it's best to do so out of view of innocent bystanders, to say nothing of new romantic interests. With Zoë standing six inches from the table, my utter boneheadedness is unspooling before my eyes. I sheepishly mention the car problem to her, and—in case I thought things couldn't get any worse—she starts to scream.

"What? How are we supposed to get there? What the hell are you thinking? You didn't tell me you were going out on a *date*!"

I start to say it's not so much a date as a spontaneous rendezvous, but I sense that my splitting of hairs won't go over well, and I stop myself. She's as furious as I've ever seen her.

"Why weren't you answering your phone?"

Zoë's perfectly reasonable question stumps me. I seem to keep burying my head in the sand, hoping that when I surface all will be well. It's not working.

"Where are your friends?" I ask lamely.

"THEY'RE OUTSIDE!"

I look behind me, and, sure enough, four lanky, long-necked high school boys are standing awkwardly out on the sidewalk, craning for a view of the ruckus inside.

As a doctor, Bob is clearly accustomed to managing crises involving distraught patients and their families. But I'm guessing he had no med-school rotation in how to handle heat-of-the-moment dramas between apoplectic teenage girls and mothers who have gone temporarily insane. Still, he chimes in calmly with a suggestion. Since his car is parked outside, he'll drive the five of them to the theater while I stay, finish my dinner, and pay the bill. Zoë accepts his offer but makes it clear I'm not off the hook.

"I expect compensation," she says.

"Compensation?" I make the mistake of asking. "What kind of compensation?"

"Money."

I'm mortified, and Bob looks amazed. He isn't charmed. I know I'm to blame for setting this whole hysterical episode in motion, and I also know that Zoë's behavior is execrable. But were I to say anything to her at the moment, it would only make matters worse, so I'm silent.

Zoë shoots me a look and they leave.

I don't know what to do. I look down at my pasta, now cold. Bob cleaned his plate, but his second glass of Chianti, which arrived minutes before Zoë did, is still full. I toy with the idea of chugging his wine, but instead I pay the bill.

As I shuffle home, I see that Bob has sent me a text: `Mission accomplished. She calmed down and friends were delightful. Glad to be of service.`

Wow, I think. *Nice guy.*

When I get back, my mother is in the kitchen. I offer a brief version of what has happened.

"Zoë's behavior is extreme," she says. Once she has my ear, she seizes the opportunity to offer more of her unsolicited view. "I'm very worried about Zoë. She never seems happy. Shouldn't she be happier?"

"She's a teenager," I say quickly. Anticipating a rebuttal I have no desire to hear, I take the unusual step of cutting my mother off. "Mom, you've never raised a teenager."

We're both a little stunned as we take in the implications of what I've just said. Then she looks me square in the eye. "You're right."

Part Two

Autumn

8.

Domestics

Nobody has ever before asked the nuclear family to live all by itself in a box the way we do. With no relatives, no support, we've put it in an impossible situation.

—Margaret Mead, in an interview

IN THE MIDDLE OF THE NINETEENTH CENTURY, TWO OUT OF EVERY three Americans lived on farms, and the vast majority of those households contained multiple generations. That made sense, given the continuity of the farming life, the seamless passing of land to the next generation.

Until World War II, roughly one in four American households contained multiple generations. Over the years, as the number of family farms dwindled, so, too, did intergenerational living. With no farm to inherit, there was little reason for adult children to live at home. Some sociologists argue that even when such living arrangements were commonplace, they weren't what people really wanted. Financial hardship was the determining factor. In the 1950s, as the nation recovered from the privations of the Depression and World War II, Americans began to associate nuclear households with affluence. Added to this was a strong societal emphasis on "maturity" and the desire for young couples who were starting families to strike out on their own. Accordingly, the multigenerational American household fell out of favor. At the end of the twentieth century, fewer than 15 percent of people age sixty-five and older lived with their adult children.

While contemporary survey-takers have found that a majority of baby boomers consider it their responsibility to take in an elderly parent who needs help, few actually do it. And when they do, it's usually because of the elderly parent's financial duress. Never has a social scientist cited cockeyed optimism as the motivating factor. This makes my mother and me statistical freaks. So surprised are people when we tell them what we're doing that I'm beginning to guess that for every ten thousand households of combined generations, only one is a threesome of white middle-class females carrying out a misguided experiment.

This is because most people know better than to try what we're trying. They know—as Lia warned—that everything can turn into a tug-of-war, that battlefields can be as small as a utensil drawer, plump with meaning. They know that after a while you start to hate yourself, as you see yourself revert to age six, or ten. These are the same realistic and sensible people who say, "I'm fine visiting my mother or having her visit me. But forty-eight hours is the most I can stand."

Sure enough, as quickly as my mother appeared in our daily lives, that's how fast things have begun to unravel. *Really* unravel. Zoë, who only two months earlier cleaned the apartment and greeted her grandmother with flowers, has begun to keep a wary distance from her, which, of course, hurts my mother's feelings. But Zoë is hurt too. She thought she'd have a warm, fulfilling relationship with her grandmother and was unprepared for my mother's hastiness to judge, her circumlocutions, her tone deafness around kids. And, having heard nothing but carefully worded encouragement for years, Zoë was particularly unprepared to have her cello-playing criticized by my mother.

Zoë has now stopped practicing her instrument altogether. It lies in its case in a corner of the living room. She doesn't give it a second look. She stays in her room most of the time, on her computer. I hope it's schoolwork, but I suspect it's Facebook. As for me, I haven't done any actual work, the kind that brings in money, for the past few weeks. I've taken on a fascinating assignment researching and editing a book for a well-known Silicon Valley venture capitalist. He pays me by the hour, and if I don't work, I don't get paid.

My mother makes careful note of every shared expense. If she pays for something we've agreed to split, such as a session with Lia, her request for reimbursement, which she sends to me via email, is made as soon as possible. My mother is appalled by how expensive everything is in San Francisco. In particular, her cleaning lady in San Diego charged nothing compared with cleaning ladies here. She does concede that Blanca, the cleaning woman recommended to us by our landlady, does a nice job in the kitchen. She's particularly impressed by Blanca's skill with a trash can and invites me one day to take a look. We stand together over the trash can, peering in at Blanca's handiwork. The white trash bag is folded so skillfully in and around the hard-plastic liner, you'd never know it's there.

My mother's need to focus on the minutiae of not just her own but other people's everyday lives, which she had so successfully exercised on Norm, now has no outlet. When she lived five hundred miles away, I found it amusing. Such behavior may be extreme, but it wasn't directed at me. Now, living under the same roof, it feels as if she's in my business every minute. Laundry is a favorite focus, requiring her constant vigilance: The lid to the washing machine must remain open; otherwise, mold and germs will collect. Dish towels will gather bacteria if not put immediately into the dryer.

The kitchen is the worst. My mother is unhappy that it is not hers alone. And at the same time that she watches my every move, she believes I think that everything she does is wrong. But then, how could she not? I had quickly established myself as the only true cook of the household and therefore the one in charge of the kitchen. My mother used to cook when she and Norm were together—simple, nutritious meals—but when their health began to fail, cooking was one of the first things to go, in favor of microwaving, which is what she still does. I once opened her oven in San Diego to find she was using it to store a large bowl.

My mother tells me she was an enthusiastic cook and baker when we lived in Rochester, and no doubt she was—at least for a while. But I have no memory of her whipping up cookies or cakes, or anything else for that matter, in the Rochester kitchen. I do, however, remember a scene that occurred in the small breakfast room behind the kitchen. I hear her screaming at my father. I see a plate flying at the wall, a piece of their wedding china, classic Ashford-gray Wedgwood painted with silver figs.

I learned cooking from watching others through the years, then trying things out on my own. Food became, for me, the ultimate symbol of warmth and nurturing. By paying attention to what I'm cooking, I like to think I'm paying attention to the people I'm cooking for. And for an enthusiastic cook, "a kitchen of one's own" can become a place of pride and creation. There's a great feeling of comfort to be found in an orderly kitchen. I learned this from Matt and his mother, Denny. Wooden spoons and cooking tools and salad servers go in one large ceramic pot on the counter, everything metal in another. Whisks have their own container, which also resides on the counter. Salt lives in a tiny wooden dish, and garlic in a pedestal bowl Denny made for me in 1973, when I was fifteen. This is how it is. And no matter where I live, this is what my kitchen counter will look like. My mother clearly gets the message, because whatever psychological sleight of hand I have employed, it is enough to get the kitchen looking exactly as I want it. As for the refrigerator, I've staked my claim there, too, and my mother has retreated conspicuously to keeping all her own perishables in one drawer. Food, and everything involved in its preparation and storage, has become the stage upon which I carry out my acid corrective against my mother.

There are moments when I allow myself to appreciate how painful all these power plays must be for her. Two months into living under the same roof and our relationship is bringing out a mean streak in me I scarcely knew existed. More than anything, what my mother wants is my attention, and I discover soon after she arrives in San Francisco that it is the one thing over which I have complete control. I become stingy with it. If she has a question, I allow her to ask it but make certain to appear absorbed in another task while she does. If she needs me to help her with something, I do it grudgingly, stiff with duty.

Such are the petty ways I exact my revenge, without really allowing myself to think about what I'm doing. But what am I seeking revenge for? My mother's failure to model how to cook or set up a kitchen? Of course not. The causes go much deeper, deeper than I want to admit, because that would require facing up to how much I longed for her in my childhood and how angry I still am at her desertion. The revenge is all about demonstrating that I've done just fine without, and despite, her.

9.

Back on the Road

California is a tragic country—
like Palestine, like every Promised Land.

—Christopher Isherwood, EXHUMATIONS

"DOING A GEOGRAPHIC" IS A TERM RECOVERING ALCOHOLICS OFTEN use for acting on the impulse to start over by moving to a new town, or state, instead of making any internal changes. It's the anywhere-but-here part of the disease that says, "Remove yourself from this, go someplace new, and everything will be better."

Two years into our Florida stint, my mother pulled a geographic as radical as the move from Rochester. The new plan was to head for California. She enrolled in the mathematics graduate program at the University of California's shiny new campus in San Diego, and as soon as our elementary school let out for the summer, she put us into a new Buick station wagon—a gift from her parents—and drove us across the country. My assessment at the time, from a seven-year-old's vantage point, was that my mother hadn't been having much fun. I knew she hated the mosquitoes as much as we did. San Diego, she told us, was mosquito-free. And she must have presented the plan to us as a continuation of our big adventure, this extended road trip we were on.

You'd think we'd have protested at yet another move. After all, having been duped before, we were in no position to believe that the next move would be any different. But I have no memory of being unhappy about the news. Because that's what often happens when an alcoholic parent is doing a geographic. She pulls you in and, before you know it, you, too, believe in the promise of the new place. And you fall in love with it, too, sight unseen. We packed the car with Archie comic books for me and several volumes of Nancy Drew mysteries for Sarah, whose literary taste seemed so grown-up to me at the time. The three of us delighted in ticking off each state—Alabama, Mississippi, Louisiana—after reaching its westernmost edge. But the drive across Texas seemed to last a lifetime, and the sheer tedium of traversing the vastness of that state seemed to sap my mother's spirit.

As with the first move, we stopped at cheap motels, one of which had a pool with a high dive. Somehow my mother got it into her head that Sarah and I should conquer it. She wanted Sarah to dive the twenty feet into the water. I, she said, could simply jump. Sarah balked at first, then pulled herself together quickly and dove. But I was terrified. I stood on that trembling board, its sandpaper surface chafing the bottom of my feet, for what felt like hours, crying, my legs knocking together with fright. My mother refused to stand down, and finally I jumped. She wrapped us in towels and gave each of us a ballpoint pen as a reward. I remember thinking afterward, at age seven, *What was she trying to prove?* I see now that our courage was hers, our flight off that board a proxy for her own leap into a new life. That's why we couldn't let her down.

When we arrived in San Diego, we checked in to the Travelodge near the airport. My mother told us that she would find us a wonderful place to live. After seeing some of the possibilities, Sarah and I asked my mother to please rule out an apartment complex in nearby La Jolla—named, appropriately enough, the La Jollans—that we had passed a few times while driving up the hill to UCSD. The buildings were as dingy and brown as the dry hills that surrounded them, and Sarah and I both took an immediate dislike to the place. But my mother rented an apartment at the La Jollans anyway, because living there meant we could walk to school. Once we nested in the new place, we were fine with it. My mother set up the television in our bedroom, and she bought us our own bookshelf for my comic books (which I cataloged and shelved with a librarian's precision) and the many volumes in Sarah's Nancy Drew collection. The complex had a swimming pool and, best of all, nearby woods and a range of bald hills that were ideal for endless exploration. Our favorite thing to do was slide down the steepest hill on large pieces of cardboard, a California version of sledding that kept us occupied for hours.

My mother began her new life as a graduate student, while Sarah and I set out for yet another school. Every morning we walked the half mile to Scripps Elementary School. We made new friends. In Florida, the teachers punished misbehavior by hitting children's upturned wrists with a ruler. In San Diego, no such thing was allowed. And my mother was right: We never saw a mosquito.

Not surprisingly, my mother's troubles had followed us west. She had failed to grasp, perhaps, that when you flee you can't leave yourself behind. The set had changed, but the basic script remained the same. As we had learned to do in Florida, Sarah and I watched for small things that might trip a switch in my mother and send her into a binge. In San Diego, it began with a cake. She had met a man, and she was smitten. One weekend morning she decided she would make him a chocolate cake and that the three of us would go to his house to give it to him. Perhaps she pictured in her mind's eye what he would see—the striking young mother and her irresistible little girls, bearing a freshly baked cake. Her happy anticipation was infectious, and by the time we got into the car, we were on a jolly outing. When we arrived at the man's apartment complex, my mother carried the cake up the walk to his door and rang the bell. The man opened the front door but kept the screen door between him and us latched. He was very handsome. He had a towel around his waist, giving me a fine view of his strong, hirsute chest. I don't remember the words that were exchanged, but I do remember a sense of terrible awkwardness between the two grown-ups. In less than a minute, we were back in the car, and so was the cake. Upset and humiliated, my mother drove us home.

Not long after, she bought an unfinished table, painted it a glossy orange, and set it out on the back patio to dry in the Southern California sun. Within an hour, the noontime sun had not dried the paint but caused a collection of blisters to form. Then one of the cats jumped on the table. My mother lost her temper. She screamed at the cat. She screamed at us, went up to her bedroom, and didn't come out—for a night, or two nights, or some number of days and nights that I no longer recall. We were back on our own. Finally she emerged. The table was still outside on the patio; I thought we should have fixed it for her. But how? My mother looked pale.

"Do you know what today is?" she asked accusingly.

We shook our heads.

"It's my birthday." Then she turned her back to us and stumbled her way up the stairs.

It was at that moment that I first experienced what it felt like to take on guilt for a crime I wasn't aware of having committed. It wasn't only that it was my mother's birthday and I hadn't known or done anything about it, but I must also have felt that our oversight was what had sent her into a drunken tailspin that just seemed to go on and on. And it was on that day, too, that I began to feel responsible for someone I didn't know how to take care of.

Since that day in 1965, I've been very aware of my mother's birthday and have tried for years to please her with gifts she might enjoy. By and large, I've succeeded, and she always seems to appreciate my thoughtfulness, pronouncing each gift "just what I needed but didn't think to buy for myself." I savor the praise.

MY MOTHER'S SEVENTY-EIGHTH BIRTHDAY is nearly upon us. This is the first time we've been together on her birthday since I was ten years old. As it happens, a friend of mine is going to be in town for a book tour, and he's giving a reading the night of my mother's birthday. It occurs to me that it might be nice to throw a party for him, and, since my mother hasn't yet made any friends in San Francisco, it might also give her the chance to meet people in a festive setting. I couldn't have been more mistaken. When I tell her the plan, I can see she's offended at my making a party for someone else on the day of her birthday, even though she doesn't say anything outright. By that time, however, there's nothing I can do. The invitations have been sent out. I'm hoping that the ideal present will help right the ship, so I'm on the lookout. A week or so before my mother's birthday, while at a nursery, I spot a topiary dog—a delightful, life-sized terrier covered in ivy. I know at once that it's the perfect gift for such a passionate dog lover.

My mother's preoccupation with dogs started in the early 1980s, when she and Norm started raising a series of German shepherds and German shepherd mixes. My grandmother had owned standard poodles and named them all, without exception, after characters in Mozart operas—Lorenzo, Zerlina, etc. My mother followed suit, not just naming them after Mozart operas but once even choosing the same name—Papageno—her mother had used.

During most of my mother's years with Norm, the dogs became her reason for living. She hovered and worried, took them to dog school, fretted over their diet, cooked them fresh chicken, and was soon an expert in all things dog. When it came to dog sitters, dog walkers, dog trainers, and medical procedures for the dogs, no expense was spared. Around the house were sprinkled the obligatory family photographs, but for the most part my mother's emotional lens was focused on the dogs, and so was the camera. Roll after roll of film was devoted to dogs on a leash and off, dogs sitting, walking, running, jumping, eating, sleeping. When the time came to put them down, she grieved intensely. The attention, care, and time my mother devoted to her dogs was so much greater than what she had given her children that it was hard for her to let the discrepancy go unremarked. In an oblique stab at apology, she told me several times over the years that raising dogs was her second chance at parenting.

Now that my mother no longer owns a dog, I feel more charitable toward her canine-loving ways, and an early birthday gift of the topiary terrier seems perfect. When I present it to her, a white ribbon around its stiff little neck, she loves it and decides she wants to name it. Her first suggestion is Cherubino, the Mozart-inspired name of one of my grandmother's poodles in the 1960s.

"Don't you think we're done with those Mozart opera names?" I ask. She agrees and runs through a few more possibilities before settling on "Porter." She keeps Porter outside her front door at the lower level and buys him a special watering can. I'm pleased.

For weeks she has been admiring my wristwatch—a simple Swiss-made timepiece that Matt gave me many years ago. She wants one like it. We decide to go off to Bloomingdale's for a birthday shopping trip for her. It's understood that a watch will be another birthday gift to her.

Zoë, in the meantime, has been lobbying for a fall shopping expedition. So I strike a deal with the two of them: It's established that this is to be her grandmother's birthday trip, but Zoë can accompany us and try on clothes by herself. I instruct Zoë to call me from her dressing room when she's ready for me to inspect her items.

We arrive at Bloomingdale's and, according to plan, Zoë sets off for the third floor. As I watch her hurry away, it occurs to me that I've forgotten to give her a dollar limit. My mother and I stay down at accessories and head straight for the watch department. She sees nothing she likes and certainly nothing resembling my watch. Just as we're about to abandon the watch counter, a Gucci dress watch catches my eye. I point it out to my mother, who urges me to try it on—and I do. I've never owned a fancy watch or even had one on my wrist. I rotate my forearm a few times, admire the watch, fantasize about owning it, then take it off and hand it back to the salesman.

At the earring counter, we're helped by a young woman who possesses an infinite store of patience. My mother examines a dozen different earrings before finally deciding on a pair. Just as we're moving on to scarves, my phone rings. It's Zoë, who's ready for me to come up to her dressing room to check out her selections. By this time, not one but two nice saleswomen in the scarf department are assisting my mother.

"I have to run up to see what Zoë's picked out," I say.

My mother looks at me matter-of-factly and says, "I'll take a taxi home."

"No, you will not take a taxi home. This will take only a few minutes." I turn to the saleswomen. "She is not to take a taxi home."

The young saleswomen look amused. "You are not to take a taxi home," one of them says to my mother, with mock sternness.

I rush up the escalator to Zoë's dressing room. The kid is surrounded by clothing, and she's got my number. She knows I feel bad for spending the entire time with my mother, not her, and she knows I'm distracted and can't take the time to veto any of her choices—which means I lack not only the time but the guts to say no.

"Whatever," I say, and rush back down to find my mother, who is ready to look at coats.

It's another testament to my willful optimism that I failed to see how sideways this little field trip could go, how forcefully I would be pulled from both sides. In fact, before we set out, I was sure we would have a lovely afternoon, during which we'd accomplish our separate goals and move closer to one another, because that's what families do. But once again I've failed to understand how much these deceptively simple rituals rest on a foundation of love, respect, and a willingness to give and take. My efforts at righting the tilt of this canted trio keep backfiring. It's at times like this when the intervention of reality is most painful, when my urge to create a family feels tragic in its hopelessness.

10.

Money

Family history, of course, has its proper dietary laws. One is supposed to swallow and digest only the permitted parts of it, the halal portions of the past, drained of their redness, their blood.

—Salman Rushdie, MIDNIGHT'S CHILDREN

WE'RE SEATED IN LIA'S OFFICE, AND MY MOTHER SAYS THERE'S something she'd like to talk about right away.

"Katie sits on her wallet," she announces.

I feel my face go hot. She's accusing me of stinginess, but I have no idea what's coming next. She continues, "She sits on her wallet when it comes to others, but she's happy to spend money on herself." And she tells Lia the story of my fascination with the expensive watch.

I'm stupefied. "But I didn't buy it," I say.

"No, you didn't," she says. So what is this about? As I will discover, this is but the first of many indications that my mother has fastened on money as an issue—perhaps *the* issue—that is dividing us. Come to think of it, as issues go, it isn't new. It's a festering sore of a topic. For my part, I think my mother's priorities are all wrong. I'm angry that she spent tens of thousands of dollars on her dogs while paying precious little for my education and that she's continuing the pattern by contributing nothing to Zoë's education either. And now I see that she views *me* as self-indulgent, perfectly willing to think about dropping $700 on a trinket for myself but—but what? I'm stumped.

We're hardly the first family to be haunted by money issues. High-profile fights over the family coffers are in the news all the time. And they aren't reserved for the Helmsleys and Astors and assorted landed gentry duking it out over inheritances the size of a small African country's economy. Money plagues families rich and not so rich, famous and obscure. Just because there's less money to fight about doesn't mean it's less of a flash point. While for many families money is a way to manipulate others and exercise power, in my family's bloodstream it's even more toxic than that: It's the virus that always lies dormant, erupting occasionally into full-blown painful lesions.

I caught drift of this problem in our family early in life. Perhaps unintentionally—perhaps not—my mother made certain of that. When I was twelve, I sent a birthday gift to my grandfather. My mother wasted no time in reporting to me that her parents decided I had done this not out of love or thoughtfulness but in order to get a shot at their money someday. Their reaction was obnoxious and paranoid, but for my mother to have told me about it was still further off the mark.

Kate Levinson, a psychotherapist in Northern California, specializes in the topic of women and their relationship to money. In her book, aptly titled *Emotional Currency*, Levinson wrote that if we have enough money to cover our basic living expenses, much of the angst we experience around money stems from what she calls "our inner money life." For women, it also represents a tangled skein of emotions. We use money to act out feelings we're unable to acknowledge or express in other ways. Nowhere does this play itself out more poignantly than in family dynamics.

The topic of money has clouded my sister's entire view of life. When Sarah was truly impoverished, she complained that she never had enough money, and although she is now settled in a lovely large house, with a stable marriage and a husband who has a good job, she hasn't stopped worrying. Year after year, I've been poised to buy gifts for her, only to have her change her mind and tell me that what she really *needs*—instead of the tub of Patricia Wexler skin-regenerating serum or the boots from Zappos.com that she's already picked out—is the cash equivalent and could I please send a check instead. She doesn't really need the cash, of course, but money handed to her by family members symbolizes something deep.

For most of her adult life, Sarah has fretted that my mother will strike her from her will—with good reason. Over the years, in reaction to Sarah-inspired upsets, my mother has spent thousands of dollars on lawyers, instructing them to excise Sarah from her will, then put her back in once the storm blows over. At the same time, she once told me she was planning to leave $100,000 to her dog trainer, in case her dogs outlived her.

The source of my mother's troubled way with money isn't hard to trace. My grandparents used money as a bludgeon. Money certainly didn't bring them happiness, but, as Helen Gurley Brown once put it, at least it helped make them miserable in comfort. They could have been generous toward their daughters, but they weren't. When my mother's sister once asked them for a loan, they agreed but informed her they would require interest at a rate comparable to what a bank would charge.

My grandfather died in 1986, and my grandmother died three years later. It was up to my grandmother to make the final decision on bequests. She once said she didn't "believe in inheritance." Accordingly, in the end, she sold her house, as well as all the rare books, the artwork, and nearly all of her property on Cape Cod, and donated most of the proceeds to Massachusetts General Hospital and Harvard Medical School, where she had conducted her research. Her longtime live-in maid, a lovely Irish woman who had devoted most of her adult life to my grandmother, received a pittance of a few thousand dollars. My grandmother left her beautiful Steinway piano to one of my grandfather's colleagues at MIT.

As for my mother and aunt, my grandmother left a trust in their names. But she didn't actually leave it for them. Her two daughters were given not the full amount of the trust but the *interest* on the principal. My grandmother's final instructions—giving a sizable sum to two institutions, then putting the rest of the principal out of reach of her children while tantalizing them with interest payments that reminded them how much they weren't getting—seemed designed to inflict pain, to humiliate. Over the years, if my mother needed, say, a new car, she had to appeal to the Boston lawyer my grandmother had named as executor, who would release funds for the purchase. No doubt this exercise in parental sadism had a profound effect on my mother's feelings about money, about inheritance, about what parents owe their children—and on what is happening between us right now.

I, too, have a troubled relationship with money. I hoard it one week, then splurge on, for example, an expensive vacation for Zoë and me the next. I've always made certain I'm working and solvent. Still, I constantly worry and fret about money and can see myself as one of those old ladies with bills stuffed in a drawer, living on Arrowroot biscuits. Zoë inherited her expensive taste from her father, Matt. (His family and I used to joke that he was descended from an aristocratic branch of the family no one had ever heard of.) No supermarket shampoo for my daughter; only "product" sold at the salon. At restaurants, if she intimates that she'd like to order an expensive main course, I shoot daggers at her until she retreats to a cheaper dish. If she pushes me a little too far about a purchase I consider unreasonable, I blow up and lecture her about how hard I have to work so she can buy her designer jeans. None of this is terribly rational, I know.

In Lia's office, my mother isn't finished. She tells Lia that she paid for Cheryl to come up and help unpack, and she resents the fact that I haven't offered to contribute. My mother has been stewing about this for some time but never mentioned anything until now. She didn't ask me to chip in, and if she had, I probably would have—or I might have decided to unpack myself. It was my understanding that this was a gift, an acknowledgment that I was upending my own life to accommodate hers. I'm speechless.

Perhaps Lia considers it too soon to focus on the meaning of money in our relationship, for she seizes the opportunity to point out that money is only one of the many issues we're coping with. She asks us what we're doing with our assignment to create distinct boundaries and guidelines around the issues of time and space as well as money. We tell her we've been trying to come up with ways to give me the time and space I need to get my work done and to live my life. As for money, we split every household expenditure; Cheryl's bill is the notable exception.

Lia nods approvingly when she hears of our progress, but the Cheryl topic is left to smolder, because my mother has another subject she'd like to bring up: Zoë. "I find Zoë uncivil and incredibly rude," she says. "And horrid," she adds, just in case "uncivil and incredibly rude" didn't get the point across.

Lia tries to zoom out to the big picture, to get my mother to see things more objectively. "There's something really fascinating about teenagers," Lia says, "if you can get beyond being hurt by them to trying to understand what makes these kids tick. It's not about loving or hating you. She's testing you, for sure, because you're a rival for her mom's love, and the question is, Are you able to love her, in spite of all that?"

My mother ignores the suggestion that she try to see beyond the narrow horizon of her own hurt feelings. "It's uncomfortable for me just to go up to the kitchen or to be down in my little cellar listening to them." By "them," I assume she is referring to Zoë and me.

It's too late in the hour to start in on this train wreck of a topic, so I deliberately change the subject.

"It's Mom's birthday today!" I say.

Lia's face brightens. God bless her. None of this can be easy to listen to. "Happy birthday!" she says to my mother. "What are you doing to celebrate?"

A loaded question, although Lia doesn't know it. I've been preparing for Thad's book party, and after our session, because I still have to buy food, we'll be going shopping on the way home. Clearly miffed that she doesn't have my full and undivided attention on her birthday, my mother goes into martyr mode for Lia.

"I'll be helping Katie shop for the party she's giving her friend," she says, "and that's fine with me." Sometimes, she plays the part of the stereotypical Jewish grandmother—the one who, when the lightbulb burns out, says, "Don't worry about me, I'll just sit in the dark"—with the skill of a seasoned Borscht Belt actress. *

At the end of the session, all Lia can say is this: "I'm going to tell you again how difficult this is. It's so difficult that I'm touched just by the fact that you are trying."

By the time my mother and I get home, the car loaded with party provisions, our mutual unhappiness poisoning the air between us, I'm determined to find some way of pleasing her. Maybe I haven't expended sufficient effort for her birthday. Even though I did give her a watch, I did so by reimbursing her for one she bought online after we failed to find the precise design at Bloomingdale's. This made the whole thing feel awfully businesslike. So, after dropping my mother off, I run out to buy her an exotic orchid from a specialty orchid store. Then I stop at another store and buy her another birthday card, this one made out of chocolate. I take the orchid home and put it on the kitchen table with the festive chocolate bar propped up against it. My mother comes into the kitchen and walks right past it. I have to point it out to her. She seems a bit confused by the chocolate, but delighted by the orchid.

At the party that night, everyone is taken with my mother, who has dressed up in slacks, a silk scarf tied around her neck with enough flair to impress a Parisian, and handsome black boots. For much of the evening, she's surrounded by a small clutch of people. "She's so lovely," people say to me. As the party is winding down, someone sits down at the Steinway and we all sing "Happy Birthday" to my mother, who looks genuinely pleased. I'm amazed, but I shouldn't be: To this day, step into any crowded room and my mother's face is the one you'll see at the center of the gathering.

II.

Halloween

Most people experience love, without noticing that there is anything remarkable about it.

—Boris Pasternak, DOCTOR ZHIVAGO

I ONCE HAD A CONVERSATION WITH A WOMAN SEATED NEXT TO ME on an airplane who, it came out, had lost her husband when her child was young, just as I had. She had only one question for me: Did I stay in touch with my in-laws? Hers lived far away, she told me, and she found visits a melancholy chore. Not wanting to paint too rosy a picture for her and make her feel even worse by comparison, I simply told her that, yes, I did visit my in-laws regularly, as I wanted my daughter to stay connected to her grandparents, who loved her very much.

While what I said was true, my desire to remain close to my in-laws runs far deeper. Matt's parents, Dick and Denny, have been a big part of my life since childhood, and I adore them—always have. I simply love being with them. Beyond that, there's this: Denny and Dick had four boys and lost two. This is a loss of such unimaginable magnitude that even now I have trouble writing it down. Both Denny and Dick, especially Dick, seldom speak of their dead sons. But I know the pain they must feel, and if there is one small thing I can do to lessen it, I will.

Which is why at least once a year, every year, no matter what, I take Zoë to see them.

The day after my mother's birthday, Zoë and I are on an early flight to Austin for a visit. When Zoë was born in 1993, Matt and I were living in Austin and having what can only be described as the sweetest time of our lives. Matt worked at the University of Texas; I was a contributing editor for *Newsweek*. Small pleasures sated us, especially anything to do with watching Zoë discover life. Matt's family had been in Austin, in the lumber business, for several generations, and much of the Lyon clan was now back in town, including Dick and Denny, who had settled in a house they built on a plot of family land out on Lake Travis. Matt and Zoë and I lived just south of the Colorado River in a big yellow house built in the early 1900s by a distant relative of Denny's, the aptly named Mr. Greathouse. The house had not one but two staircases. Our family gatherings at Dick and Denny's lake house were frequent, raucous, and happy. Zoë, blond and spirited, was doted on by one and all. Her main memory is of Denny as a Mother Goose figure, cooking and baking for her brood. Mine is of constant laughter. After we moved away, we returned often for holidays. Austin still feels not just familiar but familial. I've long since given up on having roots of my own, but I appreciate the deep roots Matt had there and am always happy to take my little native Texan to visit her grandparents.

When we arrive, it's as if nothing has changed. In mid-October, Austin is no longer scorched by heat. On the cusp of the new season, the city is awaiting that first "blue norther," the cold snap that ushers in the Texas winter. Both Dick and Denny, now living in a house close to Matt's brother Alex, are far less mobile than they used to be, especially Dick, who is afflicted with a progressive muscle-wasting disease and seldom leaves the house. But they still slip easily into their old roles. Denny immediately sets herself to the grandmotherly task of making Zoë feel enveloped in love. Dick sits opposite me at the dining table and we discuss the state of the world and the demise of journalism. What Zoë and I have in this home is what we had been hoping for in San Francisco. Denny asks Zoë question after question. She lets Zoë finish her answer, then latches on to something Zoë has said and uses it to develop the next question—the sign of a true listener.

"How are your teachers?" Denny asks.

"You'd like Jesse," Zoë says, referring to her history teacher, who is now Zoë's pal.

"Oh, really? Tell me about Jesse."

"He's so funny," Zoë starts to say, then she's off on a tangent, the words tumbling out of her. "Denny! Have you seen the Kwanzaa cake video?"

Denny dips her head and looks up at her granddaughter from over the top of her glasses. Her tone is grave but her eyes are twinkling. "The Kwanzaa cake video? No, I have not seen the Kwanzaa cake video."

Zoë pulls out her iPhone, and for the next three minutes, grandmother and granddaughter are hunched over the two-inch screen, laughing to the point of tears at Sandra Lee's "Angel Food Harvest Cake for Kwanzaa." Each insane ingredient announced by the perfectly serious Ms. Lee is cause for a new burst of mirth.

"Is that really canned apple-pie filling she's pouring into the middle??"

"Wait, are those corn nuts??" asks Denny when Sandra Lee suggests decorating the cake with "acorns." Now Denny is squinting hard at the screen. "Oh, my. Those *are* corn nuts!"

Their chemistry is something to behold. When Zoë was seven, for some reason she started to call Denny "Pearl." Denny calls her "Precious." Every card Denny sends to Zoë begins with "Dear Precious." As far as Denny is concerned, Zoë is a precious gift—and always has been.

The feeling is mutual, and the evidence of this is ever present. When Zoë is with Denny, her brattiness melts away. She speaks to her grandmother sweetly, respectfully. And on this trip, in particular, sitting in Denny's warm and familiar kitchen, I'm struck by the contrast between how my child acts toward this grandmother versus the one back in California. I always sleep well at Dick and Denny's, and this trip is no exception. In San Francisco, I've been lying awake late at night, my mind churning, wondering if this experiment in living with my mother will drive me mad. Every night in Austin, in one of the house's dark bedrooms, I enjoy a sleep better than any I've had in weeks.

On the plane on the way home, Zoë asks, "Why is it just so easy with Denny?" I tell her that what Denny gives her is unconditional love.

SOON AFTER WE RETURN, my mother's expensive birthday orchid dies. First it sheds its flowers—which wither, then float to the kitchen floor—before dropping its fat green leaves. Once they lose their purchase on the stem, the leaves fall one by one and hit the floor with pitiful little thwacks. Determined not to read too much symbolism into the demise of the plant, I take it back to the store. The proprietor tells me I've probably "shocked" the poor thing by placing it too close to a window. She replaces it with a similar orchid, which I put in the dark living room. About a week later, that one, too, enters the leaf-shedding throes of orchid death. The tragedy goes unaddressed by my mother.

Zoë seems more visibly irritated than ever by my mother's presence in our lives, especially after spending a few days in Denny's easy embrace. At dinner one night shortly before Halloween, Zoë and I are discussing how we'll decorate the house.

"I don't like Halloween," declares my mother.

"What?" Zoë asks, clearly dismayed. Zoë has always loved Halloween. She loved not only the trick-or-treating she did with us but the ceremony of giving out candy at the front door. And she and Matt often came up with impressive costumes for her. A few months before he died, Matt was inspired to create a Zoë-sized red bell pepper out of papier-mâché.

"How can you not want to give candy to little kids?" Zoë asks my mother in a tone that implies that there can be no acceptable answer.

"Norm and I would turn out the lights and go upstairs and watch a DVD."

I know what puts my mother off. It's not that she wants to disappoint innocent little kids. Her heart isn't black. Her Scrooge-like attitude toward Halloween is born of fear, fear of the older kids who make the trick-or-treating rounds long after the cute Pocahontases and mermaids and Batmans have gone to bed. Those big kids come barely dressed up, hold out pillowcases, and all but demand their candy—and sometimes money too. I try to explain this to Zoë, but—preferring the Cruella De Vil interpretation—she isn't listening. Nor, it seems, is my mother.

"I guess I'm just a disgusting person," my mother says, and she gets up and goes downstairs. Zoë looks at me, rolls her eyes, and says nothing. I remain silent, too, feeling paralyzed, incapable of altering the destructive pattern my mother and daughter fall into so readily, wondering if we will ever manage to break free. Should I be doing something? Would either of them listen to me if I tried?

Halloween arrives, and Zoë and I buy bags of candy and decorations. We wrap the gate and portico in orange and black streamers and hang a skeleton above the front door. Zoë tells me she has invited three friends to our house to eat candy and watch scary movies on TV, which I think is an excellent plan. For my part, I'm determined to have something resembling a social life, and I make plans to see Bob that night.

Zoë and I are wrapping the last of the streamers around a column when I tell her I'll be going to a movie with Bob.

"Oh, Mom, that's great!" she says. I silently rejoice that she seems happy to know I'm going on a date. "What movie?"

"He wants to see the Michael Jackson movie."

"Oh, yes, you should really see that! I've heard it's great." She doesn't ask why a couple of fuddy-duddies would want to see the Michael Jackson movie, and I'm touched that she's taking such an interest in my evening.

As I'm heading out, at about 7:00 P.M., I tell my mother that Zoë will be at home with her friends, watching movies. She seems fine with the plan.

"When will you be back? Around ten?"

"Something like that."

Just as I'm pulling in to the parking garage near the movie theater, my phone rings. It's my mother, calling to report that a pipe under the kitchen sink has burst and there is "a flood" on the kitchen floor. The subtext, of course, is that I need to come home right away to help her mop it up. But I resist. I talk her into calling Dave, the neighbor who is acting as property manager. She sends Zoë across the street, and Zoë soon returns with Dave in tow. I've bought myself a couple of hours. When the movie is over, I check my phone and see there are eleven calls from my mother, along with four voice-mail messages, as well as a lone text message from Zoë, tapped out at 8:35 (`When are you coming home?`). *Oh, my,* I think. *What's happened with the sink now?*

My mother wasn't calling about the sink.

As it turns out, while we were sitting in the movie, a few dozen teenagers were descending on the house. Apparently the news spread like a brushfire, via text messages, that there was an "open house" (code for "alcohol") at Zoë's house. Within minutes, the place was aswarm with high schoolers.

By the time I return my mother's call, the kids are gone, but I can hear Zoë screaming in the background, while my mother is mildly incoherent.

"There's alcohol in this house, and she shut me in the bathroom," my mother says.

For a moment, I assume that the alcohol she's referring to is the port, cognac, sherry, and rum I keep in the high cupboard, and I think, *So what? And the bathroom? What is she talking about? I leave for three hours and they both go insane?*

A split second later I realize she's referring to alcohol that has been brought *into* the house.

One of the kids, a sixteen-year-old with a reputation for heavy partying, had brought a "twelve-pack" of magnum-sized bottles of Bud Light and two large bottles of vodka. The kids had cleared off the kitchen table to set up their "bar" and were just opening for business when Zoë panicked and went downstairs to tell my mother what was happening. My mother came upstairs, screamed at the teenagers, ordered them out of the house, confiscated the alcohol, and decided to get rid of it. With the kitchen sink out of commission, my mother marched into the powder room off the kitchen and started pouring beer down the miniature sink. While Zoë wanted the party over, she saw no reason for my mother to take the alcohol. Furious, Zoë apparently then slammed the door of the bathroom—with my mother in it. I tell my mother I'll be home right away.

Before I can even rise from the bench where Bob and I have been sitting, Zoë calls. "Mom, she's crazy! I can never show my face in school again!"

"Don't be ridiculous. We'll sort this out as soon as I get home."

There will be no after-movie drinks with Bob. And from the expression on his face, I'm beginning to wonder if my hopelessly complicated life might be enough to send him back to his spreadsheet to check out the alternatives. Instead, he takes me by surprise. "Would you like me to come with you?" he asks. A moment passes while we both consider this. "Then again," Bob says, recalling the restaurant fiasco, "maybe not. The last time I met your daughter it didn't go well."

This makes me smile. "Yes, that may be a bad idea." And with that, I hurry to the car.

By the time I get home, the house is eerily quiet, with only subtle signs of the earlier carnage. All lights are on, the bathroom door flung open, its light ablaze; a few candy wrappers lie on the floor. The kitchen table is stacked high with red plastic cups.

My mother comes up from the basement, looking especially intense. And spent. She opens the garbage can, pulls out the vodka bottles, still full, and puts them on the table. Zoë enters the kitchen, looking just as miserable as my mother. I seat them at opposite ends of the table (why was one of my favorite espresso cups on the table with two Ping-Pong balls in it?), and my mother immediately launches in on Zoë, who starts crying—and screaming at her grandmother. It's clear that all Zoë cares about at this point is her reputation at school. From whatever safe redoubt he has found for continuing the party, the kid whose liquor my mother confiscated is already sending angry text messages, demanding the return of his liquor. No, I tell Zoë, he isn't getting it back. He's *sixteen*. What they're doing is *illegal*. What her grandmother did was the right thing. Does she get that? She stares at me piteously.

I take the two bottles of Smirnoff and three more big bottles of Bud Light downstairs and pour them out in the bigger sink in the laundry room. As I stand there, watching the clear liquid swirl down the drain and the beer foam collect, I think about the many times I did this very thing when I was a young girl, or watched while Sarah did it. As we emptied our mother's bottles, we knew we were risking her wrath, but we were too desperate to care. And only a few hours earlier, by plunging into a mob of partying teens, my mother did the same thing. And she was doing it for her granddaughter. I am grateful.

12.

Inventing Normal

If merely "feeling good" could decide, drunkenness would be the supremely valid human experience. *

—William James,
THE VARIETIES OF RELIGIOUS EXPERIENCE

SOME PEOPLE ARE SUCH QUIET, BENIGN DRUNKS, YOU'D NEVER KNOW they're smashed. My mother was not among them. Like many children of alcoholics, I was terrified of the effect alcohol had on her. My clearest memories of my mother's drinking are from our time in San Diego. When she drank, she grew mean. She would emerge from her bedroom once or twice a day, looking bloated and terrible, to rail about something. Sometimes she was clothed but often she was not, and she neither noticed nor cared. Her fury usually took the form of invective hurled at my absent father. I've forgotten many of the specific charges but do remember one thing she said to me during a particularly ferocious attack of rage: that my father spent so much time at work, she had to beg him to come home to have sex with her so Sarah would have a sibling—not something a mother would usually tell a young child.

She didn't plan the outbursts. She didn't lie in bed and in her stupor have a thought that enraged her, then come sailing out of her bedroom on a wave of fury. What she really wanted to do during those protracted binges was escape entirely—from the world, from us and our needs. But her own needs—for more liquor, to use the bathroom—brought her out. And once she was in the room with us, her inhibitions stilled by the alcohol, she let loose. Sometimes we'd hear her at night, going to the kitchen to fetch more wine. She drank stronger things, of course, but my main memories are of beer and wine. Cheap red wine. She had no interest in food, so we would make sandwiches and take them to her room. If she was awake she'd sit up, her eyes swollen half shut, her face ashen and puffy, and take the plate. If she was checked out, we'd quietly put the food on the floor next to her bed. When three or four days passed with no sign of her returning to us, we occasionally resorted to extreme measures. Sometimes we simply poured the wine down the sink, and sometimes we replaced it with water and red food coloring. Sometimes we hid the car keys. Whatever we did triggered explosive anger. She would demand the keys and when we finally gave in would drive herself—regardless of her state—to the liquor store. The sound of jangling keys and beer—even soda—cans popping open haunted me well into my adulthood. Sarah's painful memories were contained not in a sound but in a smell. For years Sarah spoke of the stomach-churning effect that the acrid smell of our kitchen sponges had on her as a child. A sponge should stand for cleanliness. To Sarah, ours signified only squalor, neglect, and the lingering odor of liquor.

Still, Sarah and I didn't know enough of life to understand that our own could be better. After leaving Rochester, I came to see our downhill spiral as part of the natural course of things, which is perhaps the way many kids try to square themselves with the world. Of course, we knew that not everyone's mother went from having a husband to having a series of boyfriends. And we knew that other people's mothers were more, well, predictable. The books we read in school featured mothers in ruffled aprons cinched tight at the waist, baking cookies with which they greeted their children upon their return from school. In my main daytime fantasy, my mother wore the same half apron around her waist, and she bore a plate of chocolate chip cookies. Always chocolate chip. Now I wonder if every child of a messed-up mother nurtures an apron-and-cookies fantasy. As an adult, I chanced on a letter written by the poet Anne Sexton to her daughter Linda, four months before Sexton killed herself: "You and

Joy always said, while growing up, 'Well, if I had a normal mother . . . !' meaning the apron and the cookies and none of this typewriting stuff that was shocking the hell out of friends' mothers . . ."

Even as I sensed I was being deprived of something important, I also sensed that my mother was in the grip of something very powerful. Who could look at the effects of alcohol on her and possibly conclude anything else? Alcohol's most hideous quality is the viselike grip with which it seizes its victims. And I believed then, as I do now, that my mother had no intention of being the agent of sorrow and hurt, that she was doing the best she could, that she wanted to take care of her girls but got tripped up—by the burden of expectations, by a marriage that wasn't what she thought it would be, by the hardship of raising two kids on her own. Once alcohol entered the mix, she didn't stand a chance. And neither did we.

MY MOTHER HADN'T BEEN in the UC San Diego mathematics program for long when she brought home a new man for us to meet, a fellow grad student named Dieter. He was very tall, especially when viewed by imps like us, and when he stood next to my mother she had to crane her neck to meet his eyes. Those eyes contained a twinkle of mischief, the mischief of an overgrown child. Sarah and I could tell at once that he was nothing like the men she had known in Florida. For one thing, Dieter was more than a decade younger than my mother. For another, within an hour, he seemed to want to spend as much time with Sarah and me as with our mother.

There was far more than age and height separating my mother and Dieter. She was a thirty-four-year-old divorced Jewish woman with two children, he a twenty-two-year-old mathematics exchange student from Germany. But they seemed to have a deep connection from the very beginning. He had probably never met anyone like her—quick, funny, and full of life. His English was halting, and Sarah and I giggled like maniacs while coaxing him through what he was trying to say. He called my mother Helainchen—little Helen.

Within a week of our first meeting, we were a tight foursome. Dieter kept his apartment in Pacific Beach but spent most of his time at our place. He lived for adventure. On an impulse, we'd all pile into his VW bug and head off. We went horseback riding. We went to see the observatory on Mount Palomar. We drove east to the desert, north to Disneyland and south to Tijuana. When my mother's sister came to visit, we all got in the Buick and drove to Las Vegas. Suddenly life was good, even glamorous. We were poor but didn't know it, or maybe we did know, but we didn't care, because my mother had stopped disappearing into her bedroom.

Years later, it was these periods of sobriety that allowed me to construct a magical view of the mother I could have had, for during the best of the Dieter Years I had glimpses of her. She still didn't prepare meals, and there were still no cookies waiting for us when we returned from school. But if Sarah or I—or both of us—entered a room, we itched for the moment her eyes would find ours, because it was in that instant that her face would light up with love for her daughters, and she would open her mouth into a huge smile, as if seeing us was the happiest surprise of her life. From across a room she sometimes shaped her mouth into a kiss and sent a loud and extravagant smooch straight at us. Those were the times we lived for, and when Dieter entered our lives, those times became our norm. Dieter was fun, but he was also strict, and he pushed us to do our best in school. Anything less than an A on a report card and he raised an eyebrow. He hung a small chalkboard on the wall next to the kitchen table, and at mealtimes he quizzed us on geography and math. We loved it.

My mother and Dieter were a good match intellectually, and together they gravitated to computer programming, a brand-new field in 1966. They learned Fortran, the programming language of the day; our apartment was strewn with IBM punch cards and large printouts with lines of Fortran and assembly language, even binary code (the ones and zeroes a machine can understand). They were a duo of early geeks.

When I was in fourth grade, my mother and Dieter decided not to live together, exactly, but to move much closer to each other. As a very proper young German, Dieter believed that cohabitation was too much of a step, but de facto cohabitation was okay. If he had his own apartment, at least nominally, he wouldn't have to tell an outright lie to his straitlaced mother back in Hanover. But instead of waiting for the school year to end or finding something in the same school district, my mother took us out in the middle of the school year to move ten miles up the coast to Del Mar. This just when we had managed to stay nearly two full years in one elementary school, and one we both liked at that. This time I made a fuss. But my mother and Dieter hardly heard me. Once again, Sarah and I said goodbye to classmates and we all moved in to a drab little apartment complex, where my mother and Dieter rented two apartments side by side and threaded an intercom system through the adjoining wall. Dieter and my mother stayed in one apartment, and Sarah and I were next door. In the ultimate display of nuclear family togetherness, we got a puppy, a Scottish terrier we named Angus.

Our apartment building was surrounded by empty lots, which were all that separated us from the ocean. Within a couple of decades, those stretches of undeveloped land—prime coastline real estate—would be built upon, with upscale apartment complexes and million-dollar houses with ocean views. But in 1967, those barren lots were our magnificent private playground. I had a tomboy streak and recruited neighborhood boys onto an ad hoc softball team. Dieter and my mother installed a tetherball pole, which acted as a magnet for kids in the neighborhood. For the first time in years, we were enjoying what felt like a normal, quasi-suburban existence, with us at the center of everything—the popular kids with the endless playground.

My mother began pushing for marriage, but Dieter wasn't ready. To buy himself some time and some space for reflection, he followed his graduate adviser, who was moving to the math department at Princeton. Once Dieter was gone, Sarah and I longed for him, but loss and change were now familiar to us, and we had gotten pretty good at it. We soon came to realize, however, how central Dieter was to my mother's stability. Within a few months of his departure, she fell apart. She took up with a physicist from UCSD we didn't like, and we moved out of the apartment with the walls adjoining Dieter's into an apartment upstairs. She resumed her drinking. We were devastated. Sarah and I came up with a signal. The first one home from school would check to see if our mother was at work or at home and in bed. If it was the former, the blinds were opened, an invitation to bring home a friend. If the blinds were closed, the message was this: "It's bad in here. Keep outsiders out."

Dieter was now in and out of our lives. Sometimes he left because of studies that took him elsewhere, but more often it was after one of his and my mother's frequent breakups. When he went to Ohio for more graduate work, he took Angus with him. We treasured Dieter's presence for many reasons but mostly because, when he was around and he and my mother were happy, she stayed sober. I came up with my own little set of equations. Life plus Dieter equaled Sober. Life minus Dieter equaled Drinking. And it was an equation we could rely on. So whenever trouble between my mother and Dieter started to brew, Sarah and I braced ourselves, because we knew that soon we would lose not just him but her as well.

My mother and Dieter eventually split up for good. In 1974, after nine years of emotional storms, my mother met Norm and left Dieter. But it turned out that I did not lose Dieter after all. Although he severed all contact with my mother, he remained close to Sarah and me, and I often turned to him for advice in the years that followed. Dieter stuck with programming, started a computer graphics company that grew successful, and became a wealthy man. When I was in high school, studying Latin, he'd insisted I drop the dead language and pick up German. If I learned German, he said, he would send me to Germany, which is how I came to spend a year there, learning to love the language as well as the art and literature. Two years after my time in Germany, he paid for my journalism school. Dieter eventually married, and his wife Maggie accepted me with grace and ease. After Zoë was born, Dieter assumed I would ask Maggie and him to be her godparents—and I did.

I ALWAYS BLAMED MYSELF for the binge that ended with our swift removal from San Diego. I was ten and taking horseback-riding lessons on Saturday mornings. I loved the routine of it, the smell of the stables, the horse named Butterscotch I rode every week, the extra hour of riding that I talked my mother into.

Perhaps what I loved most, however, was the stability I thought it introduced into our lives. Once a week my mother was obliged to drive from Del Mar down the coast to the stables in La Jolla. And she picked me up too. I was sure that my regular schedule was the linchpin holding my fragile mother together. Somehow I talked myself into believing that my desire to go riding every Saturday conjured up a sense of responsibility in her and kept her sober. Of course, the far more likely explanation for her sobriety during that period was Dieter, who had come back from Princeton for an extended visit. But I wanted to believe that I had some control.

My mother's lengthy sober phase emboldened me to demand still more of her attention. More than anything, I wanted her to come join me for lunch at school and meet my teacher, Mr. Cook, for whom I nursed a small infatuation. Of the many teachers I had experienced in my short career as a student, Mr. Cook was the star. He had been Sarah's teacher and, wanting everything my big sister had, I was overjoyed that he was now mine. I had my hand in the air constantly and quickly became his pet. I won the spelling bee almost every week. He threw math problems at us just to see how far our minds were willing to go, and I took the best of them home to my mother and Dieter to see how quickly they could solve them. My mother and Dieter sent me to school with math puzzlers for Mr. Cook.

Then I broke my leg. I was skateboarding down my favorite incline in the deserted parking lot behind our apartment building when a front wheel on my board hit a small pebble and jammed. I flew off. My leg was fractured in two places. A neighbor from across the courtyard put me in her car and drove me to the Scripps Hospital emergency room. She tracked down my mother and Dieter, both of whom materialized at once, or so it seemed.

A few days later I was back at school, and Mr. Cook was happy to see me. The first thing he did was use my accident to impart a physics lesson to the class. I had illustrated Sir Isaac Newton's first two laws of motion: As an object in motion, I remained in motion (that's the first law). Unfortunately, my skateboard, acted upon by a sudden external force, did not join me. Its rapid deceleration neatly demonstrated the second law.

What Mr. Cook didn't discuss was how my accident was going to affect the equations I had devised to account for my mother's relationship to alcohol. Although Life plus Dieter equaled Sobriety, I had come to believe that my weekly riding lessons figured into the equation too. With a cast on my leg, I was no longer able to take the lessons. Then

Dieter went back to Princeton and, with no Dieter and no weekly obligation to meet, my mother started a period of heavy drinking, the worst Sarah and I had seen.

Early one morning Sarah, now twelve years old, came into the living room and shook me awake. She was holding a bottle of pills in her hand. "She won't tell me how many she's taken." Sarah was frantic.

I followed her into the bedroom. My mother had become one with the bed, as if she had fallen into quicksand and all but her hair was submerged.

I spoke to the head of hair. "Mom. How many pills did you take?"

"A lot," she mumbled. I managed to get her to tell me that it wasn't just pills but half a bottle of hard liquor as well. My sister took charge and called my mother's parents in Boston. My grandfather said he would fly to San Diego at once.

What happened immediately thereafter is a blur. I have no memory of my mother being taken to a hospital. Nor do I recall exactly when my grandfather arrived. Whenever it was, probably no later than the next morning, he handled the situation with businesslike efficiency, focusing on logistics. Having concluded that my mother was in no position to care for Sarah and me, he had decided to send us to our father in Rochester, and he took us to our school to say goodbye and clear out our desks. Mr. Cook must have been surprised, to say nothing of my classmates, who watched the scene uncomprehending. As for me, I had grown accustomed to my friendships having a deadline. But it was an unspoken deadline, as I never knew when exactly I'd be leaving one group of friends and expected to find new friends at the next stop.

This time we would also be expected to fit into a new family, for my father had just remarried, to a British woman named Vivienne, who had three children of her own. When my mother took the pills, Sarah and I were still absorbing the news of the recent marriage, and now, never having even met Vivienne, we were about to move in with her. (Years later, Vivienne said that she and my father first learned of the events when my grandfather called and said simply, "The girls are on a plane.") Sarah and I were each allowed to take one suitcase of possessions. Unsupervised in the task of packing, I chose not clothing, pajamas, stuffed animals, or toys but schoolwork. Into one small piece of luggage I crammed the entire contents of my desk at school, along with more notebooks, ruled paper, pencils, vocabulary lists, my social studies book, and school photos. I was under the impression that I would be returning soon.

My mother came to the airport with my grandfather to see us off. I remember that she looked beaten down and miserable, but I have little memory of my own condition. Did I cry? Was I sorry to be leaving my mother? Relieved? I don't know. Nor do I know what happened to my mother after we left her with her father. Years later, Sarah recalled that my mother was furious at her for calling my grandfather. It's unlikely that my grandfather, who hardly spoke to my mother even when she was well, said much of anything to his sorry mess of a daughter before returning to Boston. It could be that he told her to get herself into a rehabilitation program. And did she? Or did she go back to bed? I don't know. And I doubt she does either.

Sarah and I flew across the country alone. Because of my broken leg, the flight attendants took pity on me and moved us to first class, where we sat at a round table and played cards. My father and new stepmother picked us up at the Rochester airport. Vivienne was tall—nearly six feet—blond, and striking. She wore heavy mascara, a thick layer of blue eye shadow, and large hoop earrings. For the six years I lived with Vivienne, I never saw her come to breakfast without having first applied her makeup.

Years later, for a writing workshop she was taking, Vivienne produced this description of the day we entered her life: "The two girls looked so lost and bedraggled and pathetic in ill-fitting clothes as they struggled down the steps of the plane. Katie looked even more forlorn than Sarah, as she had her leg in a cast. They really looked like a couple of waifs and I had a horrible feeling that they had been quite neglected. I was terribly unsure how to go about trying to relate to them. They appeared to be quite dazed and Everett seemed even more ill at ease with them than I was. My heart immediately went out to them and I resolved to do my very best to try to make things better for them." For the first week in Rochester, Vivienne wrote, I didn't speak.

13.

Dam Break

And we forget because we must
And not because we will.

—Matthew Arnold, "Absence"

"HAVE I EVER TOLD YOU WHY I LOST CUSTODY OF YOU AND SARAH?"
A week after the Halloween incident, I'm waiting in the customer lounge of the local Toyota dealership, where I've brought my car for maintenance, and my mother has just called my cellphone. This is a real bolt out of the blue.

"I know why," I respond, and I lower my voice. "But we can talk about it later. I'm at the car place." In environments like this, where the other people in the room are quietly reading newspapers and tapping on their computers and iPads, a cellphone might as well be a megaphone.

"No, I'd like to tell you now." While I struggle with what to say to stop her, she interprets my silence as an invitation to continue. "It's because I had a man in my bedroom."

"Mom, this is really not a good time; can't we talk about this later?" She agrees, and I hang up.

I'm not ready to have a conversation like this. Even if I was, how are we ever to talk about those events, given how skewed her memory appears to be? It's true that when she lost custody, men and bedrooms figured into it. But she says the words "man in my bedroom" so innocently, as if the guy were there to hang a light fixture. It would be like Nixon's saying he'd lost his presidency because of "some fellows in an office building."

It isn't until a few days later, when we go see Lia, that my mother and I pick up where we had left off. Perhaps we both know we need to wait until we are in neutral, safe territory, operating under professional supervision, to have such an exquisitely painful conversation.

Until now, neither of us has dared kick loose so much as a small rock from the rubble that is her—our—past. My mother and I have both lived under a mutually agreed-upon, unspoken pact that we never discuss what happened, which allows us to pretend that nothing actually did happen. But ever since she brought it up when I was at the car place, I've felt like something big is about to crash down on top of us, and now, in Lia's office, I'm nearly certain of it.

Sensing the same, Lia rolls her chair back an inch or two, as if to retreat from the very question she is about to ask.

"You've said there is history," she says. "I was hoping we wouldn't need to get into this, but I think we should. I'd like to know more about what happened in the past."

My mother starts to tell her version of the story. Because I'm sure she'll either get it wrong or answer incompletely, I jump in to take over. Then I stop myself. "No, you go ahead," I say.

"I lost custody of my children," my mother says. "I was divorced from Katie's father. And when they were eight and ten they went for a visit."

When we were *eight and ten*? When we were first taken away from her, which was a full two years before she officially lost custody, I was ten and Sarah was twelve. How could she have allowed precious years with her children to slip straight out of her memory bank? I start to correct her. But then I stop myself again and let her finish. "They went back to visit him, and he sued for custody, and I lost custody on the grounds I had been sleeping with a man."

She's finished. She and Lia both look at me. I say in a voice close to a whisper, "That's not what happened." They both look surprised.

And they wait for me to say more. Resting my gaze on my lap, I start to tell the entire story, and it's like a dam break: the days in bed; the ups and downs with Dieter as the barometer of her drinking, and her moods; the horseback-riding lessons and the broken leg; the incident with the pills that caused us to call our grandparents for help. And we hadn't gone to Rochester for something so benign as "a visit." We'd been airlifted out like embassy employees under siege, and sent to live with my father and Vivienne, who immediately enrolled us in school there.

The entire time I'm talking, I am thinking that I don't want my words to hurt her, that I want to protect my mother, to let her know it wasn't her fault. At the same time, there's no stopping me, because another part of me wants her to hear every word of this. To *make* her understand. How can the story of my childhood, the story I've told to friends, to the men in my life, to therapists over the years, be so different from the version she has chosen to carry with her?

By now I'm sobbing, and I can hardly speak. So I stop.

I look up at my mother. Her face is a terrible crumple, her mouth forming the small breathless "O" people sometimes wear when hit with bad news.

"Katie," she says. "I am so sorry."

And with that she is telling me something else: *She doesn't remember*. Forty years have passed, and for all of those years I thought that this crucial chapter of our lives, which has dogged Sarah and me every day since, was one that my mother and I simply chose not to speak of. Now it turns out that these are events she can recall only in their roughest outline; the more granular aspects are beyond her. I had guessed there were parts she might not remember, or that her recollections might differ from mine, but it's only now that I understand how deep my mother's memory loss runs. This recognition comes to me like a sudden strong breaker onto a beach. It's part of the legacy that alcoholics leave their children. Children often remember not merely every detail of the binges but also the events leading up to them, to say nothing of the wreckage left behind. For the parent, however, the episodes may be just one big cognitive blackout.

It's time for the session to end, and we shake ourselves back to the reality of where we are. It is 2009, not 1968, and we are not in Del Mar. We are in a therapist's office in Berkeley. Lia says quietly that she hopes we can talk about this a little more next time. I welcome the distraction of digging through my handbag for my checkbook, while Lia pulls out her calendar to set a date for our next appointment.

In the car, my mother and I are mostly silent, acting as troubled married couples often do following an explosive therapy session. When we do talk, we focus on trivia.

"Do you need anything at the store on the way home?" I ask.

She shakes her head. "No thanks."

"Do you mind if I stop for gas?"

"No, that's fine."

In the blank space between these polite exchanges, I'm thinking not about my mother and me but about Sarah. I wasn't the only one who lived through that maelstrom of a childhood. Sarah was present, too, for all of it. Did she remember what I remembered? Has she, too, sat in the office of a professional listener, weeping as she recounted the events leading up to the day my grandfather put us on a plane for Rochester? And why have we never compared notes?

As soon as we get home, I send my sister an email to let her know that our mother is now living with Zoë and me, that she's been through a lot but is basically fine. It's the first I've told my sister about the events of the past six months.

Sarah was an alcoholic for years, starting as a teenager. Eventually she beat it back and stopped drinking altogether when she was in her late twenties. She even published a book titled *Nice Girls Don't Drink*, a poignant compilation of interviews with women who were recovering alcoholics. Like my mother, my sister tried A.A. but didn't last long. Sarah's interviews are with women who, like her, got sober without A.A.

Throughout her twenties and thirties, Sarah filled what must have been a large emotional void with passionless promiscuity. But in 1997, when she was forty-two, Sarah married a musician who was devoted to her from the minute they met. Since the late 1990s, Sarah has been living in a small town in northern Massachusetts, in a large and lovely old house she and her husband share with multiple cats. My sister is a quiltmaker with a fine eye for gorgeous fabrics.

My news prompts a flood of friendly emails in response. My mother and I send Sarah a late birthday gift, and we enter lengthy, complicated three-way discussions about the upcoming holidays, our gift wishes, her gift wishes, Zoë's gift wishes. It feels good to be back in touch. Yet I'm wary. As close as we were as children, our respective relationships with our mother have cleaved us. While I've had, if anything, an overly close connection to my mother, Sarah's relationship with her grew so tortured over the years that my mother decided that Sarah was a destructive presence in her life. Her solution was to get an unlisted phone number, which put me squarely in the middle of their troubles. Now, seeing the two of them back in touch, I'm thrilled. After years of pent-up need for my mother's attention ("I've missed eight of Mom's birthdays," Sarah tells me in one plaintive email), Sarah is sending boxes filled with various things: handbags purchased from eBay; used books; earrings and bracelets she might have taken straight off her own ears and wrists. To Zoë she sends a tattered copy of Dodie Smith's *I Capture the Castle* (Sarah's and my favorite book) and several seasons of *Weeds* DVDs from Amazon.com. My mother and I send Sarah gifts she has requested, and we are all basking in the warm feelings of this renewed contact. But my mother and I also worry, because we know that Sarah's manic episodes, in which she soars before she crashes, usually end badly.

Sure enough, several weeks into our rapprochement, Sarah takes offense at my mother's diplomatic attempt to tell her she really doesn't need any more gifts, and she emails me repeatedly about the perceived slight. I'm thin-skinned, too, but Sarah has always possessed something closer to a membrane—so fine it's nearly translucent. Not knowing what to do, I do nothing. Predictably, as night follows day, as swiftly as it came, the rapprochement ends, and Sarah stops communicating with both of us.

SARAH AND I COME by our sensitivity honestly, as I've had occasion to note several times since my mother moved in. For weeks my mother has been excited about a performance she wants me to attend with her at the Jewish Community Center, a klezmer concert performed by a duo from Buenos Aires. I tell her I'd love to go, and I mark it on my calendar.

But the day of the concert, Zoë informs me that there's a volleyball game that night at her school, and although she's not on the team, she'd like me to go. Fine, I tell her, but I'll have to leave early to get to the concert on time. No problem, Zoë says. I go downstairs to tell my mother that, since there's a volleyball game at Zoë's school and I'm going to go watch some of it, I'll meet her at the JCC instead of walking there with her.

An hour before we're to leave for the game, I hear my mother call up to me from the base of the stairs.

"I really think I'm too tired to go out," she says. "I'd rather just stay home and watch a DVD. Do you think you can get someone else to go to the concert with you?"

Zoë, who has heard this, emerges from her room. And this is the scene: My mother stands at the bottom of the tall staircase, Zoë is at the top, and I'm halfway up, literally and metaphorically sandwiched between the two.

It occurs to me that the last time I felt wedged like this between my mother and my daughter was nine months ago, when my mother had knee-replacement surgery. Knowing that Norm would be of limited help in such a major ordeal, I had flown to San Diego, with plans for Zoë to join me the next day. During the three hours of surgery, I sat in the brightly lit waiting room. After my mother was finally rolled up to her room, I stayed for several more hours, watching my mother drift in and out of drugged sleep.

When I picked Zoë up from the airport the next night, she complained of stomach pain. Early the next morning, she woke me to tell me she had spent the night sitting up because it was too painful to lie down. Several hours later, Zoë was being wheeled in for an emergency appendectomy. I found myself in the same surgical waiting room on the same couch I had occupied just two days before. But now it was late Sunday afternoon and I was alone in the room. I couldn't find a light switch, so I lay on that small sofa in the dark, rested my head on the arm, and waited.

Forty-five minutes passed before the surgeon emerged. "That appendix was ready to come out," he said. "We didn't do it a minute too soon." Zoë was taken up to the same floor as my mother. Only a long hallway separated their rooms—convenient, I thought, but so very strange. Here they were, these two people on either side of me, both in need of care and attention. My bed for two nights was a reclining chair in Zoë's room. She wanted me close enough so that she could reach my hand with hers. If I left the room for five minutes, Zoë complained it was too long, but I told her I had to look in on my mother periodically. The nurses on the floor grew accustomed to seeing me shuttle between the two rooms. During one of those late-night trips, a nurse smiled at me and, in a tone better suited to a chance encounter at the grocery store than an exchange on a sterile hospital ward, asked, "How's the family?"

Now, on this staircase, I'm locked between the same two people, but this time there is no imminent escape in the form of a plane ticket back home. I *am* home.

"What's going on?" I ask my mother.

"You probably want to go to the volleyball game."

My mother is again speaking in code, and I think I get it, because this is very similar to the game I used to play when I was a child: What can I do to ensure that I am her priority? How do I get her to care? Only now the tables have turned. Now that I have an offer from Zoë, my mother is worried I'll renege.

Actually, I don't want to go to the entire volleyball game, but I do want to see some of it, and thirty minutes seems the perfect amount of time. "No," I say in a measured voice. "I'd like to go to the concert. With you. I said I'll meet you there, and that's what we're doing."

Zoë, of course, has not cracked the code, or even understood that there is a code. She chimes in from her sentry position at the top of the stairs. "Why did you lie?" she asks my mother. The child has zeroed in on my mother's indirectness, and she's out to bust her for it. She has grown increasingly intolerant of my mother's hidden meanings.

Before my mother and I have a chance to process Zoë's pointed question, I hear my child gasp. "Mom! Did you give her your watch?"

I look at my mother's new watch, the one I gave her for her birthday, which closely resembles my own. "No. I did not give her my watch," I say, emphasizing each word.

My mother looks as if she has just swallowed poison. Slowly, she removes the watch from her wrist and holds it out to Zoë. "No, dear, look at it. Come here. Look. It's not your mother's watch." Her voice is cracking, and she's visibly wounded, but because of the way she utters the word "dear"—a word I haven't heard her use before, and one that is clearly not intended as a term of endearment now—there's an instant when I'm put in mind of the wicked queen extending her arm to Snow White, offering her the deadly apple. The image stops me cold, partly because it's obviously out of sync with the reality of what's going on. Here's my mother under attack and on the verge of tears, yet I'm so caught between her and Zoë that I can't accept my mother's vulnerability.

Zoë doesn't budge from where she's standing.

I instruct my mother to meet me at the JCC in a couple of hours. She goes downstairs. Meanwhile, I'm furious with Zoë for provoking a fight again, and I insist she apologize.

"I'll apologize, but I still want to know why she lied."

"Just apologize," I snap.

Zoë goes as far as the top of the stairs, and I hear my mother start to come back up. I rush over. Zoë has offered a quick "I'm sorry." Still, she can't resist. "But why did you lie about not wanting to go to the concert?" My mother, who had been expecting a true apology, starts in on Zoë about her behavior.

By now I've given up on my attempt to restore civility. "You're both acting like eight-year-olds," I say.

This infuriates my mother. "Bullshit!"

Zoë stalks away. My mother descends the stairs once again. I call down to her that I'll meet her at the concert.

I leave the volleyball game with plenty of time to get to the JCC, where I find my mother waiting for me in the lobby. She has on her new coat from her birthday expedition, a nice pair of boots, and a scarf knotted to perfection. She looks happy to see me, and I think maybe we can salvage this night after all. We take our seats. My mother's feet are barely touching the floor. It dawns on me that I have never been to a live performance of any kind with my mother. There is so much we missed sharing, so many normal mother–daughter experiences we never had.

The Argentine musical duo is great, switching among flute, clarinet, saxophone, harmonica, accordion, and piano to combine jazz, contemporary music, and traditional tango with the Jewish folk sounds of klezmer. I can see that my mother loves it. I look out over the sea of gray heads and think, *Oh, can't she find a playdate somewhere in this room? There must be someone in this place, a kindred soul, maybe another smart, neurotic septuagenarian.*

As we walk home, my mother wants to chase the topic of Zoë, but I refuse. Lia has suggested we bring Zoë with us to the next session. If we're going to work out our three-generations-under-one-roof, Lia believes, we need a mediated discussion with all three of us present.

WHEN WE ARRIVE AT Lia's a few days later, she has pulled an extra chair into her office from the waiting room. Zoë seats herself between my mother and me, clutching her cellphone—a teenager's Binky—while my mother and I take our usual seats. My mother has come bearing an olive branch. Addressing Zoë directly, with a delivery that sounds carefully rehearsed, she says, "I might not be good with kids, but I'm hoping so much that our getting together can give me the tools to make things work with you. If you'd help me, I really would appreciate it."

But Zoë isn't going to make it easy. "I have so much other shit going on," she says. She's playing tough and squirrelly. "I don't have the emotional time and energy to deal with you and the way you perceive me. I'm sixteen and going through a lot. I can't worry about your emotions and how you feel about me."

I had predicted Zoë would sit in stony silence, but I should have known better. And she isn't finished. "My mom and I have been a twosome for so long, it's really really hard for me to see her give you her attention."

At this, Lia steps in. "Although it's true your mother has responsibility toward you, she still has strong feelings for her own mother."

It was a nice try, but Zoë isn't to be stopped. She turns straight to my mother. "I've come to resent you for the way my mom grew up. That's where a lot of my resentment comes from. It doesn't sound like you were a particularly active mother. I have never gotten the impression that you and my mom had anything near the relationship we have. And now you come and insert yourself."

Lia is a little taken aback by Zoë's candor. "Your grandmother was totally helpless at that point," she says. "She didn't have the ability to pull herself together. She was lost. And that takes a lot of courage to admit. She's clear now, she's sober, and she's committed. She wants to have a relationship."

Emboldened, my mother adds, "I was a very troubled young woman."

Lia turns to me for my reaction. "All I want is for these two to get along," I say lamely. I feel like a house sparrow trying to keep its purchase on a branch while being buffeted by gale-force winds from two directions.

"I don't want to be forced into conversation," Zoë continues, and turns back to my mother. "Also, I don't necessarily want your opinion when we're talking."

There's a hard edge to my daughter that I've never seen before.

My mother is wearing a tortured smile.

Lia interjects. "How can we give this a chance to work?"

"What can I do to get to where you're willing to just be polite to me?" my mother asks her granddaughter. "Or how about just human?"

Zoë announces that she'd like to be the one to set the ground rules on the where, when, and how of interaction between her grandmother and herself. "When we're in the kitchen, wait for me to speak to you. If I want to talk to you, I'll talk to you. I just feel too pressured to engage when I don't want to."

While Zoë's rudeness is appalling, I notice that she has gradually inched her chair toward mine, and now she has taken hold of my hand; she's caressing it, kneading it. My heart swells for my child. I want to pummel her and wrap my arms around her at the same time.

Lia tries to cast this outrageous proposal in a more positive light. "Helen, you're trying to make friends, and she's not ready to make friends. She's saying, 'I'm getting used to you. I'm getting used to your presence.' It's very difficult, what you're trying to do, but also a great opportunity."

Neither my mother nor my daughter appears to be welcoming this great opportunity. But perhaps they can be forgiven for their willed deafness, as Lia's comment, well meant as it was, suggests that she hasn't been listening to what Zoë said either. Zoë is clearly not getting used to my mother and no longer sees her presence as an opportunity for anything but competition and conflict. Lia, I'm coming to understand, may well be a wise and experienced therapist, but with us she's in over her head. Her practice centers on helping families puzzle through life's twists and turns as people age, not helping adult children of alcoholics resolve decades-old issues now coming home to roost, accompanied by undisguised hostility from a take-no-prisoners teenage only child of a widowed mother. Lia signed on to help us adjust to the practical aspects of merging households, and now she's being asked to help us work through forty-five years of accumulated pain.

The drive home is excruciatingly tense, and mostly silent. As soon as we're in the door, it's as if the boxing referee has clanged the bell; each of the battered combatants retreats to her corner of the house. Feeling helpless, I take refuge at my computer, and within minutes an email from my mother pops up in my in-box. She wants to know when, exactly when, I told Zoë about her past.

I go downstairs to talk to her and find her seated at her computer.

"If you told Zoë about my terrible past recently, after that sweet reception she gave me, then some of the hostility might make sense," she says. "But if she knew about it before then, why the warm welcome?"

"Mom, Zoë has known these things for many years," I say. My mother seems to think that the person she was no longer exists, that the past should remain past, and that by sharing information I had betrayed her and poisoned my daughter's feelings toward her.

"Your past *isn't* just your own business," I say. Zoë has always known about my childhood, I tell her, because my story is part of my daughter's story, just as my mother's story is part of mine. Whether we like it or not, we carry these narratives with us, either explicitly or implicitly, and pass them on, along with the family china, the recipes, and the antique chests. I had chosen to make the story explicit, in the belief that Zoë needed to know about the forces that had shaped my life, because they would in some way continue to resonate in hers.

"When Zoë got to high school, where kids really start to drink, I educated her about her heightened risk because of the genetic component. There are a lot of people on both sides of her family who've been alcoholics, and there's a good chance that Zoë could have inherited the tendency. So I've told her what she needs to know so she can make better choices. She needs to know that she might not react to alcohol the way other kids do." As for Zoë's warm welcome, I tell my mother, I believe it was genuine, but it faded when Zoë began to feel jealous and territorial.

My mother has been sitting quietly, listening as I speak. But what is she really hearing? What I don't tell her is that I think Zoë was hoping for a real relationship with her grandmother, that she would have treasured a net gain in the relatively small universe of people who make her feel loved and cared for. Instead, my mother's inability to connect with her, her hastiness to judge, and the claims she has made on my attention have all left Zoë feeling that she has lost rather than gained something with this new arrangement. My mother's jaw is set tight. And at that moment, I know the two of them are not going to work this out.

14.

Amherst

What do *girls do who haven't any mothers*
to help them through their troubles?

—Jo March in Louisa May Alcott, LITTLE WOMEN

IN 1968, THE YEAR SARAH AND I BECAME STEPCHILDREN, THERE WERE eight million American stepchildren under the age of eighteen. By the end of the 1990s, that number had risen to fifty million, and the re-divorce rate among remarried parents had risen along with it.

Blended families face a number of challenges that nuclear families are spared. Everyone in a stepfamily is recovering from a loss. The adults have no prior investment in their stepchildren, and the stepchildren usually have no history with one another. There are bound to be rivalries and resentments, accusations of favoritism, with or without foundation, and the pitting of stepchild against stepchild, parent against stepparent. All those evil-stepmother prototypes that populate our literature have deep psychological roots in our collective experience—though, of course, there should be evil-stepfather figures too.

For those reasons and more, when Sarah and I arrived on their doorstep out of the blue, the good people living at 460 Oakridge Drive in Rochester, New York, must not have known what hit them. Suddenly, by no one's choice, we were a family of seven, and all five children were already in, or close to entering, the dreaded teenage years. My new step-siblings, two boys and one girl, were so close to Sarah and me in age that the five of us spanned only five years, from ten (me) to fifteen (my step-sister).

The dynamic was difficult from the start. The fact that no one had time to prepare for the new arrangement was the least of it. Vivienne's three children, particularly her fifteen-year-old daughter, were going through their own adolescent trials. And my father had little patience for Vivienne's sons, who were indifferent to school and insolent to him. For my part, I was beginning to develop a protective ability to distance myself, which made me much more adaptable to new situations than Sarah was and turned me into a lifelong observer. The ability to stand outside a scene eventually helped me become a journalist. At the time, however, it simply helped me survive. Sarah had no such talent for distancing herself, and she paid the price. At twelve she was entering puberty. She would develop into a beautiful swan, but as a preteen with bad acne and frizzy hair, she had no way of knowing this. Sarah missed our mother and was miserable living with four strangers.

I, on the other hand, always eager to be accepted and craving stability, was ready to try out Vivienne as a possible mother substitute. Not long after our arrival in Rochester, I told Vivienne I was going to start calling her "Mom," and she was touched. Sarah had no such intention. She knew exactly who her mother was, and she told me that if I began to call Vivienne "Mom," I would be betraying both her and our real mother. Before long, Vivienne was back to being "Vivienne."

Only a saint could have loved and cared for us as if we were her own children. And we certainly didn't make things easy for Vivienne. Whether it was the food she made (classic British dishes like shepherd's pie and Scotch eggs), the regular mealtimes to which everyone was summoned every night, or her other expectations about what constituted proper behavior, it was all foreign to us and we often balked.

We stayed in Rochester just long enough for us to finish the school year. That summer, we all moved to Amherst, Massachusetts. As much as my grandfather disliked my father, he respected him as an educator and recommended him for a job as one of the founding deans of Hampshire College. In August 1968, our blended family of seven set off in a beige VW van and drove the six hours from Rochester to Amherst. On my lap was a Florsheim shoe box, a dozen holes punched through the lid. I had developed a fascination with cocoons and was hatching not butterflies but, for some strange reason, tent moths. During the six-hour ride, I kept my nose buried in *The Borrowers*, a five-volume children's book series I was tearing through, about tiny peoplelike creatures who lived in the crevices of houses belonging to human beings. They lived on borrowed time, in constant fear of being discovered. I could relate.

As we drew close to Amherst, the van tooling up and down the gentle hills of western Massachusetts, I put my book aside and took in the scenery—Grandma Moses villages with white churches, town commons, and classic Colonials separated by acres of farmland. The plan was for us to meet up with the Lyon family upon our arrival, in a parking lot in the center of Amherst. My father and Dick Lyon had already met, and the two men wanted their wives and children to get to know one another, since, as family members, we were all going to be part of this exciting new experiment in higher education. Dick was to be the first overall dean of Hampshire College, my father its first dean of natural science and math. It was in that parking lot next to the Amherst Town Hall that I first set eyes on the six Lyons—Dick and Denny and their boys: Christopher, Matthew, Jeremy, and Alex. The Lyons pulled up in their International Harvester Travelall, and everyone piled out of both vehicles, with the exception of Sarah, who, growing unhappier by the day, refused.

Under my arm I held my shoe box, which I was guarding carefully; Denny told me years later that the instant she saw me climb out of the VW bus with that shabby box in my hands, she loved me as her own. The adults started chattering away and we kids stood awkwardly, waiting for them to finish. The four Lyon boys were close in age, except the much younger Alex, an outlier in age as well as temperament. They were all energetic, but Alex had an unruly streak that kept his mother on constant watch. Twelve-year-old Matt, blond, beautiful, and shy, was the quiet one.

My father and Vivienne bought a big comfortable house just north of the town center, and the Lyons moved in to a house right across a cornfield from us. The two families grew close. The Lyons were different from most families. Instead of "Mom" and "Dad," the four boys called their parents "Dick" and "Denny." The entire family intrigued me, but Denny held me spellbound. I had never known anyone like her. A dancer and a potter, she seemed the most exotic person I'd ever met. She kept her potting wheel in the basement of their sprawling house, and she made tortillas by hand; that skill alone would have been enough to put me forever in awe of my future mother-in-law. Sarah and I thought we understood Mexican food. We had come from San Diego, after all. But the Mexican food we knew was Old El Paso—preformed corn tortillas and taco seasoning in the yellow-and-red cans and packages. A Texan by birth with a little Native American blood mixed in, Denny made the dough for her tortillas from scratch, then flattened it in a tortilla press. And she had a cupboard filled with exotic spices. Her kitchen was like an artist's studio, her spatulas and wooden spoons, her whisks and her ladles, standing up like so many paintbrushes in the large ceramic pots she had made herself.

Denny was my idea of a tribal elder. It was as if when I met her she had already been alive for hundreds of years. At age ten, I had yet to encounter anyone who could have been described as spiritual, and here she was, her long brown hair framing her narrow face. She was only thirty-seven, but wisdom and clarity of purpose were already etched in her features. Denny swept me off my feet every bit as much as her son would a few years later. This was the woman who, together with Matthew, would show me, a refugee newly arrived from a land of turmoil, not just how to love but how to love big and deep.

Denny and all her boys were artistic and handy with tools. Dick, on the other hand, was, like my father, a pure intellectual. Like my mother, Denny had dropped out of college to marry. She followed Dick to Cambridge, England, where he was studying philosophy. They were married in All Hallows by the Tower in London. Theirs was the first American wedding to take place in the church since 1797, when John Quincy Adams married Louisa Catherine Johnson. Once they returned to the States, Dick became an itinerant academic—one university for his master's, another for his PhD, another for a job as a junior faculty member. When I first heard about their constant moves, I thought, *Are they like me?* But, no, this family was different. Rather than feeling uprooted every time they moved, the happy, stable Lyon boys welcomed each move as a new adventure.

By the time I entered sixth grade at Crocker Elementary in Amherst, I had attended seven different schools in four different states, and I had mastered the difficult art of being the new kid, which meant I had perfected the art of ingratiation. At my new school, I became a sixty-pound heat-seeking missile, quickly identifying the popular kids and securing a spot among them. Soon, my life settled into something resembling normal. I not only grew used to my stepmother's cooking but came to treasure the routine of a dinner eaten every night at roughly the same time with the same people. Even the weekly household chores she assigned us seemed part of this reassuringly regular life.

In Amherst, when she was in ninth grade, Sarah blossomed and I was more in awe of my big sister than ever. I sat in our room and watched while she set her hair, put on makeup, got ready for dances, and talked on the phone with a series of boyfriends. Having lost so much of her childhood being a surrogate mother to me, she was no longer paying me much attention, but that was fine. What I didn't understand then was that what seemed to be normal teenage-girl behavior was in fact the start of Sarah's gradual shift into a full-blown pathological obsession with men.

While I bobbed like a cork on a stormy sea, Sarah got smacked by every wave and continued to pine for our mother. She phoned her frequently and reported to me that my mother's voice was often cheerful and steady. Perhaps with her daughters out of the way, my mother had found the wherewithal to pull herself together.

IN THE SUMMER OF 1970, when I was twelve and about to enter eighth grade, Sarah and I went for an extended visit to San Diego. My mother had moved to a tiny bungalow in Mission Beach, a gritty little place on a finger of shoreline. Her sandy dwelling was surrounded by similar houses inhabited by surfers and beach bums with lean, tanned bodies and hair as light as the sun itself. Sarah brought along her friend Dina for the first part of the summer. There wasn't much for us to do but go to the beach and ride bikes up the boardwalk to Belmont Park, the local amusement park. Every day, Sarah and Dina put on their bikinis, went to the beach, and flirted with older boys, who invited them to parties. I was beset by envy and begged for inclusion, especially when it came to the parties. So they stuffed tissues into my size-A bra and took me along.

That summer, we reverted to our old eating habits. Instead of Vivienne's roast beef with Yorkshire pudding, we ate butterscotch pies, Minute Rice, and fried bologna. Oddly, my mother gave in immediately to my pleas for a kitten. Like most children, I wasn't thinking about what having a kitten actually meant or what would happen at the end of the summer when it was time to leave. I was simply thrilled to have it.

To our profound relief and delight, our mother remained sober that summer. She was in good spirits, even though she and Dieter were very much on-again off-again in those days. Since he was away for that summer, they were definitely off for the duration of our stay. But instead of falling apart, she was calm and happy. She even engaged in all the rituals we associated with a functioning mother: She frosted her hair; she dieted, put ice cubes and saccharin in her black coffee, did her Jack LaLanne exercises, and played her Joan Baez and Peter, Paul and Mary records. When she and Sarah were out together, strangers thought they were sisters, which never failed to put a big smile on my mother's face.

We three girls slept in the living room on various makeshift beds. The only bathroom was in the back of the house, off my mother's small bedroom. When my mother had a man over, walking through her bedroom in the middle of the night to pee felt too awkward. So we peed into a glass jar and tossed the contents onto a bird of paradise outside the front window.

Throughout the visit, there must have been a few mentions of whether we would like to stay in San Diego permanently, and this possibility—which did not seem out of the question, given my mother's apparent stability that summer—must have been conveyed to my father and stepmother. My father's reaction was subdued, but Vivienne wouldn't hear of it. Years later, I learned that while my passive father would probably have let my mother keep us in San Diego, Vivienne urged him to bring us home to Amherst.

My mother turned uncharacteristically quiet. Soon it was conveyed to us that our father had decided we should return to Amherst and that he had made airline reservations for our return. Then, late one afternoon just before we were supposed to leave, my mother came home and announced that she had obtained temporary custody. *What? Why?* Sarah seemed ready to stay with my mother. She was spending her time at the beach, hanging out with boys, and my mother not only gave her fourteen-year-old daughter no flak about this but seemed to approve. They were closer than ever. But I wanted to go back, and for the first time in my life, I broke ranks with my sister. Vivienne was hardly a demonstrative or warm woman, and she had made her preference for her own children clear. Still, I craved the order and continuity she and my father now represented.

My mother's expression turned sheepish when she saw how shocked I was. But her tone was righteous. She told us we would be better off with her. After all, she was our mother. She loved us. Of course, I loved her too. But I had a life in Amherst. I had friends there. I had my own bed—and a built-in desk for doing my homework. I panicked. Somehow I decided that the only obstacle to our returning to Amherst was the lack of a proper home for my kitten, which was bigger now and no longer quite so cute. The day after my mother announced her custodial gambit, I went to the Mission Beach boardwalk with the cat in my arms. I was hugely relieved when I found someone to take it. Now there was nothing holding me back.

Which turned out to be true, though for reasons having nothing to do with the cat. In 1968, soon after we moved to Amherst, my father had obtained temporary custody of us. (In his order, the judge had referred to my mother's "illness" with enough delicate disapproval to make the reference worthy of Tennessee Williams.) My mother's hasty action in San Diego must not have been enough to supersede that order, because she finally agreed to send us home in time to start school. Both my father and stepmother picked us up at the airport, and when we pulled in to our driveway, I was overjoyed. I reveled in the cleanliness of the house. I appreciated the spotless red carpet in the hallway leading to the staircase that in turn led up to our large, orderly bedrooms; the fresh tracks left by the vacuum cleaner gave me inexplicable solace. For the rest of my life, staircases, especially those with thick banisters and sturdy newel posts, would symbolize stability. And promise.

At the same time, I sensed that however intact it all seemed, something wasn't right. My father and stepmother fought constantly. Vivienne openly favored her own children, picking on Sarah in particular, while my father complained bitterly about my stepbrothers' laziness and general good-for-nothingness. Still, I convinced myself that it wasn't so much *whom* I wanted to be with but *what* I wanted to be with: the big open kitchen with a built-in fireplace and cabinets Vivienne had painted in bright mod yellow, purple, and orange; the school bus that stopped at our corner; and my clutch of friends at school. The Amherst house proved there was an alternative to my mother's lifestyle, which required me to pee into a jar so as not to come upon adults having sex.

Within a few days of our return, my father and stepmother told us that my mother was suing for custody, as well as back child support for the years we'd been living with them. As soon as Sarah and I arrived in Rochester in April 1968, my father had stopped paying. Now my mother's parents had talked her into staking a legal claim to the support. They had hired an expensive Boston lawyer named Brooks Potter, while my father and stepmother found a less expensive but tenacious lawyer named Selma Rollins.

On the day of the hearing—September 11, 1970, the day before Sarah's fifteenth birthday—my father and stepmother took the five of us out of school, put us in the van, and drove the eight miles to the Hampshire County Superior Courthouse in the town of Northampton. Having all the children present had been Vivienne's idea. She was intent on conveying the impression of a happy, cohesive family—a ruse, given the tension at the time, but a pleasing montage to offer up to the judge.

My mother, accompanied by my grandfather and Mr. Potter, was dressed conservatively in a long gray wool dress—also an effect aimed at the judge. I remember being struck by how unlikely such an article of clothing seemed. I was accustomed to seeing her in sporty slacks and the occasional minidress, not Amish-inspired attire. In fact, the playacting on both sides was hard to ignore. Here was Vivienne, who on her best days was a cold fish of a mother, acting like Gaia herself. And then there was my mother—yes, the same one who boasted of her sexual conquests to her young daughters—dressed like Maria von Trapp.

Sarah and I weren't invited into the courtroom, but our feelings were apparently something the court wanted to take into consideration.

I was interviewed in a separate room, apart from Sarah, and asked where I'd like to live. I remember expressing my preference to remain in Amherst. I was asked to draw a diagram of the layout of my mother's bungalow, which made it clear that there was only one route to the bathroom: through my mother's bedroom. This architectural detail apparently sparked the judge's interest and concern. Selma Rollins was aggressive, if not downright cruel, in her determination to characterize my mother as unfit. By the time my mother emerged from the courtroom, she was ashen. My protective instincts must have kicked in, because I remember rushing to her side. But I don't remember much else.

The judge was a conservative man raised down the road, in the farming town of Hadley, a swatch of a place known for its fine asparagus. He handled many of the divorce and custody cases in the county and no doubt had seen his share of scandal, but perhaps no behavior quite so blatant as my mother's. There was plenty to chew on in our sorry tale, but he had focused on one thing: the diagram I had drawn. The placement of the bathroom and the implications of that placement were to become the central fact around which all else pivoted.

The judge awarded permanent custody to my father and stepmother. This was a slap in the face to my mother, coming at a time when women were almost always awarded sole custody, out of the belief that the mother was the most appropriate parent to raise a child. When deciding custody cases, courts embraced this sentiment, which was known as the "tender years doctrine." (It wasn't until later in the 1970s that a major shift in custody law reversed that well-entrenched preference for the mother, and the tender years doctrine gave way to a different standard, known in legal circles as the "best interests of the child.") In 1970, the maternal preference was set aside only when the mother was found to be "for some reason . . . unfit for the trust." The principal reason for my mother's unfitness was, of course, her drinking, which gave rise to a branching tree of unacceptable behaviors.

After the judge's ruling, my mother and grandfather and the Boston lawyer huddled briefly in the hallways outside the courtroom. Then they were gone.

Sarah was crushed at the outcome. Her allegiance to our mother throughout the court proceedings had been unwavering. I was pleased

15.

Stirrings

We love but once, for once only are we perfectly equipped for loving.

—Cyril Connolly, THE UNQUIET GRAVE

MATT LYON WAS A BEAUTIFUL BOY WHO GREW EVER MORE STRIKING over time. He had long, delicate fingers, high cheekbones, and thick curls of blond hair that he pulled back into a ponytail. He was like Tadzio, the fourteen-year-old boy from *Death in Venice,* who represents the very ideal of youthful beauty. And for me, at age thirteen, Matt went from being one of the Lyon boys to my object of single-minded obsession. Throughout the spring of eighth grade, I held my crush on Matt close, telling no one about it. And then, by some miracle, during a weeklong school camping trip at the end of the year, Matt noticed me. He started to single me out, ever so tentatively gravitating to me. We didn't say much to each other—we were too shy for that. But on that camping trip, everything else melted away as we focused on our intense mutual awareness. On the last night, he crawled into my tent and lay silently next to me, my hand in his, while my tent-mate slept. An hour later he was gone.

by the ruling but also ashamed of myself. I had been proven a traitor to both my mother and my sister, who now sat glum and silent in the farthest backseat of the van. Not only had I expressed a preference for my father and Vivienne, but *I had produced the damning diagram*, complete with the inconvenient bathroom that served as Exhibit A. Still, even as a twelve-year-old, I sensed that Sarah and I were collateral damage. Our feelings were beside the point.

Then summer arrived. I had been planning to go to California to see my mother and was waiting for her to call with details. I never called her myself, though I did write her letters. I had been crushed too many times after dialing her number and hearing her answer the phone drunk and clearly disappointed to hear the voice of her daughter. She called us sometimes but only if something pressing—usually involving logistics—needed to be conveyed. A week or two before I was to leave for California, she called to say she couldn't have me come after all. She "wasn't up for a long visit." Perhaps she was drinking, or getting over a binge, or felt she might tip over into one, or just plain didn't have the emotional room to have me there. Whatever her reason, I was devastated. My stepmother had been standing near the phone, and when I hung up she consoled me, tut-tutting as she went. The subtext was clear: My mother was an unreliable, unpredictable, selfish woman, and that judge in Northampton had made precisely the right call.

I persuaded my father and stepmother to send me to a theater camp on Long Island instead. The night before I was to leave, magic happened. I was staying in my stepsister's room on the lower level of the house, because she was away, working as an au pair in Belgium ("Anything to get out of there," she told me years later). The back door opened directly to the lower level of the house, and my stepsister's room was just inside the door. Hearing a tap at the back door, I opened it, and Matt came in and climbed into my bed. My recollection is that we simply lay there, too terrified to do more than hold hands. At around midnight, we heard footsteps coming down the stairs. It was my father, coming to check on me. Matt dashed into the closet, my father opened the door, peered in, then shut it again. Matt emerged from the closet, tiptoed back to the bed, and finally left at 5:00 A.M.

I spent much of my summer on Long Island preoccupied with thoughts of Matt, wondering what would happen in the fall. I wrote him several times, but he didn't respond. I began to wonder if I had dreamed our night together.

While I was at camp, Sarah, who had fallen in with a group of college kids, hung around Amherst, then decided that she was going to visit my mother regardless of her state. Sarah wanted desperately to get away from home. The atmosphere was poisonous. My father, who was now repeating the pattern established with my mother ten years earlier, spent most of his time at work. When he was home, he and my stepmother fought frequently, usually about Sarah, whom my stepmother had come to dislike and distrust. So Sarah set off to California with a new boyfriend I had yet to meet. All I knew was that he was an Amherst College student named Derek.

At the end of the summer, after both Sarah and I had returned, she invited Derek to dinner. Before he arrived, she told me all about her beau: so smart and wise and mature, and, best of all, she said, "Mom loves him!" My stepsiblings still hadn't returned from their various summer getaways, so when Vivienne set the formal dining room table, it was for just the five of us. The moment the boyfriend entered the house, I knew the evening would not go well. Tall and gaunt, he wasn't merely unshaven; he was dirty. He wore a blue work shirt and jeans that looked as if they hadn't been washed in weeks. After an uncomfortable silence, Sarah ran up to him and threw her arms around his neck. He kissed her passionately. I squirmed. It was all so discordant. Sarah had reached the height of a young woman without having shed the soft features of childhood. And here she was, engaging in a kiss that was like something in a movie she was too young to see.

My father and Vivienne made an effort, asking him polite and uninteresting questions. "You attend Amherst College, Derek? And when do you graduate?"

"I guess when I feel like it," the boy-man answered. He had attacked his plate of food as if it were prey, utterly without appreciation.

At Hampshire, where he taught undergraduates, my father had seen plenty of college students like Derek. They'd been to Woodstock and dropped acid and opposed the Vietnam War and despised authority. But this one was in my father's house, eating my father's food, and sleeping with his fifteen-year-old daughter. Things turned from awkward to unpleasant. My father began to lecture Derek. He had made a decent home for his two daughters, he said. He suggested that Derek look around and appreciate it. Derek then delivered a speech of his own. He told my father that this cloistered and stifling place was not the best atmosphere for Sarah, that she was old enough to be independent. Then he announced the apparent reason for the visit. "Sarah isn't happy living with you. I think it would be best for her if she came to stay with me."

I recall that my father's face registered pure astonishment. Vivienne reverted to an annoying habit of drumming her fingers against the table.

"Where are you planning to live, for God's sake, and since when are you so unhappy here?" my father asked Sarah, who in turn looked to Derek for support. But he said nothing.

"Well, we're always yelling at each other, and you have such stupid rules. Derek's smart, and he's made me see that I can't put up with the shit you guys feed me anymore. I need a life of my own with someone who really cares," she said. She was crying. Derek remained silent. I despised him.

Now Vivienne spoke up. "Your father asked you where you were going to live, Sarah."

"I guess I'll live with Derek in his fraternity, right, Derek?" Derek nodded.

At this, my father exploded. "A fraternity house? You mean you want to go with this freeloader and be somebody's girl in some frat house? You want to go off with this long-haired lump of nothing who doesn't have enough goddamned decency to come into this house in clean clothes?" I was silently amused by his focus on Derek's clothing. But I knew my father was right. Sarah had to stay, and someone had to persuade her.

"Sarah," I said meekly. "You have to go to school." She glared at me.

By now Derek was standing at the door. "Sarah," he said, "you can either stay and listen to your old man spout garbage or you can come with me."

Then, in contrast to his primal outburst of a few minutes earlier, my father grew formal and grave. He gave his daughter an ultimatum: "If you leave this house, you deserve no further support or attention from us."

Vivienne was still tapping the table. I looked at her and instantly knew that my father wasn't the bad guy here. It was my stepmother. She had long since identified Sarah as the troublemaker, and now she wanted my sister out of the house. My passive father was merely carrying out orders. Clearly he and Vivienne had discussed "the Sarah problem" behind closed doors, and my stepmother must have been pressuring him to get tough with her.

Sarah hesitated for a moment, then followed Derek out. I wanted to run after her, but I didn't. I had learned this much about growing up: Watch your back; let someone else get hurt; keep your own skin out of the game. Nothing further was said. My father went into his study and shut the door. I heard his typewriter. Vivienne went into the kitchen and started doing dishes.

I walked out of the house and across the cornfield, turned right on North Pleasant Street, and knocked on the Lyons' kitchen door. Denny opened it. Matt was seated at the kitchen table, eating slices from a loaf of packaged rye bread. He looked up at me and smiled. Our first kiss took place a few weeks later, in the cornfield, not long after the combine had been through for the harvest, leaving behind a hay-strewn carpet. When autumn peaked, Matt and I, undeterred by the cold, met nearly every night after dinner in that pitch-black cornfield, the stars sprayed like foam across the night sky. Sometimes we had a perfect slice of moon. Both of us impossibly shy, we threw ourselves into our explorations with ample enthusiasm but few words. Every silent roving of our hands was a small pledge to each other. The quiet was filled with the nylon rustling of Matt's down jacket, which he had bought with earnings from his after-school job at Watroba's, the neighborhood market. That jacket kept both of us warm. When winter arrived, we moved to Matt's upstairs bedroom and spent hours there. Remarkably enough, our virginity remained intact. Years later, I asked Denny what she was thinking during those evenings when she was downstairs in the kitchen and we were up in Matt's bedroom with the door closed. "I wasn't thinking, darling," she replied. "I was praying."

FOR SARAH, THE DAY she left the house with Derek marked the onset of years of chaos and misery. Clouds of trouble followed her wherever she went. Her move to the Amherst College fraternity, Theta Xi, a brotherhood of dope-smoking hippies, was just the beginning. It was there, I believe, that she began to drink heavily. "Drunkards beget drunkards," observed the philosopher Plutarch nearly two thousand years ago. Contemporary scientists have confirmed that nod at genetic vulnerability with scores of studies. The bottom line is that alcoholic parents are four times more likely to have children who become alcoholics.

Against my stepmother's strict orders, I went to see Sarah at the fraternity. I stole food from our kitchen cupboard and took it to her. But I hated being there. There were empty wine jugs around the room, and whenever I went, Derek was nowhere to be seen. When I got home from those visits, Vivienne eyed me with suspicion. "You've been to see Sarah, haven't you?" she once said. I denied it, but my lie was transparent. My stepmother could smell the place on me.

After a few months, Sarah moved to a foster home in a nearby town, where she lived with a family named the Sullivans. I rode my bike to visit her there, and she seemed happier than she had been in the fraternity. But the next thing I heard, from my father and Vivienne, was that Sarah had "seduced" the husband and had been thrown out. She returned to the fraternity.

Logic dictated that Sarah's absence would prompt my father and stepmother to fight less, but they fought more. I took refuge from the strife at home by going to Matt's house, where I quickly became a fixture. When the Lyon family went on camping trips in the Travelall, I went along.

Dick and Denny were friends, partners, lovers. Even then I could recognize that this was a couple better together than apart. Denny made Dick a better version of himself, and vice versa. I studied their behavior, so different from that of my own parents. When Denny spoke, Dick paid attention to his wife's words with the respect he might give a colleague at work. When Dick listened to Denny, his body was perfect stillness. And Denny was the same. For many years after their quiet, esoteric teachings, Dick and Denny were the two people I thought of whenever I tried to conjure an approach to real love and marriage. Matt in turn taught me how to love. It was as if he noticed that I was missing a limb, which he was determined to find and reattach. Dick and Denny's certainty about how to love trickled down to their children. I was befuddled as to why Matt Lyon, who had the pick of any girl at Amherst High School, would choose me.

But he did, and he was convinced we would spend the rest of our lives together.

The summer before my junior year of high school, however, I went to visit my mother on my own. She was living in yet another San Diego beach community, called Pacific Beach. Her binge drinking was out of control—a week of sobriety followed by a week shitfaced in bed. One morning, she totaled her car while trying to drive home from the liquor store. She was so discombobulated that she thought nothing of it and wandered back to the apartment on foot, bag of booze in hand. She was unhurt and, as far as I could tell, unfazed. When I asked her if something had happened, she just looked at me, confused, and mumbled something about her car.

Dieter was out of town, and he and my mother were going through one of their periodic breakups. I called a friend of theirs for help. He had a key to Dieter's apartment and took me there to sleep for a night or two, then he returned to my mother's, sorted out the car mess, and stayed with her until she sobered up. In retrospect, I should have gotten on a plane and returned to Amherst. Instead, I escaped to the San Diego tennis courts, where one day a fellow player who, at twenty, was five years older than I, tried to pick me up. Feeling vulnerable yet proud of my apparent powers of attraction, I reported the incident to my mother. Rather than offer me any guidance, any words of caution about being involved with someone so much older, she immediately took me to her gynecologist to be fitted for a diaphragm. The doctor was kindly and unquestioning. When I left the examining room, my little rubber dome packed tidily into its pink plastic case, I was excited to be a new pledge in my mother's sorority, caught up in her thrill at the idea that I was going to lose my virginity.

Once deflowered, I promised the tennis player I would break up with my boyfriend back home. In a fit of selfish cruelty, when I returned to Amherst at the end of the summer, that is precisely what I did. Furious and crushed, Matt stopped speaking to me altogether. I wrote him letters over the eighteen years that followed, but he never replied, and I was sure he had tossed them out, perhaps without reading them.

Then, in early 1992, Matthew Lyon reentered my life. He hadn't married, but I had, to a talented fellow reporter. The only real source of disagreement in our marriage was children. My husband once told me that it wasn't so much that he didn't want children; he just wasn't sure that he wanted to have children with me—someone as focused on work as he was—since he had no interest in sacrificing his journalistic career for the sake of being a parent. And he was right: Our marriage was fine day to day, but if children had entered the picture, it would have required long-term concessions that neither of us was willing to make.

In late 1991 I published a piece in *The New York Times Magazine* that caught Matt's attention. He was thirty-five and living in Austin. Dick and Denny were in Austin now, too, and Matt was at their house for breakfast one Sunday when he saw the article. "Is that our Katie Hafner?" he said to Denny.

Certain that we were meant to be together, Matt got in touch with me, and when he heard that I was having misgivings about my marriage, he wooed me fervently. At the time, I was commuting every few months between New York and Berlin, where I was writing freelance pieces for *The New York Times* and researching a book. Over a period of months, Matt sent a postcard or letter to Berlin every day. An inveterate clothes shopper, he shipped off dresses and blouses he hoped I'd like. When I was home in New York, he sent a large bouquet of yellow tulips; written on the card was just this line from an e. e. cummings poem: "love is the whole and more than all."

It's no accident that in middle and old age people often circle back to their first love. It's a way of returning to a time when we felt safe, before real life intervened, before there was any true intimation of mortality. There's a voice in our head—irrational, but there nonetheless—that whispers, *If only you had stayed with this person, life would have remained simple. None of the bad things would have happened.*

While Matt was trying to win me back, he came to New York, and we spent one intense weekend together. On his last night in town, we sat in my car and for a full hour he wept, mostly over his older brother, Christopher, who had died three years before, at age thirty-four, of a melanoma caught too late. He was also crying over what it felt like to be together again: His heart was back in a dwelling place that he had once believed was meant to be. And the same was true for me. Matt had offered stability where there was none, and here he was again, offering that and more. Not only did he want children, but he had always assumed I was the one with whom he would have those children. In this life we love who we love. That Matthew felt this with such clarity took my breath away. And for that very clarity, I loved him back. Why not deposit my own uncertain heart into the hands of someone so sure of his own? I was once again in love with Matt Lyon and began to wonder if there was ever a time when I wasn't.

Before finally deciding what to do about my marriage, I asked Matt to come with me to San Diego, to meet my mother for the first time. For years, I had been telling her about my relationships with men, and she never shied from telling me what she thought. I knew that she had no special affection for my husband the journalist. When I had told her the news of our engagement, her response was, "He'll make a great first husband." After we married, she grew increasingly unhappy about him, and he returned the feeling. He once sent a signed copy of a book he had written not to my mother but to my grandmother (who, ever the snob, worshipped him because he wrote for *The New York Times*, years before I did). This was a slight my mother never forgave.

The San Diego visit went splendidly. Matt arrived bearing lovely gifts, and as my mother and I stood at the baggage-claim carousel, watching the handsome Matthew wait for his bag, my mother looked at me and said, "You hit the jackpot."

I got divorced, moved to Austin, married Matt, and promptly got pregnant. Dick and Denny welcomed me back into the fold. When Zoë was born, Denny told me that her job as Zoë's grandmother was to spoil her, not with things but with love and attention. I returned to work after just a few weeks, and for the first several months of Zoë's life, Denny spent the days with her only granddaughter. She brooked no contradiction to her method of infant care. One day when Zoë had a cold, I came home to find my daughter swaddled in blankets. "I'm sweating it out of her," Denny announced. Had anyone else mummy-wrapped my infant in ninety-degree heat, I'd have objected, and strongly. But since it was Denny, I didn't question it, and, of course, Zoë's fever broke that night. Denny remains convinced that those early months created a special bond between them, and I agree.

For many years I believed that Matt and his family saved me. And for years I've thanked whoever or whatever it was that summoned those Lyons back into my life. But I've gradually come to understand that it wasn't just Matt's family that saved me. Matt and Denny and Dick and the rest of their big brood were there, but it was I who knew to seek them out. So in a way, I saved myself. Even—or perhaps especially—when things were at their most chaotic and painful, my natural tendency was to gravitate to sanity, while my sister tilted toward tumult and chaos. Who can know what combination of genes, neurotransmitters, birth order, phase of the moon, or divine intervention determines such things? But I was clearly the lucky one.

Part Three

Winter

16.

Mount Everest

We are a constant stumbling-block to all the tomfooleries and excesses of the outside.

—Carl Jung, in a letter

IN A FIT OF OPTIMISM AT THE BEGINNING OF ZOË'S JUNIOR YEAR IN high school, just when my mother was coming to live with us, I had written her name on a form as the grandparent of record. Apparently my mother's outlook had been equally sunny. At around the same time she must have checked a box on a reply card indicating she would attend Grandparents Day, because in late November Zoë found a notice in her school mailbox, along with some materials to give to the grandmother who had RSVP'd to the invitation. Now my disenchanted daughter tells me she's determined to avoid an encounter between her classmates and the infamous woman who shrieked at them and confiscated their alcohol on that disastrous Halloween night.

"She's not coming," Zoë says as the day approaches. "I fear for her safety."

When Grandparents Day arrives, hoping my mother has forgotten about it, I set off for a trip to Costco with her instead. She tells me she'd like to drive us there. But first she wants to practice her parallel parking.

I'm not feeling very patient but agree to help her with it, because—and, while she has explained this point to me umpteen times, I am just now beginning to absorb it—she won't feel truly free to explore the city with her car until she knows she can also park it anywhere.

While we circle the neighborhood in search of a suitable practice spot, she talks nonstop. The first thing she wants to bring up is Lia.

"Lia is ageist," she says.

"Ageist? What do you mean?"

"She treats me differently than she treats you," she says. "If I take out my checkbook, she says, 'Oh, you're sooo organized!' in a condescending way, like she's praising a child. But if you take out your checkbook, she doesn't say a thing."

"Oh, really? I hadn't noticed that," I say. "I'll watch for it next time."

She's moved on to the matter at hand—the parallel-parking lesson. The topic has obviously been on her mind. She has a two-page, nineteen-point primer that she found online and printed out. I can tell she has read it carefully—probably more than once—because she keeps referring to its teachings.

As we continue to circle, my mother analyzes her relationship to the challenge of parallel parking, comparing herself to me.

"You're adventurous, and that's why you're so good at it," she says. It's true that after years of city driving, I'm now very good at getting myself in and out of spots so small they look like a crane would be needed for the job. But adventurous? Mountain climbing is adventurous. Helicopter skiing is adventurous. Parallel parking, which requires little more than practice, is not. Then I remind myself that this *is* my mother's version of mountain climbing. The whole move to San Francisco has been her personal Mount Everest, and she will not have reached the summit until she learns to maneuver her car into a parking space.

She sees a spot and decides to go for it. As parking spots go, this one seems pretty roomy—a relative cinch. She pulls her car up alongside the car in front of the spot. So far, so good. She recites a few lines of parallel-parking lingo from the instruction sheet, but then, just as she's backing up, she stops, paralyzed with fear.

"Let's do it another time," she says.

"Wow, you weren't kidding when you said you can't parallel park."

My mother takes this in good spirits, offering a kind of compliment to Zoë in response. "Unlike me, Zoë has a parallel-parking personality."

"What?"

"She has a lot of physical competence and confidence."

My mother's words sweeten my day. Ever so cautiously, she is expressing her admiration of Zoë and me for what she sees as our skill and adventurousness. And I'm admiring my mother in return: for the steps she is taking to change her life, to move forward at such an advanced age.

MY MOTHER AND I return to Lia in early December—without Zoë—and this time it's my birthday that's around the corner. I've told my mother and Zoë that there's only one thing I want for my birthday: a gift that comes from the two of them. I don't care if it's a tube of toothpaste, as long as the two of them have called a cranky truce, gotten together, and found a gift that is from them to me. I relayed this request to each of them separately; neither looked thrilled. This could be another futile attempt to force them into détente, but I know that a team effort would please me no end.

At Lia's, we rehash the session with Zoë, and all agree it was a disaster.

"I have the feeling that a great many of Katie's friends know what a terrible childhood she had and what a bad mother I was," my mother says. "It feels like everyone who comes into the house says, 'There she is. There's that bad mother.' I should wear a sign that says 'leper.' "

She goes on. "I don't like that young woman I was. That was one unhappy cookie, not being able to face the day and get out of bed. But why the short honeymoon period with Zoë? Why the warm welcome if she's always known about our tragedy?"

Lia jumps on this. "You take a lot of what that kid is doing as something really personal," she tells my mother. "You cannot see that she's just basically a kid. You can but you don't, because you are so raw. In order to stop being so reactive to her, you need to give yourself the room to be with yourself, to soothe the pain for yourself, even to mother yourself. The reason you couldn't be a good mother to your daughters was because you had been deprived by your own mother. Maybe it's time to be more understanding of what you need. You need to ask, 'What is it that I want? Where am I going? What am I trying to accomplish?' "

This is more therapy-speak than we've heard from Lia to date. Usually her strategy is to tell us just enough to allow us to arrive at our own interpretation. But the last visit must have sent her back to the manual or to search her computer for "what to do when nothing's working," and now she's decided to lay it out for us. I nod, because I think I understand what she's saying. But this isn't working for my mother. Lia is using a language of the emotions that my mother simply doesn't understand. Even if Lia doesn't see this, I do. I see my mother chafe. She starts to wring her hands and says nothing.

On the way home, my mother says, "You seem to understand what Lia's saying, and I don't have a clue." Then she says, "I think I prefer the unexamined life."

This is something that I, too, might have said as recently as six months ago. Now, however, I see that it was living the unexamined life that brought my mother and me to this place.

BOB AND I HAVE continued to see each other, and while we're compatible in many ways, we also have some very real differences. Unlike me, Bob enjoyed a carefree and happy childhood, which he spent in one house in an affluent town on Long Island. His parents, he tells me, are normal, loving people who paid for his college and medical school education, contributed to their grandchildren's college funds, and, on the occasion of each grandchild's eighth birthday, went on special trips to destinations of the child's choosing. In all of these ways, he and I are so different that Bob might as well be telling me he was raised on the moon.

These misalignments don't stop at our upbringings. Bob informs me that *Seinfeld* is his most important cultural touchstone, that in fact most of life's big topics—love, friendship, work, religion, family, and various rites of passage—have been addressed in a *Seinfeld* episode. ("*Seinfeld* is like the Talmud. All truth lies therein.") I confess to never having seen the show. Not only is *Animal House* his favorite movie, but he has no qualms about telling anyone he meets that it's one of the best movies ever made. I've never seen *Animal House,* either, and I'm not entirely sure what it's about.

My musical tastes veer in the direction of classical, Cole Porter, and bossa nova, while he likes Billy Joel and Barry Manilow and idolizes Bruce Springsteen. I read books; he doesn't. When I first mentioned my love for Kafka, he responded, "You mean the guy with the bug?" Bob is a passionate golfer who started playing as a boy. Addicted to tennis, I've never stepped foot on a golf course. In other words, on Match.com both of us would have promptly clicked to the next prospect. But none of this seems to matter much, for there is some connection of heart, humor, and outlook on the world that overrides our differences.

For my birthday, Bob wants to treat me to an overnight stay at a spa/resort in the Napa Valley. He comes to pick me up the day before, and as we're about to leave, my mother comes upstairs to say hello to Bob and goodbye to me. She has met Bob a couple of times, and each time she has asked him about orthopedic surgeons for her left knee (the unreplaced one), which is now bothering her. She tells him that the surgeon he recommended never got back to her. In what I've come to recognize as Bob's modus operandi when it comes to addressing my mother's medical questions, he responds not with indifference exactly but with doctorly reserve. "Why don't you try one more time, and if that doesn't work I'll send him a note," Bob says. I'm learning that this studied blandness is common among doctors when they're asked for advice outside a clinical setting, and his response seems fine to me. But I see that my mother has taken it as a slight. She falls silent.

My mother has sent me off with a birthday gift from her and told me to open it that night. Bob will appreciate it, she said. As instructed, I open it after we return from dinner. There is no card, and the object itself has been wrapped in plain tissue and placed in a large gift bag. I dig into it and remove the tissue to reveal something that looks very familiar. It's a long red-and-white flannel nightgown from L.L.Bean with a smocked, high-button top. It looks familiar because I already own that nightgown; my mother gave me its identical twin a few years earlier, when I was going through a terrible time. When she sent it to me the first time, I was touched beyond words. It was exactly the comfort item I needed, and somehow she had known this. But this time, sitting with

Bob on a fancy four-poster bed in Napa, what am I to make of the fact that her gift choice is a nightgown whose prototype was quite possibly the night frock worn by Granny on *The Beverly Hillbillies*? And what does it mean that she has told me that Bob will appreciate it? I don't want to go there.

As we're driving home the next day, Bob asks me if I'd like to accompany him to Florida in March, to a surprise party for his father's eightieth birthday. This is certainly unexpected. I hardly know this man. Our time together has been nice, but I wasn't aware of just how far beyond spreadsheet-entry status I'd progressed. I'm wary of doing anything too hastily, and a cross-country trip to meet the family is a big step. I tell him I'm honored by the invitation and I'll think about it.

After our lovely but too brief overnight trip to the wine country, Bob drops me at home. The house is quiet. It's my birthday. I've clung to my hope for a gift collaboration between Zoë and my mother, but when I enter the kitchen, I see nothing. No present, and no cake, not even a cupcake. My mother hears me in the kitchen and comes upstairs. She wishes me a happy birthday and asks how the getaway went.

"It was fine," I say.

"How did you like my gift?"

I start to say it was very sweet, but then I tell her the truth. "You gave me that same nightgown a couple of years ago."

"Really?" she asks, taken aback.

"Yes. You don't remember?"

I change the subject. "I'd love to have a birthday cake."

"You want a cake?" she says, looking genuinely surprised.

Suddenly I'm a child again and I'm over the moon because my father is in San Diego for a visit. We're living in the apartment complex in La Jolla, and Dieter has yet to enter our lives. My father and mother take me out to dinner at a fancy restaurant. It's my birthday. I'm finally eight. For these few hours, I'll be with both my parents, on my very birthday. We'll go home later and there will be cake and presents. And everything will be right with the world.

Halfway through the meal, they tell me there's something I should know. Today, November 5, isn't actually my birthday. It's not for another month. They explain: I was born a week too late to enter kindergarten, so they forged my birth certificate. With some heavy eraser work and a typewriter similar to the one used for the original certificate, my father changed *Dec. 5* to *Nov. 5.* And voilà! I was out of the house and in school a year before I should have been. They tell me they kept up the lie because they were so deep into it with the schools. And, of course, they didn't want to confuse me when I was too young to understand.

By now I'm crying, sobbing. I'm not really *eight*?! My parents shake their heads. No, not for another month. I cry harder. Everything is ruined. Shocked by my outburst, my mother takes me home to our apartment, where there is no cake, and no gifts. Because it's not my birthday.

Now my mother is standing by her door, looking at me. "I'll go down to the bakery with you if you want to get a cake."

"No thanks."

"Well, I'm not much of a cake eater anyway," she says, and heads back downstairs.

17.

Drinking a Little

I'll ne'er be drunk whilst I live again,
but in honest, civil, godly company.

—Slender in William Shakespeare,
THE MERRY WIVES OF WINDSOR

PART OF THE PROCESS OF ENTERING INTO A RELATIONSHIP WITH BOB means we're stepping into each other's social lives. As a busy physician at the University of California, San Francisco, Bob has many social obligations related to work, especially around the holidays, when there are parties to attend. As we mingle our way through one of them, held at an elegant Pacific Heights house, Bob makes a point of introducing me to his UCSF colleague Louann Brizendine and her husband, Sam Barondes. Both Sam and Louann are psychiatrists, and in the midst of our small talk, I tell them about my living arrangement. They're immediately curious, their questions so disarming that I tell them more. Within minutes, we're huddled on a window seat in a corner of the dining room, with the rest of the party melting away. I'm leaning into Sam and Louann's sympathetic probing with my head down, studying the pattern of the room-sized Oriental rug under my feet as I tell them about my childhood and my mother's drinking.

Sam asks me a pointed yet obvious question: "Does she still drink?"

I don't quite know how to answer Sam's question. "Well, I'm not sure," I say. "I think she drinks a little." When we moved in together, I explain, I noticed that she had a stash of cheap wine in a cupboard in the laundry room downstairs—bottles of Two-Buck Chuck from Trader Joe's and cartons of Franzia chardonnay from Safeway. My hunch is that she buys the wine in bulk much as she buys paper towels in bulk, not because she is storing up for a binge but for reasons of frugality. And I'm guessing that she has a glass or two at night, the purpose of which I believe is to help her sleep. Although I've thought about measuring the levels at regular intervals, I can't bring myself to and have simply chosen not to worry. She doesn't drink during the day, and at dinner she doesn't drink wine unless it's to take a small sip of something good I've opened, just to taste it. As I speak, I see a slight shift, a new look of curiosity in the eyes of both doctors.

"Oh!" says Sam, taking in the new information and running with it. "So she uses it as a sedative. That seems fine. But it's very unusual for an alcoholic to be able to drink in moderation. It's not unheard of, but it's very, very unusual." Louann, who writes bestselling books about how the brain works, nods in agreement. She explains something about the technical reasons that partial abstinence is so difficult. Her explanation involves dopamine pathways, pleasure receptors, and enzymes, most of which goes straight over my head.

Sam gives me his card. "If you want to talk more about this, give me a call."

FOR MANY YEARS AFTER my mother quit her heavy drinking, she still claimed that she had never been a true alcoholic. She would refer to her past out-of-control drinking as "whatever the problem was." But Marty Mann, the first female member of A.A., once wrote that "an alcoholic is someone whose drinking causes a continuing problem in any department of his life." My mother's drinking eroded her professional career and caused the loss of her children, to cite two of life's more significant departments. I think she qualified. But, given the times, one might understand why she would have been in denial about it.

In the 1950s and 1960s, it was barely acknowledged that there *were* any women who had problems with alcohol. Even Alcoholics Anonymous, which came into being in the 1930s, at first opposed the admission of women out of the belief that "nice" women couldn't be drunks. A.A. eventually changed its policy, and by the early 1970s, when it had nearly a million members, one in every three new members was a woman. Yet society as a whole was slower to recognize that gender was no barrier to alcoholism.

While my mother may not have been willing to call herself an alcoholic, she nonetheless tried A.A. several times over the years. The only requirement for membership in A.A. is "an honest desire to stop drinking," and that was certainly a box my mother could check. But A.A. didn't stick. My guess—and I'm only guessing, because this is an area my mother is still unwilling to discuss with me—is that she is one of the many people who give A.A. meetings a try but finally say, "That's not me." Although she lived in San Diego, my mother was still not entirely at home in the confessional California culture, which might have made it hard to find kindred spirits among those who attended A.A. She also had the unusual ability to go for long periods of time where she could take a drink without going on a bender, which runs counter to A.A.'s binary perspective—that you're either wet or dry. There's no in-between.

My mother's wariness around A.A. could also have had something to do with its religious overtones. A.A.'s two basic texts are crammed with references to God. And that's just the written material. At the end of many A.A. meetings, members join to recite the Serenity Prayer:

God grant me the serenity to accept the things I cannot change,
Courage to change the things I can,
And wisdom to know the difference.

What are atheists like my mother supposed to do with that? While this has made many people skeptical of A.A., it's also a way in which

A.A. has been misconstrued. A.A.'s culture encourages members to find not God per se but a power greater than themselves. In A.A., you connect first with yourself, then with another alcoholic, then with your higher power, whatever you decide that is.

A.A.'s insistence on a higher power might have been a problem for my mother, but the Serenity Prayer wasn't. She once told me that she carries it with her "always." Given her antipathy toward all things religious, I was sure she was joking, but she insisted she wasn't. Whatever clash there might be between my mother's staunch atheism and A.A.'s spiritual emphasis, she apparently gets comfort from that piece of paper, with the Serenity Prayer printed on one side and A.A.'s Twelve Traditions on the other.

The other thing that helped her stop the excessive drinking was finally being free of her own mother. It turned out that what my mother really needed—to be blunt—was for her mother to die, which happened in 1989, when my mother was fifty-eight. On the day that she heard my grandmother was dying, she lost the desire to escape. "It was as if a spigot had been turned off," she has told me repeatedly over the years, her voice laced with a mix of bitterness, relief, and a little guilt. All it took was the news of her mother's impending demise and she was freed from her ethanol-laden shackles. It's almost as if *that* was my mother's spiritual awakening.

THE FIRST TIME I really learned anything about A.A. was in my thirties, when I read a book titled *Getting Better: Inside Alcoholics Anonymous.* I was intrigued by the author, Nan Robertson, a tough *New York Times* reporter I had long admired. Robertson broke ranks with A.A. anonymity hard-liners and wrote the book using her real name. At the end of the book, Robertson tells her own story, much as she told it at A.A. meetings through the years. After many years of heavy drinking, she finally broke down in 1975, while working overseas. On assignment in Portugal, after drinking heavily with other foreign correspondents, she cabled her editor in New York to expect a long descriptive story. She then sat down at her typewriter and was unable to compose a single sentence for the first time in three decades of reporting. *Unable to compose a single sentence.*

When I read that, the reality of just how destructive alcohol can be—from the alcoholic's perspective—sank in. Robertson immediately returned to New York. Recovery came later.

Robertson was a woman whose professional success I aspired to, who had lived through hell and emerged still a wonderful reporter. (She went on to win a Pulitzer.) If Nan Robertson could beat it, why couldn't my mother?

Alcoholics Anonymous was one of the main reasons Robertson stayed sober. She wrote: "I discovered in A.A. that I would never be alone again—that I could get help and support within moments of stepping out of my front door or picking up a telephone. You cannot imagine the relief, the way the burdens roll off. There is no therapy more powerful than just sitting in a meeting and listening to the lives of other people who, you realize, have all the same problems you do—and then telling them about your own."

I see the point of what Robertson says. And I could certainly have benefited from a similar kind of support, had I ever gone to Al-Anon, the A.A. spin-off for family members of alcoholics. After all, I've read the so-called "Laundry List" of personality traits commonly found among adult children of alcoholics, and I recognize many of them in me: We judge ourselves harshly. We have low self-esteem. After years of living in the midst of family soap operas, we become addicted to excitement. We tend to deny our feelings. Still, even with a mother and a sister who were alcoholics, even after reading Nan Robertson's book, I decided that I had no use for the process. I'm sure it had something to do with thinking I had moved on, gotten over it, when nothing could have been further from the truth.

ONE AFTERNOON TWO WEEKS after the holiday party, my mother is out of the house and I call Sam Barondes, who had offered to give me some further information about alcoholism, particularly as it pertains to my mother's form. He tells me about the volumes of research that have been done on partial abstinence, explaining that there's a slippery-slope phenomenon that occurs in the brain, making it extremely difficult for an alcoholic to have one or two drinks and not need more. Excessive amounts of alcohol diminish the brain's natural capacity for producing feelings of pleasure and calm, while increasing the dependence on artificial means of doing so. The general consensus is that addiction is best managed by total abstinence.

Alcoholics, drug addicts, and even smokers struggle with what Sam calls "triggers." "You pick up the glass, and all kinds of stuff starts happening, all these conditioned associations with whatever you are addicted to," he says. This has been studied a lot with cocaine. Just show cocaine addicts the paraphernalia—mirrors, razor blades, scales—and their likelihood of using the drug skyrockets. "It's very seductive and very hard to extinguish," he says.

For my own part, my body has always simply had a limit, an internal mechanism that says "enough," usually after a second glass of wine. I've spent a lifetime watching how much others drink at meals. I'm judgmental, rigid, and scared. So painful are my associations that when I see someone pour a third glass of wine or order a second scotch and soda, I feel dread, and I withdraw. I know that alcoholics generally have no idea when or how to stop. And this is what makes partial abstinence so unusual.

Sam presses me on how much alcohol my mother keeps downstairs. With the phone in my hand, I descend to my mother's place and notice, perhaps for the first time since we moved in, just how cold, dark, and cryptlike it is down there. The poor woman is living in a frigid tomb. I turn on the laundry room light, open the cupboard, and report what I find: two large cardboard containers of Franzia, both full, and a few other bottles of cheap white wine, all of them unopened.

While I'm standing there, staring into the cupboard, something tells me this is a ridiculous mission—and an inappropriate one. What I'm doing feels like a terrible violation of my mother's privacy. I close the cupboard door.

"Does she get up at a reasonable hour in the morning?" Sam asks while I'm climbing up the stairs.

"Always."

"Is she alert and active throughout the day?"

"Yes, a lot more alert and active than I am." This is a woman who recently started taking courses at the Fromm Institute for Lifelong Learning, which offers courses to seniors and holds its classes at the University of San Francisco. My mother takes two different bus lines several times a week to attend classes in physics, game theory, and landmark Supreme Court decisions. In fact, she's at one of her classes right now.

"Leave it alone," Sam says. "She may be one of those people who has used a great deal of alcohol but never became addicted. That would fit with your observation that she's now able to drink a little and not escalate to massive continuous drinking. The important point is that there's no evidence that she's getting drunk." Case closed.

After we hang up, I'm seeing my mother in a new light. I think of the times since moving in with me that she has taken a small sip of the wine I'm serving with dinner, and that's all she drinks—one small sip, just to taste it. She seems uninterested in drinking more. I'm relieved—and proud.

While I'm still in the kitchen, the doorbell rings. It's a package delivery—a large, heavy box from Amazon.com, addressed to me. I open it and find a brand-new Cuisinart, an appliance I've always wanted but never allowed myself to buy. The note inside tells me it's a late birthday present from my mother. I'm truly touched.

I've just extracted the heavy machine from the box when my mother walks in the door.

"Mom, what a gift!" I say when she enters the kitchen. "Thank you!"

Her eyes are bright. "You're welcome, sweetie. It was something I thought you could use." It's been a while since she's called me "sweetie." Lately it's been a frost-laden "Katie"—or nothing at all.

She's in an exuberant mood, eager to tell me about her classes. While she talks, I fuss over my new gadget, trying out different blades, flipping through the recipe booklet, happily envisioning all the foods I can pulverize.

"That's so impressive," I say. "Will you get a degree?"

"In what? Old lady?"

I laugh.

After a while she goes downstairs and I hear her practicing on the Yamaha upright piano. She's working on a Bach invention, and over the weeks she has slowly but unmistakably picked up speed and dexterity. She started by playing each hand's part separately, and now she's putting her hands together, letting one measure glide into the next, a sign that she's looking ahead in the music. Maybe it's a metaphor for what she's doing at this stage of her life.

My friend Carolyn has invited us to a Hanukkah dinner, and I throw together a salad. Zoë chooses to stay home. My mother and I set off. Carolyn lives on the other side of the city, at the top of a steep hill. I park about a block away and we both get out of the car. As we start to make our way up the formidable incline, I look over and see that my mother has stopped moving. Her head is down.

"Mom, what's wrong?"

"I'm having trouble," she says. "I should be able to do this, but my body isn't cooperating." I offer her my arm, but I'm carrying a large, bulky bowl, which makes it hard to support her. Worse, the steepness of the hill throws her off balance and I can see she's visibly shaken. I think about getting her back in the car and driving her to Carolyn's front door. But I decide to just stay with her, urging her on, as she inches her way up the sidewalk. She becomes uncharacteristically quiet as she takes in what is to become a watershed moment: the unhappy realization that her body can't do something that it once—only yesterday, it seems—achieved with ease. After dinner, I pull the car around to the front of Carolyn's house. But the rise from the house to the curb where I'm waiting is steep as well, and my mother's steps are small and tentative as she makes her way toward me.

18.

"How Weird"

Cheer up, the worst is yet to come!

—Philander Chase Johnson, EVERYBODY'S MAGAZINE

MY FATHER'S MARRIAGE TO VIVIENNE LASTED ONLY FIVE YEARS. In 1973, just a year and a half after Sarah left, Vivienne asked my father to leave as well. I was a junior in high school and set adrift. My stepsister was in college, Vivienne had sent her two boys off to a fancy boarding school nearby, and I stayed in the house alone with Vivienne, while my father paid her for my keep. That was the summer I went to visit my mother, got involved with the tennis player, and broke up with Matt. Once my father settled in a new place, I moved in with him, feeling rooted nowhere at all.

Since childhood, Sarah and I had given our father a free pass on life. We grew up worshipping him, all the more because we felt unfairly wrenched from him as small girls. My mother's rants against him only made me love him more. I seldom mentioned him to her, however, because I didn't want to hear her roll call of justifications for leaving him. I preferred an idealized picture.

In my twenties I came to view my father more realistically. He had been largely absent both times that we lived with him. I later came to understand my mother's frustrations with a husband who coped with domestic strife by escaping into work. At the same time, I came to appreciate his agile and steady mind. I believed that it was his optimistic nature I had inherited, his steadiness of spirit I had to thank for my own internal gyroscope. And the more I appreciated my father, the harder it was for me to believe that my mother had settled for someone as drab and monosyllabic as Norm. My father, for his part, wasn't one to hold a grudge, but well into his seventies, his good-natured face clouded over at the mere mention of my mother. I knew little about how to read that cloud, but clearly his marriage to my mother was an episode in his life best left alone.

After retiring from Hampshire College, my father settled into a rich and full life in Williamsburg, Massachusetts, a beautiful small town in the Berkshire foothills. His house was filled with musical instruments, synthesizers, and various pieces of scientific equipment. His library consisted of more than four thousand volumes, many of which he had read more than once. He built bookshelves in every room, even the bathroom. The historic house doubled as a B&B, which he ran with an eccentric but well-intentioned hand. He learned to fly planes in his sixties and used the earnings he made from a sideline tuning pianos to pay for occasional flights in a little Cessna he rented from a local company. When he was in his seventies, he got a second PhD, in musicology.

After I left New England for college, my father and I stayed close and spoke often. He was my reliable source of bad puns and inane jokes, my word man. He drummed into me the difference between "further" and "farther," and "liable" and "apt." His eccentricities increased with age, and people found them charming. Denny once told me that when she was still living in Amherst, she occasionally bumped into my father at the local market, and he was always buying something "interesting," like a single rutabaga or a bag of quahogs.

When Zoë came along, my father was thrilled; he manufactured any excuse to visit Austin to see her, and she adored him in return. She was "Poopsie" to his "Popsie."

On a summer morning in 1998, my father and I chatted on the phone. He told me of the flight he was planning for the next day, and, while I could tell he was excited, I could also hear the fatigue in his voice. He was being treated for bladder cancer, and the treatments made him tired.

I told him that a flight in mid-afternoon, a time of day he should probably spend napping, might not be a good idea. He brushed it off. "I'm fine, dear," he said, then had to hang up because he had guests coming and bread in the oven.

The next afternoon, as my father was flying with a local photographer to take aerial photographs of a music festival in the Berkshires, the Cessna crashed into the woods. Both my father and his passenger were killed. Near midnight, a search party found their bodies and the wreckage from the crash and went to Sarah's house to break the news. My sister then called me.

It was the first time I had lost a close family member. My mind was filled with nothing and everything, so overwhelmed that it just went blank. Matt called Dick and Denny and put me on the phone with them. In Denny's voice I heard not just profound sympathy for me but the deep fondness she and Dick had always had for my father. Then my mother called. Sarah had told her. Her reaction puzzled me. "How weird," she said about my father's sudden death. Not tragic, or awful, or shocking, but "weird." I listened for sadness in my mother's voice but heard none.

The day after the crash, Matt, Zoë, age four, and I flew east. The entire town of Williamsburg was in mourning. A shrine of sorts had been erected in front of the library, where residents had placed flowers from their gardens. When we walked into my father's house, we found he had left the door unlocked and the oven on.

In the next few days, the buckets and vases outside the library multiplied. People returned to straighten them up and freshen the water. Everywhere I went, I felt not just my own shock and grief but the shock and grief of an entire town. People came to the house to tell me they had known my father. They had been to his house for dinner and heard his stories, his endless repertory of jokes, his scientific and political ideas. They had known when he had visitors and when he was out of town. They knew he was worried that the tomatoes he was growing wouldn't ripen before the first frost. They had argued with him at town meetings and read the letters he sent to the local paper.

In certain circumstances, when a death is accidental, when a loved one dives into the too-shallow pond, steps off the curb without seeing the car, drinks another shot before getting behind the wheel, we hold fast to the notion that, but for an urgent clearing of the throat, we could have prevented it. I'd have done anything to roll back the tape to our phone call a few days earlier. In the new version of our conversation, I'd have pressed my father about his fatigue, insisted he rethink his plan. If that hadn't worked, I'd have called Neil, the photographer—this part of the scenario didn't actually make sense, since I didn't know Neil's last name or where he lived—and told him my father was too tired to fly. If only I had called out.

In the months that followed, I made a few trips back to Williamsburg—first for the memorial service, then to help Sarah sort through my father's things. One night, alone in my father's house, I found more than half a century's worth of meticulously labeled folders, beginning with letters from the 1940s, from MIT, Columbia, and Cambridge, offering him positions in their graduate programs and physics labs. Eventually I stumbled upon a collection of legal papers, dating back to my parents' initial separation in 1963. My father had neatly filed every document: the papers from the instant divorce my mother obtained in Mexico, complete with an English translation; my mother's official 1965 petition for divorce; letters between my father and the social worker overseeing Sarah's foster-home stay; and letters between the lawyers on both sides of the custody battle.

Alone in his house, I sat down on his bed and looked through the file. There were no real surprises—until I came upon a letter from Brooks Potter to Selma Rollins. Much of my parents' marital endgame had revolved around money, of course. But for all those years I had also secretly hoped that my mother's highest priority in the legal battle was Sarah and me, that she wanted nothing more than custody of her beloved daughters, that money was a side issue, relevant only as it related to her ability to take care of her children.

I was wrong. Ten days after the hearing, Potter wrote a three-paragraph letter to Selma Rollins. "That was quite a day we had in Northampton. It would have made a good television script," he wrote, as if they were a pair of old fishing buddies who had gotten caught in a squall, not legal adversaries determining the course of two young girls' lives. After congratulating Mrs. Rollins on her victory, Mr. Potter informed her that he would not be appealing the custody judgment. He did, however, plan to contest the decision denying payments to my mother.

My first impulse was to shove the papers into the folder and put the file back in the drawer. Instead, I took the entire file folder and packed it into my suitcase.

19.

Huge, Angry, and White

Good Morning—Midnight—
I'm coming Home—
Day—got tired of Me—
How could I—of Him?

—Emily Dickinson, "Good Morning—Midnight"

IN 1996, WHEN ZOË WAS THREE, WE LEFT AUSTIN AND MOVED TO CALIfornia, where I was sent by *Newsweek*. Matt landed a job as head of public affairs at the University of California at Berkeley. After a couple of years I was recruited to *The New York Times,* to work for a new technology section called "Circuits," writing on a topic that fascinated me: the intersection of technology and society. I woke up every morning in love with my job. My editor, Jim Gorman, seemed to walk straight out of a dream and into my life. He was imaginative and funny and careful about not taking anything too seriously. He also understood what it meant to have a family. When I told him that Zoë's class was planning a special field trip to a nearby farm on the day a story was due, he said this: "Katie, five years from now, what will you remember? That your story was a day late, or that you didn't go on Zoë's field trip?" I went on the field trip, and the story turned out fine.

I worked from home, and more often than not the messages on my work line were from Jim. Zoë grew used to hearing them and absorbed the rhythms of my job. Sometimes after dropping her at school, I would go into my home office, punch the playback button on the answering machine, and hear my child's tiny voice parroting my editor's baritone: "Hi, Katie, it's Jim [then a pause]. The story's good [another pause] . . . but I didn't like the lede," she would finally announce, tossing off the word journalists use to refer to opening lines of a story. "So I'm sending it back to you with a new lede. Tell me what you think." And she could be a far tougher critic than my actual editor: "Hi, Katie, it's Jim. The story [lengthy pause] . . . it just doesn't work. Call me. I'll be here until six my time."

Our life bumped along. Like most marriages, mine to Matt wasn't always easy. We were both stubborn and competitive. And Matt was much stricter with Zoë than I was, which was perhaps the biggest source of friction between us. I did not enjoy the good cop–bad cop routine, mostly because I thought he was far too bad a cop, which made me in turn overcompensate in my role.

But Matt knew how to love, and he loved me fiercely, unapologetically. Dick and Denny had taught him all about that, just by being who they were together.

For their forty-fifth wedding anniversary, Dick and Denny came to visit us in our new home in California. We took them out to dinner, and as we pondered the menu, I posed a question I had always longed to ask them: What was the secret to the longevity of their marriage?

Denny's spiritual side often expressed itself at moments like this, but now she said something at once simple and profound, completely romantic and utterly practical, something that has stayed with me to this day: "It's like this menu. You know you can't have everything on it. You have to pick one thing. And you know that if you get the chicken it will be wonderful and satisfying in a lot of ways, but it won't be the same as the steak, which you didn't order. But you made your choice."

That was it. She had said all she wanted to say on the topic. Dick looked pleased, and very content with his own choice.

In late 2001, Denny's menu analogy saved my marriage to Matt. Shortly after Zoë turned eight, Matt and I hit a terrible patch. We found ourselves fighting over things large and small. We disagreed more violently than ever over how to raise Zoë. I felt tyrannized by him, and he felt frustrated and pushed away by me. Then, whatever behavior I had internalized as a child reached up and grabbed me from somewhere very deep. Instead of turning to the menu lesson imparted by my mother-in-law, instead of staying true to Matthew and working things out, I had an affair.

Matt found out, and he was enraged. Were he here to tell the story of the night he shook me out of a deep sleep to confront me, I would be a pathetic figure, sitting on the edge of our bed in my pajamas, hugging my knees to my chest, sobbing, and—of all outlandish heat-of-the-moment reactions—blaming my mother. Her infidelities had been the model for both Sarah and me. I was simply following her example. *She* was the one without a moral reference point.

And this is where mother-blame is a dangerous thing. "Don't blame your parents too much!" the writer Katherine Mansfield said in a letter to a friend nearly a hundred years ago. "We *all* had parents. There is only one way of escaping from their influence and that is by going into the matter with yourself—examining yourself & making perfectly sure of their share." In my eagerness to deceive myself, to talk my way out of disgrace, I failed to acknowledge that my mother did not blindfold me, take me by the hand, and thrust me into the arms of someone other than my husband. I made that choice.

My regret was profound, but the force of Matt's anger and hurt was so great that he struck back with an affair of his own. He matched me blow for painful blow. As a child, I had witnessed so much giving up and fleeing that I nearly gave up and fled myself. Even Matt, who had loved me steadily for thirty years, began to wonder if we should stay together. That's how far to the edge of the marriage we went. Then, over a period of months, we quietly returned to each other.

Friends once told me the story of their near divorce. They were close to arriving at an amicable split when, one day after going to see their divorce mediator, they stopped for coffee at a nearby McDonald's. While sitting there, they realized how miserable they were at the prospect of being divorced from each other. One of them said, "Let's not do this," and the other broke into a wide grin. They've been together ever since. For Matt and me, there was no such McDonald's moment. We both just gradually realized that together was the way we belonged—for us and for Zoë. We emerged from the crisis singed but stronger than ever. And I knew never again to trifle with someone's heart.

Once we were back together, I relaxed as I had never done before, with Matt or anyone. Our lovemaking took on a new tenderness and vulnerability that surprised both of us. "Where did all the passion come from?" Matt asked me one night. "It's always been there," I said, my face pressed against his. "Ever since we were kids." And he nodded.

We were a happy pair, perhaps happier than we had ever been. In what seemed a quiet celebration, for only the second time that either of us could remember, Matt stopped biting his fingernails. They grew from ravaged little stubs into healthy arcs that reached just beyond his fingertips.

In the end, it was Denny's simple wisdom that kept me there with this man who knew love, really *knew* it. Both Matt and Denny offered me a different story line for family than the one I grew up with, one I was beginning to see was possible. And that story line was, more than anything, about stability—not only for Matt and me but for Zoë. I was now determined to give my child a solid base, a constancy I had never known. Indeed, Zoë was the biggest beneficiary of her parents' renewed happiness, as struggles over how to discipline her, struggles that had once seemed vitally important, began to diminish.

ONE NIGHT IN EARLY 2002, Matt had a nightmare. I hadn't known him to remember his dreams. I was the one with the graphic dreams, the one whose nights were spent spinning complex narratives punctuated by menacing figures, missed flights, unmet deadlines, jealousy, and upset. But Matt's dream was so frightening, it woke both of us up. He was thrashing around in the sheets, then he called out a loud and terrified "No!" I put my hand on his chest to see if I could gently shake him awake. He was trembling when he opened his eyes, and he told me what happened in the dream: He was at a maximum-security prison. He wasn't there as a guard, but he wasn't a visitor either. He was just there. Without warning, mayhem broke out—a riot among the prisoners—and a prisoner confined on the other side of a solid wall began heaving himself against the door. Matt knew that whoever was on the other side of that barrier intended to kill him. The "No!" had come tearing out of him just as the prisoner broke through.

I asked him what the prisoner had looked like.

"He was huge," he said. "And angry. And white."

The dream trailed after both of us the next day, and when Matt came home that night, he told me he couldn't get it out of his head.

A week later, on the day before Valentine's Day, his favorite holiday, he left on a business trip. Zoë and I had slipped a large heart-shaped gingerbread cookie into his bag. The cookie was in a cellophane bag tied with a red ribbon. He drove Zoë to school and called me a couple of hours later to check in. Before we hung up, he chuckled and told me that in the car Zoë had seemed overly curious about when he planned to unpack his bag. I confessed that there was something inside from his girls. The next day, he sent me three dozen tulips, and the same to Denny. And for the first time, he sent Zoë her own bouquet. Zoë and I each got notes telling us how much he loved us. I missed his call on my cellphone and he left a tender Valentine's message.

As Zoë and I were driving home from school that afternoon, she said, "I wish my dad would come home."

"I do too," I said.

"I'm worried he's going to die," she said. I had noticed that she was developing a worry streak, but this was a first. In the past, she hadn't noted his absence much except to hope he would return with a gift. "Don't be silly," I said. "He'll be fine."

Before he left town, he was tired. It's only in retrospect, of course, that I now think he seemed *unusually* tired. The day before he was to return, he called from Pike Place Market in Seattle to ask me if I wanted anything. I could picture him standing there in the covered marketplace, appreciating the hubbub of that latter-day agora, with its smells of fish and produce and spiced tea. But he also sounded agitated, so much so that after we hung up I called him back.

"Is everything okay?" I asked.

"Everything's fine," he said, perking up.

"I love you."

"I love you too," he said. We hung up.

Zoë had her friend Jenna over for the night. The next morning, the girls watched cartoons while I cleaned the house. I was in a good mood. Matt was coming home that night, and we were planning to send Zoë off to sleep at Jenna's house so that we could have the night to ourselves. I was struggling with the vacuum cleaner, attempting to pry loose one of the attachments, when the phone rang. It was Don, Matt's boss at UC Berkeley. Was he looking for Matt? Was there a university emergency? I was just wondering why Don wouldn't have called Matt on his cellphone when he said, "It's Matt. He collapsed on the treadmill at the hotel. But the paramedics are with him."

Matt had collapsed once as a child while playing a sport—was it football? I couldn't remember—and after blacking out he woke up in the emergency room feeling fine. I said this to Don and told him I was sure Matt would be fine. Don said to call the hotel front desk, because they would know which hospital he was being taken to. The man who answered the phone at the front desk stammered, "Ma'am, there's nothing wrong with our exercise equipment." That opaque reference to danger stopped me in my tracks. I must have panicked, because Zoë, who was sitting two feet from me, sensed that something was off. She began to cry, her wails filling the room. In her hand she held a sock of Matt's, clutching it tightly to her as she sobbed, over and over, "I want my daddy." She must have been terrified.

I had the presence of mind to call Jenna's mother, Noreen, who was blasé and assured me that her elderly parents had made multiple trips to the emergency room over the past year and were now in perfect health. She was so reassuring that I was able to shift my attention to logistics, to dealing with the infrastructure of this health emergency. I hoped if it was something more than a concussion or fainting spell, Noreen would be able to take Zoë for a few days while I went to Seattle. Noreen said she'd be right over to pick up both the girls. I called Harborview Medical Center in Seattle and was connected to the emergency room. I said I believed my husband had just arrived and gave his name. The person on the other end moved the phone away from his mouth, and I heard him say, "It's the wife."

A woman's voice came on the phone—a nurse, I presumed—and asked for Matt's Social Security number.

"What's wrong with him?" I asked.

Again, she asked for his Social Security number.

My composure vanished. "You're asking me for his Social Security number and you can't tell me what's wrong with him? Can you please tell me what's wrong with him!?"

I wasn't aware of it, but I must have been screaming at her.

Her voice rose too. "Don't scream at me," she shot back. "Your husband is very ill. And my time would be better spent with him than on the phone with you."

I said nothing.

"Do you want to speak to a social worker?"

"No!" I knew I had raised my voice, but I was unable to do anything else. "I don't want to speak to a social worker. I want to speak to a doctor."

It could have been seconds, it could have been minutes, but a doctor then came on the phone and I asked him if he could please tell me what was wrong with my husband. He said he didn't know, but he thought it could be his heart or a blood clot. He didn't bother with the "We're doing all we can" line. He asked me if I knew of any sudden deaths in Matt's family. Yes, I said. His grandfather, Dick's father, died suddenly when he was in his fifties, out mowing the lawn one day in Austin. The doctors decided it was probably a blood clot to the lungs that followed a surgical procedure he had gone through several weeks earlier. But now, as I sat there, I thought maybe it was his heart. And, of course, I knew that what was at issue here was Matt's heart.

Where the nurse had been gruff and impatient, this physician, whose name I instantly forgot, was gentle, his words like a soft pillow. I felt like I was falling into his voice. The doctor told me he was going to go back to Matt, while I remained on the line. I cupped the handset and put my mouth straight on the receiver. This random chunk of plastic, buttons, and wire became a conduit to Matt, an avatar for Matt himself. I began to speak directly to him. I said his name over and over again. Mattie Mattie Mattie Mattie. I told him to be okay, that he had no choice.

I heard Noreen at the door and, while still cradling the phone, I let her in. She gathered Jenna and Zoë, who now seemed calmer. She had Zoë pack some overnight clothes in case I had to leave for Seattle. Just as they were leaving, the doctor came back on the phone. "I'm so sorry," he said. "Your husband has passed away." He asked me if I wanted to speak to the social worker. I said yes. Noreen was looking in my direction, and I caught her eye. I made certain Zoë wasn't looking at me when I mouthed the words "He's gone." Noreen gave me a quick look, then turned to the girls, trying to usher them out the door. But Zoë didn't want to leave my side. "Is my dad going to be okay?" This wasn't a question. It was a demand. I was sitting on the couch, the phone still in my hand. My eyes settled on Noreen, who looked me straight in the eye. "Tell her everything is going to be fine," she mouthed. I must have hesitated, because she made the same signals again. "Tell her everything is going to be fine."

"Sweetie, everything is going to be fine," I said. And they left.

I heard a female voice come on the line. It was the social worker. She wanted to know if there was anyone with me. I have no recollection of how I responded or how we ended the conversation. The next thing I knew, I was on the floor in the downstairs hallway, and Matt's boss, Don, was there. I don't know how he got in. I must have opened the door for him, but I have no memory of doing so. And there he was, on the floor with me, holding me.

Out of nowhere, or so it seemed, my closest friends materialized: Candace, Steven, Amy. They took over. Candace made the phone calls. She called Sarah, and she called my editor at the *Times*. She called my mother, who, Candace reported, was incredulous, but not the way others were incredulous. Her reaction was to doubt the facts of what Candace had told her. Of course that was her reaction: She viewed the world through the prism of her own airtight existence. "Norm's had a bad heart for years and he's fine," she said. Ergo, a forty-five-year-old man in perfect shape with no history of heart disease couldn't possibly die from a sudden, massive heart attack. "How bizarre," Candace said after relating the conversation.

I called Denny myself. The chancellor of the university, a close friend of Dick and Denny's, had just called her. All she could say to me after this, the death of yet another son, was, "Katie, I don't believe in anything anymore."

By sending Zoë off to Noreen's, I had bought myself several hours to figure out a way to break the news to my eight-year-old. The task overwhelmed me. I needed help. The university put me in touch with Judith Wallerstein, a prominent expert in childhood loss. I recognized the name. Looking for something to write in, I picked up the first thing I found—a skinny brown steno pad with *Reporter's Notebook* printed on the cover—and flipped it to the first blank page. As Wallerstein spoke, I took notes quickly, in my reporter's scrawl, as if I was interviewing someone for a story. I took her words down precisely:

> Say it as simply as you can . . .
> "this morning he got sick very suddenly"
> . . . the more details, the less fantasy.
> Say "we didn't know. Sometimes you know. We didn't know. But he died. And that's terrible because we won't have him with us."

I told her Zoë was at a friend's house. Should I go pick her up myself? No, Noreen should bring her home. How was Zoë likely to react? She couldn't say for certain, but her bottom line was that when I told her, we should be alone in the room, with another adult close by.

When Noreen brought Zoë home, Amy and I were the only ones home. As instructed, Amy was upstairs and I stayed downstairs. "Is my dad okay?" Zoë asked as soon as she walked in the door.

I sat her next to me on the couch and began my speech.

"Sweetie, you know your dad was on the treadmill in the hotel—"

She interrupted me. "He didn't make it, did he?" she asked, trying out a phrase she must have picked up from television. She asked me this already knowing the answer. If anything, her tone was resigned, as if she had already prepared herself for what she had been fearing all day.

I shook my head. "No, he didn't."

She was silent for a few seconds, then asked something that took me by complete surprise. "Are you going to get remarried?"

"Well, I don't know," I said. "But I do know I'm going to focus on raising you."

Again she was quiet, then said, "I know you'll do a wonderful job," acting for all the world as if it were her role to comfort *me*. Amy suggested she take Zoë out to the grocery store and buy a few things for dinner. Zoë went to put on a jacket, and when she reappeared she was wearing one of Matt's navy blazers. It reached below her knees. When Amy took her shopping, she kept the jacket on.

The autopsy showed a near-total occlusion in the left anterior descending artery, a major supplier of blood to the heart and a conduit so vital that physicians often refer to such a blockage as "the widow-maker." It was unclear how long his heart had been diseased, but I blamed myself. I blamed myself for causing him stress during our bad patch. I blamed myself for not picking up on his fatigue or any other small symptoms he might have shown. I blamed myself for not probing a little more on the day before he died, when he called and sounded agitated. I would blame myself for years to come.

A few days later, Don brought Matt's suitcase over. Matt had tied the red ribbon from the gingerbread heart onto the handle. This meant he had found the cookie, and the thought consoled me.

A week or so after Matt died, Zoë told me that on the day he left for the business trip, they had had a fight. Matt drove our third-grader to her elementary school, up in the Berkeley hills, which had a steep set of stairs from the drop-off area to the school entrance. The way Matt and I dealt with those stairs illustrated our different parenting styles. Every time I drove, Zoë asked me to carry her heavy backpack up the stairs for her and, classic pushover that I am, I did. When Matt drove, she would make the same request. Sometimes, when circumstances warranted (rain, say, or extra items to lug), he would do it, but usually he would refuse, and when he did, these two stubborn souls got into a fight. As Zoë recounted it to me, that's exactly what happened the morning her father left for Seattle: He refused to carry the backpack up the stairs; she protested while he held his ground; she got out of the car, slammed the door behind her, then started up the stairs. But something made her turn around and look back. When she did, he was driving away.

In the immediate aftermath of Matt's death, Zoë cried only twice. A few days after he died, she noticed that her earring was missing. It was a small blue glass ball, from a pair Matt had bought for her a few months earlier at a street fair in Berkeley. She sobbed inconsolably, harder than she ever had as a baby. And this sound was different from any I had heard her make: It was the profound cry of loss. Her keening propelled me to action. Nothing could be made even remotely right until I found that earring. I hunted everywhere, until finally, on a hunch, I ripped open the vacuum cleaner bag, fished through a cloud of lint, dust, hair, and grime, and pulled out the earring.

The next time Zoë cried was at the public memorial service, which was held at UC Berkeley, for the university community. Zoë sat between Denny and me, blank-faced and still. Sergei, her cello teacher, performed two pieces. The first, which I had selected, was the last piece Matt had heard her practice—a jaunty Russian folk song, one of Sergei's standard teaching tools. Sergei had chosen the second piece: the melancholy saraband from Bach's second unaccompanied cello suite. When Sergei's bow crossed two strings together in thick double stops, creating one high pitch, another low, it sounded for all the world as if father and daughter were in secret conversation, while Sergei and Zoë were momentarily united in grief. He was less than a minute into the piece when she began to sob into her grandmother's chest.

There was also a private memorial, at a small church in Sonoma County whose architecture Matt had admired. My mother left Norm at home with the dogs and came by herself to both services. At the service on campus, she sat in the second row, behind me, Zoë, and Matt's family. She stayed at Amy's house and I didn't see much of her, but when I did, she looked uncomfortable and lost. Her discomfort might have been caused by the presence of Dieter and Maggie, whom Dieter had married in 1977. It was the first time my mother had seen Dieter in years and the first time she had met Maggie. Vivienne was there as well. One of my stepbrothers had brought her to California from Massachusetts. Under any other circumstances, I'd have paid close attention to the exchanges between my mother and all these people whose connections to her were so complicated. But I barely registered their presence.

At the private service, I spoke. I had to. The other eulogies had been about Matt's talents in writing, politics, and art. No one had talked about his most remarkable gift: his talent for loving. I wrote what amounted to a lengthy love letter and read it aloud. In it, I thanked my in-laws for the lesson of love they had imparted to their son and, by extension, to me. Denny was present, but Dick had stayed in Austin, too broken to make the trip. There was a small reception following the service, and as Denny was leaving, she hugged me hard and said into my ear, "He loved you more than life itself."

A short time later, as my mother was leaving, she requested a hug. "I want some of this love crap," she said. I winced. This comment captured so much of my mother: her awkwardness, her jealousy, her need to be loved outdone by her talent for self-defeat.

A few months after Matt died, my grief condensed itself into one focal point: my throat. I had a lump that felt like a large marble in my throat, and when I tried to eat or drink I was unable to swallow. I called a good friend who is an ear, nose, and throat doctor in Minneapolis and he diagnosed the condition instantly over the telephone. It's called *globus hystericus.* My friend explained that there is a sphincteric muscle in the throat that causes the lump sensation. It turns out to be a real condition but one whose cause is psychological, not unlike a stomachache that results from anxiety. Zoë and I called it my "grief lump."

After a few weeks, the grief lump gradually disappeared, and a profound emptiness took its place. I didn't know what to do with myself; without the three-legged stool that had been Matt, Zoë, and me, I developed an all-consuming fear of being alone. When I went back to work, I started going into the *Times* bureau in San Francisco in order to have people around me, rather than working from home. Zoë didn't take it well. Every morning when I left her at school on my way across the bay, she said, "Don't die." My mother called me at least once a day, but I couldn't tell her how scared I was.

20.

Bloodied and Raw

No one ever told me that grief felt so like fear.

—C. S. Lewis, A GRIEF OBSERVED

PEOPLE WHO LOSE A SPOUSE OR PARTNER ARE OFTEN COUNSELED BY friends and relatives, therapists and self-help books, that when it comes to rearranging your life, do as little as possible. Set your engines to idle. Don't go back to work too soon. Don't move households right away. Don't remarry too quickly—or even date for a while. And there are reasons for this. You're not in your right mind. You will act out of loneliness or fear. And frightened people often make bad decisions.

I wish I could tell you that I held true to the word I gave to Zoë on the day her father died and focused all my energy on being her mother. And I wish I could tell you that I embraced each and every one of those unwritten rules of widowhood. But I can't tell you those things. After Matt died, I went just a little bit insane. I was back at work within weeks. I sold our beautiful house, which Matthew himself had designed, and I bought another. But those missteps were nothing compared to the one I then took, a mistake that would have repercussions for me, yes, but mostly for my child, already reeling from too much pain too early in life.

Eight months after Matt died, Zoë entered fourth grade at a new school in Berkeley, a tiny music school for string players. Matt and I had started her on the cello with the intention of having her apply to this small and special school. One of the last things he got to do before he died was watch Zoë's face and hear her shriek of joy when she opened her letter of acceptance.

A few weeks into the school year, Zoë introduced me to Scott, the upper school English teacher, a kind man much loved by the kids. Tall and lean with large, penetrating blue eyes, Scott was handsome without vanity, intelligent without pretension. I suggested we meet for coffee, and after we did, he sent me an email suggesting we meet again.

In one of my first messages to Scott, I told him there were two things he needed to know about me: I was allergic to emotional pain, and my child came first. Of course, he responded. Zoë's a great kid. You're doing a great job with her.

He had two teenage kids, a son and a daughter, ages twelve and fifteen, who lived with him half the time. The other half the time he was free, and wanting to see me. The feeling was mutual, but I wasn't yet ready to let Zoë know about our connection. A friend who was in favor of the union covered for me and came to stay with Zoë one night every week, for which my cover story to Zoë was that I was in Silicon Valley, working on a series for the paper. I spent those nights with Scott.

Having Scott come into my life felt like one enormous gift. In the morning, he brought me coffee and freshly baked biscuits in bed. Once, in the middle of the night when I couldn't sleep, he lay next to me and recited *The Rime of the Ancient Mariner*, in its entirety, which took him thirty minutes. I was charmed. I had never read the epic poem and knew only enough about it to remember that "Rime" was spelled oddly. Scott had memorized it one summer while in college but had never recited it aloud to anyone before. I asked him why. "Because I hadn't found the right person until now," he said.

Scott and I revealed our relationship to Zoë one Sunday afternoon a month after we started to see each other. She went into her room, shut the door, climbed into bed, and pulled the covers over her head. Scott offered to talk to her. He sat on the edge of her bed and delivered a poignant speech: He would not be able to replace her father, of course, but he would be there for her, and he would love her. After a minute or so, she peeked out from under the covers and offered both of us a tentative smile.

We introduced our children to one another, and it seemed to go well. Zoë was happy to have a special relationship with a teacher at her school, but she was also confused. Her father had just died, and even she knew things were changing again, perhaps too soon. And how should she conduct herself around Scott? Was he a teacher? A friend? A father?

Few of my friends thought that embroiling myself in a new relationship so quickly was a good idea. Candace was conspicuously troubled. And my wise friend Amy, who was quietly appalled, tried to warn me with these words: "It's not just your relationship with Scott, or his relationship with Zoë, that you have to think about, but permutations of relationships among five different people." I might have heard hints of doubt from others as well. If nothing else, I should have heard an inner voice reminding me of the colossally unpleasant years I spent with the "family" my father and Vivienne had tried to stitch together.

When Scott gave up his tiny two-bedroom apartment to move in with us, his kids were unhappy, especially his daughter. They weren't particularly fond of my cooking, finding it too elaborate. They didn't like my house and longed to be back in their cozy little place, which is to say they longed for the threesome they had had with their father.

Not only did our children have little in common, but Scott's daughter grew openly contemptuous of Zoë. The one she really objected to was me, not because she disliked me per se but because I had disrupted the life she had for ten years so cherished with her father. But the safer object of open dislike was Zoë.

Zoë began to act out at school, which put Scott in the awkward position of needing to discipline her. It was unfair—to Scott, of course, but mostly to Zoë. That's because a child's grief is ineffable, complicated, unpredictable, expressed in ways that are completely different from an adult's grief. Adults do predictable things: We cry; we have an unfillable hole in our hearts yet we are able to articulate that; we express our pain, our anger, our guilt. We carry out our need to tell people how it happened, and with each reenactment we are working our way through to the other side. If we are in a fog, we are conscious of our fog. And most of us, however bloodied and raw we are inside, get up in the morning, make coffee, get dressed, brush our teeth.

A child does none of that. Her insides roil, too, but in a way she can't comprehend or confront. So she does other things. She talks back to teachers. She hides another kid's backpack. She kicks up a fuss about where she's been placed in the orchestra. In doing these things, Zoë was clearly wearing her grief on her sleeve.

The day after Matt died, my daughter turned to me and said, "Now everyone is going to think I'm adopted, because I don't look like you." Then, a few months after Matt died, as we walked down the street and saw an ambulance speeding by, I said, "That's what took your dad to the hospital when they were trying to save his life," and she replied, in anger, "Maybe if you hadn't had him cremated, they could have saved him."

Still, I was determined to make a new life with this man whose mind I so admired, who recited poetry to me and brought me coffee in bed every morning. And I was determined to successfully blend two families as no one in my experience ever had.

By the spring of 2003, only fourteen months after Matt died, Scott and I had decided to marry. My mother was one of the few advocates. She had quit her alcoholic binges nearly fourteen years earlier, and I had long since lifted my ban on phone calls. No longer worried about what state she might be in when she answered, I called her whenever I pleased and confided in her often and in detail. When Matt and I had had troubles, I told her about them, knowing full well that by then she had no special affection for him; he returned the sentiment, finding her opinionated and meddling. Matt had no interest in trying to endear himself to my mother, and his indifference annoyed and hurt her.

When my mother met Scott, however, she was thrilled. Already inclined to like him because of the tenderness she heard in my voice when I spoke of him, she was in awe of what she considered to be Scott's physical superbness, his powerful intellect and trenchant humor. They were united by a love of dogs and a discomfort around people. And as the years passed, surely they bonded over their shared inability to relate to Zoë. Scott never wavered from his attentive ways with my mother.

After we married, on a few occasions he and his two children even drove to San Diego on their own to visit my mother, Norm, and the dogs.

I know beyond doubt that Matt would have been confused by my remarrying so soon and definitely enraged that I had chosen a man who would hurt our child. I'm not a believer in the paranormal, yet sometimes I saw what I could only interpret as signs of his anger. I was driving to meet Scott one day, shortly before our wedding, when I heard an explosion and looked over to see that my side-view mirror had shattered—spontaneously. Still, I went through with it. Denny, for her part, kept a distance and refrained from judgment. I can only imagine she was horrified by the hasty move. I assured her that Scott was wonderful with and to her granddaughter. She insisted on coming to the wedding. My mother and Norm came, too, but they left the wedding before dark—not long after it started—lest they lose their way back to the Holiday Inn.

Soon after the wedding, Zoë's behavior at school grew worse. Scott began to view her as the source of problems large and small. I took her out of the school and enrolled her in a different music school. Now that he no longer viewed her as his, he stopped speaking to her altogether. Zoë and I lived not so much with Scott as around him. If she and I walked into a room where Scott sat, he greeted me but did not acknowledge her presence. He attended her concerts and recitals, only, he told me, because I wanted him there. After a while I stopped asking him and went alone. Once when I asked him to pick Zoë up from school, his daughter accused me of "using" him.

It wasn't until I tried to make my own blended family work that I appreciated the effort Vivienne had put into the undertaking years earlier. My own attempt ended just as badly. In early 2008, after more than four years of agonizing failure at trying to merge our two families (Zoë once remarked that it was as if the five of us were put in a blender and someone forgot to secure the top before pushing the "on" button), it finally, mercifully, ended. Zoë and I eventually moved in to our small, comfortable apartment in Pacific Heights. For the first time in many months, Zoë told me, she felt as if she was free to breathe.

I look back on that terrible mistake and I now see that it was almost preordained. The Al-Anon literature, which I had for years avoided so assiduously, describes adult children of alcoholics most tellingly: "We are dependent personalities who are terrified of abandonment and will do anything to hold on to a relationship in order not to experience painful abandonment feelings."

It would be too tidy to assign blame to Scott for the way things played out, to say that instead of seeing Zoë for the grief-stricken child she was, he punished her for it and allowed his children to do the same. That's true, of course, but while every intersecting point went sour, while we all played a part in the drama, Zoë had a starring role. She hated seeing me in love with a man who was not her father. She hated watching him absorb my attention, which she believed by all rights should be hers and hers alone. I had no inkling that two years later I would see a repeat of that dynamic, as day after day passed without a word exchanged between my mother and my daughter. It would be some time after both of these disasters before I recognized my own complicity, saw that by always trying to follow the path of least resistance I made things worse for everybody. And yet it takes a tremendous amount of strength to break the patterns of a lifetime. I wasn't there yet.

Zoë and I were alone again and just beginning to pick up the pieces of the past five years when, two months after Scott left, I got caught in a newsroom cutback and was laid off with no warning. I had dropped Zoë at school and was on my way to work when I got a call from the *Times*'s business editor, summoning me to the San Francisco Hyatt to meet with a "masthead" editor from New York, who was in town for a few hours to hand me my papers, on her way to other bureaus to do the same to a handful of other reporters.

Unemployment was everything it was cracked up to be: Horrible. And frightening. For several months I lost my footing altogether. I have no memory of this, but Denny told me later that when I called her the day I was laid off, through my sobs I said, over and over, "They're going to take my child away. They're going to take my child away"—as if, stripped of my livelihood, I would lose Zoë, who would be taken into protective custody, away from a mother who could no longer care for her.

I had never lost a job. And being laid off from *The New York Times* has a particularly cruel edge to it. Working for the *Times* is insidious that way. If you're not careful—and most *Times* reporters aren't—your identity gets wrapped up in it. You forget where you end and the paper begins. When I encountered people I had met before who had trouble recalling my name, instead of "Remind me of your name," they would nod in recognition and simply say, *"New York Times."*

The layoff also threw Zoë. She said she felt as if her father had died all over again, and her separation anxiety escalated into full-blown panic. We had been planning for months for her to go to a camp in upstate New York that summer, but as soon as I dropped her off, she started to have trouble. The camp had bad cell service, so if she wanted to talk to me—which was every minute of the day—she had to walk from her cabin to the dining hall to use the pay phone. If I didn't answer the phone when she called, it caused a terrifying panic attack, and her mind filled with images of me flatlining in a hospital or being hit by a drunk driver.

When we did finally connect, she would feel anxious again the second we hung up. She had long been seeing a grief therapist, and after he spoke with Zoë to assess the situation, he told me to bring her home. We followed through with the next planned summer event, a two-week academic program for her in Oxford. But this time I went with her. We both bought cheap cellphones and stayed in constant touch during the day. Nights I spent with her in her dormitory room, sleeping in the narrow bed while Zoë slept on the floor beside me.

It wasn't until December of 2008, seven months after I lost my job and nearly seven years after Matt's death, that Zoë was able to make it through a day without calling me to make sure I was alive.

21.

Culling a Life

If only there could be an invention . . . that bottled up memory, like scent. And it never faded, and it never got stale. And then, when one wanted it, the bottle could be uncorked, and it would be like living the moment all over again.

—Daphne du Maurier, REBECCA

IT COULD BE THE NAGGING PRESENCE OF ALL THE BOXES IN THE GArage, still crowding my mother's car, awaiting my attention, but Matt is on my mind. One night I dream he isn't dead after all, that it's been a huge mistake, the cosmic equivalent of a clerical error. The next day, with Zoë in the car, I say, "Last night I dreamed your dad was still alive."

"I've had that dream like three thousand times," she says casually. "He just comes to school to pick me up and everything is totally normal."

Different as they are, Zoë's and my dreams point to the trouble we both have when it comes to carrying Matt's memory with us. And I now see that I mean this in a material as well as an emotional sense. There have been things of his that I couldn't, and wouldn't, part with. This includes not only no-brainers like his personal correspondence and his writing but even his favorite boxers and T-shirts. The down jacket we warmed ourselves in when we met in the cornfield during our high school years, now faded and torn, hangs in my closet, next to my own clothes. Very occasionally, I bury my nose in it.

Through eight years and four moves, I have carried around some two dozen boxes filled with these tangible memories. But in the process of culling my own things during this last move, I have begun to see that Matt's boxes have taken on a distinct, mulish character of their own, refusing to be much more than a burden. I resolve to sort through them, box by box. I had already sent Matt's family the things they wanted. The goal, I decide, is to end up with a much smaller collection of things that will ultimately pass to Zoë, although Zoë, now sixteen, claims not to care. "Mom, I don't remember him. Why would I want his old stuff?" Of course she remembers him, but she needs to minimize her connection to him. For me, the boxes are comforting; they help assuage my sense of loss. But Zoë is still working her way toward acknowledging that loss.

I probably wouldn't have mustered the energy for this winnowing process had it not been for Cheryl the downsizer, who knows that sorting through tangible memories can be more difficult than grappling with the intangible ones. Objects, in their very concreteness, tell a more relentlessly truthful story than memories do.

I had started to think about what to do with Matt's possessions when Cheryl was helping us move in to the house with my mother. While I focused on unpacking the household boxes, Cheryl went at Matt's things in the garage—not to edit them but to make sure they were properly stored. Over the years the boxes had crumpled, which bothered her. She wanted to honor him, she said, and bent boxes simply wouldn't do. She washed and folded all the clothes (she told me that some had actually collected mold), then repacked everything into uniform labeled boxes, which she placed in their own little section of the garage.

Now, in mid-December, I'm finally ready to weed the boxes. But I don't know where to start, and I call Cheryl. She carries a map of the entire garage in her head and can tell me where every box is located: artwork tucked against the far wall; his writing—college papers, speeches, correspondence—immediately above; clothing adjacent to that, et cetera. What I really need to know is not where it all is, however, but how to decide what to keep, especially in light of Zoë's apparent indifference. Cheryl weighs in with some wisdom that will become my guidepost in the days that follow. "I don't know if you even have to think about what Zoë might like," she tells me. "Instead, think about what Matt might want Zoë to know about him, or what you want her to know about him."

Every morning, I take my coffee out to the garage to work on the boxes. One morning I pull down a box labeled DOCUMENTS and begin digging through it, with a recycling bag at my side. A third of the way into the box, I come upon a bundle of letters, dozens of romantic missives from a parade of ex-girlfriends. They're postmarked Los Angeles, Amherst, Connecticut, Boston, and Austin. I try not to read them but get sucked in. There was one ardent marriage proposal (from the girlfriend) and a fraught reference to an abortion. I wince. I knew about most of these women, had even become friends with two of them. (But who was *Nikki*?) Why would I want Zoë to see these? I throw them into the recycling bag.

Then I feel disgusted with myself. Here I am, standing in my garage, playing God with Matt's life, editing out the fact that other women had loved him and that there were other women he had loved. I stop for the day. That night, a friend calls and I tell her about the letters. She offers this: "The only relationship with a woman Zoë really needs to know about is his relationship with you."

The next box I open is far easier to deal with. It contains a lot of work papers, only a few of which strike me as important keepsakes. Matt's political work was mainly in speechwriting, and the man had a gift for it. I tuck the most eloquent speeches into a ZOË box.

Just as I'm working my way to the bottom of the work-related papers, Zoë pokes her head into the garage. She's all attitude. "Why are you wasting your time with this shit?" she demands.

Her coarse language is a jolt. "Zoë, do you have to use swear words?"

"Oh, come on, Mom, everyone does it. You wouldn't believe the language in high school." She stops, but only to catch her breath. "And, besides, what would you suggest I say instead?"

"I don't know. 'Crudbuckets'?"

This sends her into gales of laughter. "*Crudbuckets?* Are you kidding? You mean like, 'I got a B minus on my history paper. Crudbuckets!' "

Now we're both laughing. Then she stops and points at Matt's passes from the 1984 and 1988 Democratic National Conventions. Her eyes light up. "What are those?" she asks.

When I explain, she asks me to keep them for her. Suddenly she's interested. She spots a photo of Matt from the early 1980s. She walks away with it and reappears ten minutes later. "Mom, look at this." She holds the photograph up for me to see, and next to it she holds a recent photograph of herself. Perhaps this will help her remember her father, this astonishing resemblance between the man in his early twenties and his daughter at sixteen. Later I see that she has tacked up the photos side by side on her bulletin board.

I feel as though something has shifted in Zoë, allowing her both to connect more deeply with her father and to acknowledge the feelings of loss she has been avoiding for so long. When I eventually get around to sorting through Matt's clothes, she latches on to one of his sweaters, a nubby and soft blanket of a garment.

Over the days and weeks that follow, I develop a keener sense of what else might really matter to Zoë—and to Matt. I find another box of letters, and mixed in the stack are all the letters from me, dating back to the late 1970s after we had broken up, letters he didn't answer. He had kept all of them. He had also kept our more-recent correspondence, including a postcard I sent to him on his birthday in 1992, shortly after we were reunited. On the front was a photo of a dozen or so antique Steiff teddy bears, staring at the camera with their beady little button eyes, the way small children often do. I had clearly been fantasizing about what our children might look like: "Will they be like this?" I wrote on the card. "Blond hair and brown eyes? I hope so. Happy birthday, dear Matthew. You're right. Life is long. And big. Isn't it?" We were so wrong. Life might have been big but it wasn't long, at least not for him. I take the postcard and all my other letters to Matt and add them to the box that contains all the letters he wrote to me, which I've kept in a drawer of my bedside table.

By the end of my time in the garage, I've made my way through everything, condensing the palimpsest of Matt's life into a tidy handful of boxes for Zoë to take with her someday. This much, I think, we can manage to carry around with us for the next few years. A few of his sweaters, including that old brown one Zoë likes, live with us in the house. When Zoë wears it, her hair, now blondish-brown and really just a longer version of Matt's, flows down her back, blending into the wool. And whenever I see her in that sweater, I think that maybe life is long after all.

THE FITS AND STARTS with which Zoë grapples with Matt's death are in evidence again a few weeks later, when, for Christmas, I take her on a trip to Whistler, a ski resort north of Vancouver, British Columbia. At passport control at the Vancouver airport, the guard takes my passport, then Zoë's, and notes the different surnames. Perhaps he also sees that we look nothing alike, because he asks, "What is your relationship?"

"I'm her mother."

"And where is the father?"

In unison, Zoë and I reply, "He's dead."

I'm both surprised and impressed that she has said this so matter-of-factly and without resorting to euphemisms to soften it, like "passed" or "deceased"—fine words to use when filling out a form requiring information about both parents, but not, I believe, when asked a question as direct as the one posed by the border guard.

In the days that follow, we bask in the old rhythms of our mother–daughter dyad. We focus our conversations on Zoë: her skis, her ski lessons, her ski boots, her helmet and goggles, her hungers and thirsts, her friends, her teachers—and boys. I let her know that she should feel free to talk to me about boys. She doesn't brush me off, nor is she entirely forthcoming. I recognize this as the start of the natural—and necessary—process of separating from me, and it feels right. It's perhaps the first time in her life when she will no longer allow me to know her fully. The reverse has always applied to me as well, which has also felt right. I've never spoken with her about my sex life, and Matt and I were discreet. As a little girl, Zoë liked to crawl into bed with us in the morning but never came close to doing so at an inappropriate moment.

Years later, I asked her how she timed her entrances, and she said, "I would lie in bed and wait until I heard you talking and laughing."

One morning over breakfast in the hotel dining room, Zoë wants to tell me something. "You know, Mom," she says, "sometimes I hate telling people my dad is dead. Like when the passport guy asked us that."

"I know," I say.

Then she adds, "So sometimes I pretend he's alive. Like when I meet people I know I won't see again. Like Eric the ski instructor. Yesterday we were on the chairlift and he asked me what my dad does, and I said, 'He works at UC Berkeley.' "

This gets my attention. Just thirty-six hours ago I was applauding her ability to face loss head-on.

"Why do you think you do that?" I ask her.

"It's just so much easier," she says. "I hate how people react when I say it."

This saddens me. But as I look around at all the nuclear families in the restaurant, I can see why she would feel self-conscious. Kids her age don't want to stand out from the crowd in any way. What teenager would want to be "the kid with the dead dad"?

As I ponder this, I notice that many of the children in these families are on their best restaurant behavior. I find myself wondering about what Zoë might have learned from me. Not life lessons but practical skills, manners, and customs. So I ask her whether I've taught her anything.

"What do you mean?" she asks.

"I mean the stuff mothers are supposed to teach their daughters. Basic stuff you need to know."

"Of course you have," she says.

I ask her for specifics and she shrugs. "I don't know. Just stuff. Like putting your napkin in your lap and chewing with your mouth closed."

When I think about it, the only concrete everyday task I can remember my mother having taught me was how to tie my shoes. But she didn't teach me how to stitch a hem without having the thread show on the outside. She didn't teach me what I know about cooking bacon—that it will sneak up on you, that just when you think it needs another minute, it's done. And she certainly didn't teach me to put my napkin in my lap. But who did?

WHILE ZOË IS OFF skiing, I send Sarah an email. Since getting back in touch, I've been asking her for some basic facts about our childhood. Today, among other things, I ask her what we learned from our mother. Ten minutes later, I get a lengthy response. To the question about life skills, she tells me my mother could make a hamburger and open canned vegetables, feed us and sit us back down in front of the TV set. Sarah has more to say—so much, in fact, that the subject line of her email is "It's all very shocking so sit down." I'm not sure if I'm ready to absorb all of this.

Her email is an elaborately detailed account of the day our grandfather removed us from San Diego, and the events leading up to it. At first I skip like a virtual rock over the pond of words, alighting on a few phrases here and there: "the place was almost uninhabitable" and "in bed drunk for a week."

Then I focus. Sarah's memory, it turns out, is much clearer than mine. Once we had determined how much my mother had ingested in the way of hard liquor ("close to a quarter of a bottle") and barbiturates ("a handful of pheno"), Sarah called our grandparents. My mother was enraged at Sarah for busting her to her parents.

Next, Sarah writes something that is difficult to read, and even more difficult to ingest. Just as I blamed myself because of my broken leg, Sarah had always thought *she* was the cause of that messy, pill-laden binge. Sarah was twelve and had just gotten her first period. And that made our thirty-six-year-old, achingly beautiful mother feel old, and threatened by the blooming of her daughter, her replacement. Sarah has always believed that, for a variety of reasons, my mother blamed her two children for her misery: the responsibility we burdened her with, and the lack of freedom we represented. We were her jailers.

Sarah had a far keener understanding of the impact of our mother's alcoholism than I did, no doubt because she took more of the brunt of it. This twelve-year-old girl had suffered a forty-five-year-old's quota of disappointment and had "finally just had it." It was Sarah who could say, point-blank, that our mother had been in bed drunk for a week, that the apartment was a filthy mess. (As I look back on it, I realize it was probably at that moment that Sarah gave up once and for all on being a child; her "I'd finally just had it" was a more general resignation.) Sarah minced no words. She got it, and she always had, in a way I hadn't.

I close my computer and go for a walk.

Later that day, when I return to the computer and open my email, there are more messages from Sarah, and I'm relieved to see that she has moved on to her favorite subject: gifts for each other. Would I like her to send me a pair of pewter earrings? Yes, I say, that sounds very nice. Sarah also has a few more ideas for Zoë: Would she like a charm bracelet? Another season of *Weeds*?

Before we leave Whistler, I ask Bob if he'll pick Zoë and me up at the San Francisco airport. He's happy to do it, but an airport pickup, he informs me, crosses a significant line in a relationship, implying true boyfriend/girlfriend status. The freighted meaning of an airport pickup is a nugget he got from a *Seinfeld* episode, he explains, and I'm amused. Given that he has invited me to meet his parents for the surprise birthday celebration for his father, it seems to me we crossed that line a while back.

22.

Mother Daughter Me

The truth is that it is not the sins of the fathers that descend unto the third generation, but the sorrows of the mothers.

—Marilyn French, HER MOTHER'S DAUGHTER

BOB, ZOË, BOB'S YOUNGER SON BENJY, AND I ARE INVITED TO DINner at the home of David and Matt, the couple who set Bob and me up, and I've decided to bake a cake for the occasion—a thank-you for the uncommonly successful matchmaking. But when the morning of the dinner arrives, I'm distressed at the thought of leaving my mother behind, of telling her we're off to dinner, having her ask where, then having to explain it's a family dinner to which she isn't invited.

Even with an inner voice nagging at me—this can't turn out well—I send an email to David asking if I might include my mother, and he responds immediately: "Yes, do." When I ask her if she'd like to join us, she says she'd be delighted.

Shortly afterward, Zoë and I set off to shop at our favorite Safeway. Just as we're pulling in to the parking lot, Zoë asks me who will be at the dinner. I go down the list and tack my mother on at the end, ever so casually, hoping to slip this past her. No such luck.

"If she's there, I'll feel terrible." At first I think Zoë is angry, which, in part, she is. But there's a more complicated set of emotions here: sadness, disappointment, frustration.

"Terrible about what?" I ask.

"About everything. She just makes me feel terrible about everything."

Zoë says she won't go, she'd rather go to a basketball game at school. She and my mother are so at odds that she has legitimate cause for anger. Then she adds: "And I'm sure Bob would agree with me."

By now we're in the grocery store and I call Bob.

When I tell him Zoë is angry with me for inviting my mother, he's quiet. "You're in a difficult position," he says. For a fleeting moment I think he's going to be sympathetic. He is, but he's also ticked off. He hasn't been drawn to my mother over the past few months. He describes the vibe he gets from her as "cold" and "judgmental." He is disinclined by nature to fawn, and the bits and pieces he's heard about my childhood have made him wary of her. She picks up on it, and all of this adds to the tension between them.

"Having your mother there will alter the dynamic," he says. "You need to understand that what you do isn't neutral for everyone else. It has an effect on others." I'm coming to recognize Bob as a man who knows how to keep a cool head and offer reasoned assessments, an ability I'm both unaccustomed to and grateful for. He does this now without a trace of rancor, but his sentiment is clear.

I'm in the produce section, paying so little attention to the shopping that I'm randomly piling vegetables into the cart—pounds of broccoli and loose carrots. At that instant, it dawns on me that I've invited my mother to a dinner celebrating a relationship of which she disapproves. And there's no question Bob is right—her presence will alter the vibe, and not for the better. I close my eyes and let out a small moan. If Zoë doesn't go, Bob says, Benjy probably won't go either. I've wandered into the dairy section and forgotten why I'm here. I'm so absorbed in the conversation that I'm bumping into other grocery carts with my own. People are glaring at me; I've become a parody of an annoying person on a cellphone. I tell Bob I'll disinvite my mother. He says he's sorry that I have to do that, but it's the right thing to do, and we hang up.

On the checkout line, I tell Zoë I'm going to go home and tell my mother she can't come after all.

"Now I feel bad that you have to do this," she says, but when she hears that Bob has taken her side, she's vindicated. "I told you he would agree with me." The moment is painful, but after the Scott fiasco, I do like the fact that Bob and Zoë often find themselves as a team, even if it is a team pushing back against my decisions. "So when you talk to her, please don't lay this all on me."

When we get home, I hear my mother practicing on the piano downstairs. I go directly to see her and do exactly what Zoë asked me not to do. Sitting on the couch next to the piano, I stammer out something about the tension between her and Zoë and that it might not be a good idea for her to come tonight after all. But I simply can't bring myself to mention that Bob felt just as strongly, if not more so.

My mother says she understands, that she'll go to Trader Joe's to buy herself some dinner. But as I sit there, I see her mouth grow tight. An hour later, I'm in the kitchen making the cake and my mother returns from the store. As she puts her food away, she's banging things around, mumbling—quite audibly—something about how much trouble it is to fit everything into her one drawer in the refrigerator. She's furious.

"I can tell you've been stewing about this," I say, calling out the obvious.

"You would be stewing about it too," she says, then pauses before coming out with what she really wants to say. "The worst part is that you felt like you *could* do this."

"Mom, you're making me feel awful."

"Yes," she says. "And you should."

She's right, of course. In my attempt to anger no one, I've managed to anger everyone.

My mother isn't finished. "I can understand that there's something about me that Zoë doesn't like, but it seems that my very existence is a problem for her."

Now her anger at me is buzzing around the kitchen like a trapped housefly; it quickly lands on something in the corner of the room. I follow her eyes and see she's looking at the garbage can, which, I notice,

I've done a pretty sloppy job of lining. White plastic is poking out everywhere. My mother picks up the garbage can, carries it over to where I stand, deposits it next to me on the floor, and directs all her fury and frustration at this singular domestic failing. "Have you learned *nothing* from your expensive cleaning lady?" With that she snaps the bag into place, returns the can to its corner, and storms downstairs. I'm left speechless.

When we return from dinner that night, having had a wonderful evening, free of tension, the house is quiet, the lights are out, and I assume—I hope—my mother is asleep. As I lie in bed, the incident still churns in my mind. Why do I continue to try to create harmony between my daughter and mother, and now between my mother and Bob? Why do I keep making the same mistake?

With fatigue, oddly enough, comes clarity. Sure, part of it is my ceaseless—and by now clearly futile—desire to write a fairy-tale ending to this mother–daughter–granddaughter parable. But there's something more at play. It was the *man* thing again. I still want her approval. I've wanted her to view Bob as a prize because I want her to think I excel in the arena that matters most to her. I'm still stuck in that car at age seven, with my mother and grandmother appraising my figure—and my future.

23.

Housebroken

You do not want to believe this,
but I have no reason to lie.
I hated the car, the rubber toys,
disliked your friends and, worse, your relatives.

The jingling of my tags drove me mad.
You always scratched me in the wrong place.
All I ever wanted from you
was food and fresh water in my metal bowls.

—Billy Collins, "The Revenant"

Bob's Saturday has too many moving parts. He needs somewhere to park Smokey, his dog, for the afternoon. I offer to take the dog and to make dinner for Bob and Benjy that night. Bob is grateful for the help, and he and Smokey arrive a few hours later; he unpacks the bowls, leash, and squeaky toy while my mother and I watch. We hear a pronounced click-click-click against the hardwood floors as Smokey, a high-strung smooth-haired collie, paces from room to room, assessing the place with his nose.

"Smokey's nails are too long," says my mother.

Bob looks irritated. "Feel free to cut them," he says.

"And there's an appendectomy that needs performing in the other room?" my mother says.

Bob looks at her quizzically.

"Cutting a dog's nails isn't easy," my mother continues, in a tone that lets us know she thinks Bob has no idea what he's talking about.

When Bob leaves, Zoë and I go off to shop for dinner, and no sooner do we enter the store than I see I have a voice mail from my mother. Uh-oh. "Smokey took a huge pee right in the middle of the rug in my piano room." She is not happy. She wants me to get some Nature's Miracle, which creates an enzymatic reaction that magically neutralizes the odor. She's going on at some length about the science behind the product, but I cut off the message and call her back.

"I'm so sorry," I say.

Her tone is grim. "He made a beeline for my rug as soon as he heard the front door close. Then there was a loud sound, like a garden hose. And there he was, peeing all over my rug."

Once we get home with the groceries and the odor neutralizer, Smokey barks at us for a while, then calms down, but my mother doesn't. Not surprisingly, she has strong opinions not only about the dog but about Bob's shortcomings as his owner.

"He told me Smokey flunked out of dog school," she says. "Dogs don't flunk out of dog school. Their owners do."

I glance over at Zoë and up wells the unwelcome memory of one of my mother's dogs, a large animal named Tavi (short for Don Ottavio from *Don Giovanni*). During a visit to San Diego when Zoë was four, my mother and Norm decided they should help Zoë get acclimated to Tavi by having her feed him treats. A moment later I saw a hundred pounds of dog lunge at my child's face, heard my mother shriek, and saw Norm pull the dog back. Luckily for Zoë, while her face would be bruised for a few days and she would be left with a small permanent scar on the inside of her lip, the dog hadn't actually sunk his dagger-sharp fangs into her skin. I was furious. Not long after Tavi lunged at Zoë, he attacked a couple of dogs at the park. My mother had him put down, a decision that devastated her.

While I have no doubt that my mother is a dog expert, recalling her massive lapse in judgment with her own dog makes me want to change the subject. But my mother wants to stick to the topic of Bob. "He's very solid, he gives you a tremendous sense of stability, but he's also arrogant and dull." I suspect that my mother's real objection to Bob isn't his "arrogance" but his apparent indifference to her. I let the conversation hang.

Smokey's dinnertime rolls around and, busy cooking, I ask my mother to feed him. But she refuses, because apparently this would signal to Smokey that she is his caretaker. I try to point out to her that I doubt Smokey will form a lifelong attachment to her if she pours some food into his bowl. She still refuses. *Just act normal and feed the goddamned dog,* I think. But I don't say anything, and I feed him myself. After he has eaten, Smokey paces. He's definitely a nervous dog. Is he looking for something to herd? I pat his head. "Calmer," my mother says, "more gently." I do as she says and he grows still.

When Bob and Benjy show up, Smokey barks vigorously, already on to his new assignment of protecting my mother and me. Benjy whoops and hollers at his dog, and I have to restrain myself from telling him to be calmer with him. Because my mother is right: This is an anxious dog in need of calming input.

Bob, who possesses a fine musical ear that my mother and I both envy, likes tinkering on the Steinway, and he sits down to the piano and plays a little Billy Joel. Zoë, hearing the hubbub, joins us in the kitchen.

Over dinner, Benjy tells me he's been on Amazon.com, checking out my books. The one that interests him the most is *Cyberpunk*, a book about computer hackers I wrote twenty years ago. My mother turns to Bob. "You've read *Cyberpunk*, Bob?" she asks. Her question seems unfair. It's been so long since I wrote that book, I doubt I've ever mentioned it to Bob. He says nothing, but I can see he's beginning to simmer.

The tension my mother has succeeded in introducing quickly gets defused by the next topic: television. Bob, Benjy, and Zoë do a thumbnail review of their favorite shows: *24*, *Modern Family*, *30 Rock*. As Bob and Zoë discuss Dr. House's recent reference to Jack Bauer, I silently wonder whom to thank for bringing this man to us.

When the conversation grows especially animated, Smokey gets excited and starts to bark. Benjy pats his leg vigorously to signal Smokey to come to him, and my mother jumps in. "That will just scare him," she says, and makes a clicking noise with her tongue against the side of her hard palate, to demonstrate how it should be done. So much of my relationship with Bob is going well, but the boyfriend–mother relationship is spiraling in the wrong direction.

Once Bob and Benjy have left, Zoë goes upstairs to do homework and I clear the table while my mother starts washing the dishes.

"They have no business being dog owners; they know nothing about dogs," she says.

"What do you mean?"

"Smokey barks and they get loud and frantic themselves." She's waving her Playtex-gloved hands in the air. "And that only makes him more frantic. Smokey needs to be with people who can really work with him. I'm constantly telling them what they're doing wrong, even though I know I shouldn't be saying anything. He's a great dog in spite of them." She has made her assessment.

Then comes more commentary. "They sure do watch a lot of television."

"Yes, they do."

She shakes her head while piling plates into the dishwasher.

She's just getting started.

"I know Bob's a lot smarter than I am—"

Surely she knows this isn't true, and I try to interrupt her to tell her, but once she has the floor, she isn't about to yield it. "And I know he really cares about you, but . . ."

I can tell where this is heading: straight to Scott, who took in my mother's most recent German shepherd, and whom she visits regularly. And I'm right. "I don't know if it's that he's trivial in comparison with Scott," she says. "Scott is just so smart, and everything he says is interesting."

Oy.

I sense an urgency to her objections to Bob. "If I were about to win a Nobel Prize, he'd be nice to me, but I'm a person of no consequence."

I get as far as saying, "You're not a person of no consequence—" before she cuts me off.

"I'm not making a statement about me. I'm making a statement about Bob."

Oh.

She continues: "And you know what my father thought of doctors. He thought they were barely scientists. He thought even less of them than he thought of mathematicians."

"Well, he sure needed doctors in the end," I say, "for all that heart surgery."

"Yes, but he needed them the way he needed a plumber."

She's quiet for a few seconds, then adds, "Do you really want to be with him? He's such a lump."

A lump? Lumps don't invent entire fields of medicine or crisscross the globe giving speeches to packed conference rooms. I could point this out but I don't, because I'm no longer going to involve my mother in my relationship with Bob, which means letting go of any investment in her opinion of him. My silence doesn't register, and she continues. "He comes into the house and barely deigns to speak to me. I guarantee he made his ex-wife feel like a fixture." Where this came from I have no idea, but she says it with such conviction you'd think she's privy to information I don't have. "And in two years he'll be doing that to you. And you'll be saying, 'Mom, you were so right.'"

And with that she circles back to the man who turned her granddaughter's life into an uninterrupted misery. "You know who I think the man for you is. He's everything. I've always thought that. He's the man of every woman's dreams. If it weren't for Zoë, I'd tell you to go back to Scott now. But you could wait until she goes off and has twelve children of her own and has her own life, and then go back to Scott."

To my astonishment, her voice is breaking. "Things are so different than I had expected," she continues. "I had it all plotted out, with my friend DeeDee, before I even left San Diego, that Zoë and I would get along and start spending a lot of time together and you and Scott would get back together."

I nod, a signal that I've heard her. Then, to my own surprise, instead of letting her words hang in the air unaddressed, instead of seeking a distraction or changing the subject, I speak. "Mom, I know you're sad that it didn't work out that way," I say. "I understand that you think my relationship with Scott was the better relationship for me, but that's not my experience. My experience is that the relationship with Bob is the better one, for me and definitely for Zoë. You have, and can continue to have, a good relationship with Scott. But your relationships with Scott and Bob are separate from my relationships with Scott and Bob."

Then I'm quiet, and so is she. She's scrubbing a saucepan that has mozzarella affixed like glue to the bottom.

"Do you want me to try to get that off?" I offer. "Mozzarella always does that."

"Yes, it does," she says. "I think I can get it." I can see she's determined to clean that pot.

I put soap in the dishwasher, turn it on, say good night, and head for the stairs.

THAT NIGHT, I DREAM I'm at my old desk in *The New York Times*'s San Francisco bureau, working on a story with an impossible deadline. I'm typing frantically, with my mother seated next to me. She understands neither the story nor the pressure I'm under. Nevertheless, determined to help, she keeps chiming in with proposed wording, and no matter what I say, she won't stop. She's so close to my ear that I find myself writing down her words, taking dictation, until suddenly I stop and scream at her. Then I strike her. We're both stunned.

The dream is so disturbing and vivid that I wrestle myself awake. I know it's a reaction to her unremitting impulse to interfere. And I know it's telling me that I need to find a way of coping with that impulse of hers, of drawing the boundaries that Lia has been talking about since our first session. I began to absorb this message in a more visceral way a few months ago, when my mother's comment about co-mingling our kitchen dishes made me actually shudder. But the true implications of it are just now settling in.

My mother isn't to blame for this. I feel a solid little click of understanding. My mother butts into my life because, for years, by "taking dictation," I have invited her to do so. I feared that if I set boundaries,

I'd sacrifice closeness, maybe even lose her. But the opposite is true. By failing to separate myself from her, by failing to take firmer control of what brings us together, I've only created more opportunities for conflict. Now I see that I can—and must—have a different relationship with my mother. My mother needs to move out.

24.

Approaching White

The older you get the stronger the wind gets—
and it's always in your face.

—Jack Nicklaus

My mother is thinking the same thing. We're seated at the kitchen table, she with her decaf–Splenda concoction, I with a cup of regular coffee. We agree that we cannot live together. The immediate and face-saving reason we agree upon is physical. Her knee is giving her a lot of trouble, and each trip up and down the stairs of the house has become a painful chore. But she and I also know that, for all three of us, the emotional effluvium is contaminating the very air we breathe. So far, our "year in Provence" has been half a year of hell.

We're both matter-of-fact about this new development, and clearly relieved. What to do next? My mother wants her own apartment, but we're also both curious about independent-living places that don't require a buy-in, and we decide to go look at a few.

We've imagined these places, and we both know she isn't ready for a euphemistically named "assisted-living" facility, or at least not our picture of what life there would be like—soft, bland, pabulum-like meals served in an institutional dining room; drab, poky apartments;

activities and outings geared to the elderly. Still, it seems wise to take a look at what's available. I contact Anne Ellerbee, the placement specialist I consulted when my mother first decided to move to the Bay Area, who says she'd be happy to spend a day taking us around. She has a few communities in mind and suggests as a first stop a place called Vintage Golden Gate, which is on the west side of town, on 19th Avenue, the busy artery between the San Francisco Peninsula and the Golden Gate Bridge. My mother is predisposed against visiting Vintage because she's already been to the website and the first thing she saw was prominent mention of its dementia unit. She shot off an email to Anne, saying she hoped she was still several years from needing a dementia unit, which appeared to be the principal part of the business. When Anne assured her that "memory care" (there seems to be a happy-talk term for everything) was just a small part of Vintage's offerings, my mother relented, and we set off.

When we arrive at Vintage Golden Gate, I realize I've passed this sprawling brick building many times and never thought much about it. Vintage Golden Gate is the former Shriners Hospital, renovated and reconfigured for seniors. From the outside, it looks prisonlike, and I mention this to my mother, who agrees.

Once we've parked and started to approach the entrance, passing well-manicured flower beds, the grounds look more inviting. Anne is waiting for us in the lobby with a colleague, Susan, as well as a young Vintage employee who introduces herself as Elma. The patterned carpeting that lines the long hallway we start walking down is pleasant enough to the eye. But there's no ignoring how institutional everything is—from Elma's plastic name badge, printed in eighteen-point font, to the instrumental version of "Some Enchanted Evening" being piped into the public areas.

Elma tells us she's taking us to see a one-bedroom, and my mother stops. "I want two bedrooms," she says. Elma looks flustered. There are only four two-bedroom apartments at Vintage, she says, and they're all occupied. As it turns out, there's a 98 percent occupancy rate at Vintage.

My mother asks Elma about the demographics. She tells us the average age is seventy-four, and my mother seems to like that answer. On small ledges next to each front door, people have erected shrines to personalize the entrances: plastic flowers and ceramic animals, framed photos of family members, sports trophies from times long past, even the occasional craft room creation. We arrive at the one-bedroom apartment, and, despite the fact that it overlooks a sunny courtyard, the rooms themselves are dark, unwelcoming, and small. With five of us in there, the place feels particularly confining. I make a stab at a generous estimate—part question, part small talk.

"Six hundred square feet?" I ask.

"A little over five hundred," says Elma.

The kitchenette area is minimal; the refrigerator is half-sized, and I notice there is no stove, nothing even remotely resembling a cooktop. I point this out to no one in particular. Elma explains: "It's a safety hazard."

My mother's actual emotions are impossible to read, but it's clear that she wants to be polite and she's Googling her brain for something upbeat to say. "It has a bathroom!" is all that she's able to come up with. She says this in the high-pitched, little-girl voice she sometimes assumes when she's feeling uncomfortable.

"Well, I'd hope so," Anne says, earnestly. Perhaps my mother is trying her best to be positive; perhaps she's being ironic—hard to tell. In any case, a woman who's just found it necessary to elevate to celestial glory the presence of a bathroom is clearly not liking what she's seeing.

The rent for this sliver of a living space is $4,900 a month. But presumably much of it goes to upkeep, which includes three meals a day in the dining room, as well as all housekeeping, utilities, laundry, a parking spot, and van transportation to doctors' appointments. Unlike the average $500,000 "buy-in" at other places in the area, at Vintage there's a one-time "community" fee of just $1,000.

San Francisco rents are ridiculously high, so $4,900 a month may be a relative bargain. By the time we get to the "tea room," I'm beginning to sense that my mother's playacting is an attempt to mask her dread. We enter the recreation room, where we come upon a very elderly woman in a wheelchair, completely alone in the room. She's just finished their tai chi class but, unable to operate the wheelchair on her own, has been left stranded and is clearly unhappy about it. Elma greets her with a spirited "Hi, Jean!" but Jean wants nothing to do with us. She is waiting for an attendant to arrive and take her back to her apartment, and she complains that she has been waiting too long. She looks exhausted and put out.

"Did you press your pendant?" Elma asks her, referring to a large button attached to a lanyard hanging from Jean's neck. Jean says nothing but looks at Elma as if to say, "Do you think I'm an idiot? Of course I pressed my pendant."

Elma turns her attention away from the despondent Jean and points to the room's original murals, which depict children at play. "What a great place to celebrate life," Anne says. Jean is clearly not in a celebratory mood.

Now Anne is directing our attention to the spotless outdoor courtyard, where the plants are real.

"It looks like a lot of fun," my mother says, her voice now moving up the scale as if she's Beverly Sills. Whatever "it" is, it also looks deserted. As we sweep past the indoor and distinctly unreal palms and ferns, I ask Elma where everyone is. She tells us that family and friends come to visit residents every day. But where are they? And where, for that matter, are the residents? Is everyone napping? Or stuck somewhere pressing their pendants, trying to get someone's attention? Here in this hallway, I half-expect to see a tumbleweed roll by.

Next we get a tour of an already occupied apartment. Barbara, who lives there, is a twig of a woman with osteoporosis so advanced she has taken on the shape of a question mark. Unlike Jean, Barbara is only too pleased to see us, and she invites us to look around. She has moved here from London to be with one of her children, and the apartment is scattered with vestiges from her life overseas—a tasteful rug here, a small antique there. When my mother asks Barbara how long she has lived at Vintage, Barbara defers to Elma, who tells her it has been nearly three months now. Eventually, it's clear that Barbara isn't sure what day it is, much less when she arrived.

Our visit is over, and Elma encourages us to return someday soon for another visit and to stay for lunch. We say we'd love to and set off with Anne and Susan for the next place on Anne's list, Coventry Park, which is closer to downtown. I'm hoping Coventry Park will be better. The lobby is spare but cheerful, with a large arrangement of fresh flowers to the right of the entrance. This time our host is Hannah, a young woman who explains that the building used to house Red Cross offices but since 1998 has been an independent-living facility.

"It looks just like the Cloisters," my mother says, referring to the place where Paula had installed Norm eight months earlier. This is not a compliment, I know.

At this facility, Hannah tells us, the average age is "in the eighties." She doesn't get more specific than that, and we don't ask.

These apartments have a full-sized refrigerator in each kitchenette, as well as a two-burner stovetop. Perhaps people in their eighties have better safety records than the youngsters at Vintage.

As the tour of Coventry Park progresses, I see that my mother is now truly miserable. She's even starting to look aged, transformed into an enfeebled old woman, her back bent, her complexion pale, and her skin so thin it's almost translucent, fine veins visible everywhere just beneath the surface. Earlier that morning she could have passed for seventy, and she now seems at least a decade older.

Unaware of any of this, Hannah is busy telling us about the glee club, the Scrabble club, the bridge club, and the scenic drives on Sundays. We stop to admire the deserted exercise room, which consists of bare walls and two pieces of equipment whose function I can't discern.

"This is a nice room," my mother says in her high-pitched, Pollyanna voice. But it most assuredly is not. When we reach the barber/beauty shop, its emptiness has a particular poignancy. Do people not want their hair styled, their nails done? Where is everyone? If not now, when do these rooms fill with people? The beauty shop is the final straw for my mother, and she delivers a speech she's apparently been rehearsing in her head for the entire morning, storing up for just the right moment.

"Rather than depressed, I'm heartened," she says. "I can't tell you how I've shifted from being negative to positive. The experience today will make me want to do this sooner rather than later. But what I think is that I don't want to move in to a place like this right now. I'm still not psychologically ready. At the moment, I'm—" She pauses, thinking about how to follow this. "I'm very busy."

The other women are nodding. They may not have heard this particular speech before, but they've doubtless heard dozens of versions of the "I'm not ready" plea, some of them uttered by people like my mother, who aren't yet in need of this kind of living environment, and others who are but think they're not. Making as rapid an escape as we can, we thank Anne and Susan for their time and extricate ourselves from the plan they'd made for us to see the remaining two places on their list.

Once we return home, my mother fixes us both some tea. "I just can't do that yet," she says. "I need a few years to really live." Of course, she's right. Even if the time should come when she's in need of more support, I can't imagine my mother at a Vintage or Coventry Park. I can't see her doing jigsaw puzzles, playing bridge or mah-jongg. And I definitely can't imagine my musical hermit of a mother singing in the glee club.

I'm still growing accustomed to the idea that my mother is now unambiguously uncoupled. By unambiguously I mean not just between relationships but truly on her own. Until the day Norm went to the Cloisters, my mother was never without a man. When she was younger, she often had a spare or two waiting in the wings. Oddly enough—odd given that we are at such different stages of life—something in both my mother and me has changed, and changed at about the same time, so that we are both breaking our relationship addictions. I'm happy to see Bob, but I'm also just as content to spend many evenings in a row without him. There's no neurotic need for his attention, no hole to fill that I can't seem to fill myself. It's not that I don't want to see him. It's that I don't *need* to see him.

After Scott moved out, Zoë and I kept getting socked: the layoff from the *Times*, the onset of Zoë's anxiety attacks, her appendicitis, followed by another scary episode, the summer before my mother came to San Francisco, when Zoë had a fever so high that she landed in the hospital again. The hospital staff was sufficiently nervous about what disease she might have that we were both put in isolation, which struck me then as an apt metaphor for our life. Dire as the situation was in the moment, however, something about the fact that I was ultimately able to deal with it—and with all those other crises—without a man in my life seemed to free me from a lifetime of neediness, from a longing for protection within the structure of a relationship. I'm not sure where this new strength came from. It definitely wasn't from years of therapy on and off, which failed to help in any fundamental way. And it couldn't have been meditation, yoga, or solo backpacking trips to the Sierra, because I never did any of that. It was simply years and years of trying it the other way and having it blow up in my face.

My mother has arrived at a similar place. In her inimitable style, she says Norm has "queered" her on men completely.

"But this is a time of life I have to face," my mother goes on, while filling the teapot. "Old age is very, very depressing; there's nothing to look ahead to." She's waiting for the tea to steep, and now she's really thinking—swaying from side to side with particular vigor. "But old age is also a kind of liberation, because no one expects much of you anymore.

"I sure don't want sex," she says. I snap to attention. "I don't have a hormone left in my body. But if I came across a nice strapping forty-year-old, I might invite him to dinner and get him to move some heavy stuff and fix a few things," she says. I chuckle, and she continues.

"You know, I got an email out of the blue a few weeks ago from a man who was in love with me when I was at Radcliffe."

"Really? Who?" I ask.

"Harvey Braddock. We were in the same physics class at Harvard. He looked me up on the Internet, and he's been writing to me."

"Wow, after all these years?" I'm intrigued.

"Yes, he seemed really infatuated. I kept telling him I'm an old lady now, but he refused to believe it. This went on until just the other day. I finally sent him a picture of me to prove it."

"And?"

"Haven't heard a thing."

Now she brings up my father. I've noticed this happening more. I've also noticed that instead of inveighing against him, her old habit, she grows nostalgic, retells his jokes, recounts adventures they shared, reminisces about the year they spent in England when newly married. Today she wants to describe an elaborate word game they used to play on road trips, as well as a music game that consisted of beating out a rhythm to a song, then guessing the tune. "Did I play that too?" I ask.

"No, you were too little," she says. "But you heard a lot of music."

And now she can't resist a jab at Bob. "And none of it was Barry Manilow." I let this remark go unaddressed, preferring to focus on the new closeness we're enjoying.

FOR DINNER THAT NIGHT, I pick up enough Chinese food for the three of us, though there are no guarantees that we'll eat together. Zoë does decide to join us, but from the first words out of her mouth it's clear that she's not happy about it. I notice that she's wearing a new sweatshirt I can't recall having purchased for her, and I ask, "Where did you get that sweatshirt, sweetie?" The response—"Does it matter?"—tells me everything I need to know about her mood.

Senator Dianne Feinstein, whose granddaughter is in Zoë's high school class, came to speak at Zoë's school that morning. The senator's visit made a big impact on Zoë, who is bursting with her impressions, but she refuses to direct any of her conversation to my mother. During the question-and-answer period with the students, Zoë says, she was surprised by Feinstein's lack of candor and her reflexive support for her party's policies. "I've never seen anyone so guarded and evasive." I explain to her that politicians, especially those as prominent as Feinstein, are always on guard when they speak in public. And as a Democrat, of course she's going to defend Obama and his administration.

"That's a tough sitch, man," Zoë says, lapsing into teen-speak. My mother has said nothing. I wish I could pass my mother some cue cards under the table, prompting her on how to ask questions of her granddaughter that might elicit a friendly response. But I've resigned myself to my mother's inability to do that.

My mother finishes her dinner in silence, then gets up from the table and, without a word, goes downstairs.

"Is she mad?" Zoë asks.

I roll my eyes.

"What?" she asks, feigning innocence.

"You speak only to me then wonder why she feels excluded enough to leave the room?"

Zoë doesn't say anything. But on her face I see a struggle. She's still wrestling with the contrast between the expectations she'd had about the day-to-day life with her grandmother and the reality of it. Her face wears the same expression I saw so often when the high hopes she had for a relationship with Scott were dashed. I brought Scott into her life, and he shut her out with devastating totality. Then I took my child by the hand and led her, squinting into the sun, into this latest living arrangement, only to see the pattern repeat itself. Zoë bought flowers, made a card, and scrubbed the apartment with similar buoyancy, but, still stinging from the harsh judgment she felt from Scott, she began erecting emotional walls soon after my mother's first criticism of her music. Her lips don't move as she takes in what I've just said, but her eyes convey all I need to know.

I WAKE UP THE next morning to the sound of the garbage truck grinding its way down our street and realize I've forgotten to put the trash bins out. Still in my pajamas, I tear down the stairs and out the door, hoping to beat the trash guys to our curb. I make it just in time. But as I turn to go back into the house, I see that my car, parked just beyond the driveway, has a broken window. The contents of the car have been rifled but nothing stolen. Still, it's a mess. There's glass all over the backseat.

My mother is already in the kitchen, mixing up her signature drink. She's alarmed by the incident, and she immediately decides to sweep up the fragments. I tell her not to bother, that the glass is tempered and most of it is inside the car. But she hasn't heard me, and she's heading out the door, broom and dustpan in hand. "Just for the sake of the shoeless," she says. By this, of course, she means dogs.

After my mother returns, the conversation turns to Smokey, then, not surprisingly, to her own dogs, including Tavi, the aggressive one she put down. "It's the hardest thing I've ever done in my life," she says.

This, of course, would ordinarily make me go berserk. She has just told me that she found the death of a dog more tragic than the custodial surrender of her children. But today I'm indifferent. And with this comes a glimmer of understanding: I can pick and choose what I absorb and what I deflect. This is how the color spectrum works: Some colors absorb light, while others deflect it, depending on where they are on the spectrum. Earlier in my life, when it came to hurtful words from my mother, I was more like an off-shade of brown, absorbing most of them. Now, with experience, wisdom, and a little more self-confidence, my spectrum is shifting. I'm making a choice to be less absorptive. And her comment about the dog she put down is one for which I choose to become pure white.

25.

Single Place Mats

Life is like a sewer:
What you get out of it depends on what you put into it.

—Tom Lehrer, "We Will All Go Together When We Go"

WHILE ZOË IS OFF ON A SCHOOL SKI TRIP OVER PRESIDENTS' DAY weekend, I spend two nights at Bob's little bachelor apartment. His father's surprise party is less than a month away, and I've told him I'll be happy to accompany him. Over breakfast the first morning he asks me if I'd like to bring Zoë along. I say that it's very nice of him to think of it and that she'd probably love to come.

On his small dining table I notice a single plastic place mat. I point it out to him. "That's me in two years after Zoë leaves for college." As I'm saying these words, I find I'm not afraid of a solitary place mat. Bob's response takes me aback. Ever so gingerly, he says, "Well, you never know what might happen to us. If we're a Thing, we might put our single place mats together."

Of course, he knows we're already a Thing, that taking both Zoë and me to Florida for a family event implies big-time Thing status. Now he means a bigger Thing. "Nice," I say, sticking with the image, not quite ready to deal with its implications. "Two pathetic single-place-mat people coming together."

Later that day, I'm back home and in the dining room, where I'm working on a large editing project, papers spread across the long table. My mother comes in and I tell her about Bob's comment about uniting our single place mats. Then I catch myself. I no longer want to say anything about Bob that might invite a judgmental comment, and I wish I hadn't. Yet habits born of excess psychological baggage die slow, complicated deaths. We can't just tell ourselves we've killed them off one day and start fresh the next. Luckily, as I'm trying to figure out a nimble way to take the conversation in another direction, she does it for me, by turning it to herself.

"I've definitely reached the single-place-mat stage of life," she says. She tells me she had a dream that she was living in a tiny apartment in an independent-living facility like the ones we visited. Nothing happened. It was a still life of a dream, yet it felt like a nightmare.

"I just wanted to get out," she says.

"Maybe you're having some anxiety because of our day with Anne," I suggest. "Or maybe it's your knee. It's really limiting your mobility."

She ponders this. "Maybe, yes, looking at those places was pretty depressing. And you're right. I'm not exactly swift on my feet."

Geriatricians often say that one mistake doctors tend to make when caring for the elderly is to blame everything on age. They'll say, "What do you expect? You're seventy-eight; do you expect to feel marvelous all the time?" A favorite joke among more-enlightened geriatricians is about the ninety-year-old man who went to the doctor complaining of knee pain. When his physician handed him the standard line, "What do you expect, you're ninety years old," the man replied, "Oh, yeah? My other knee is ninety years old, too, and it feels fine."

But here and now, in my mother's mind, her knee problems cannot be untangled from the steady creep toward advanced old age. I don't say this to her, but the tiny apartment in that dream may represent many of her fears about the growing limitations of her body, which, in spite of two knee surgeries—to say nothing of years of abuse from cigarettes and alcohol—has held up remarkably well. I sense that she's worried her luck is running out.

—

MY MOTHER HAS BEEN apartment hunting with a vengeance. Her criteria for the perfect dwelling: two bedrooms, one and a half baths, decent heating, in a building that's piano-friendly, and in a neighborhood that's not too hilly, with good bus access. She has her mind set on a place with two bathrooms, or at least two toilets—in case one clogs. She is in touch with a few different rental agents, and my seventy-eight-year-old computer maven of a mom is on Craigslist constantly. But she's growing unhappy with the online listings, where the same crummy places keep coming up.

I suggest we drive around her preferred neighborhood looking for FOR RENT signs. We find one almost immediately; my mother calls the number and the manager tells us it's a two-bedroom apartment in an elevator building. With two bathrooms! The ten-story Gothic Revival-style building, constructed in the 1920s, is a beauty, in what seems to me a perfect setting. Within a couple of hours, we're meeting the building's manager. Not only is the apartment large and sunny, with freshly refinished hardwood floors and a bay window, but it's a corner unit on the fifth floor, with a view up and down Pacific Avenue, which is lined with handsome old buildings. Best of all, the rent is reasonable. She decides to take it on the spot.

On the way home, she turns philosophical. "Katie, I think we conducted a noble experiment. I couldn't have done this move to San Francisco without having this transition step. I don't think I would ever have left San Diego. I needed the fantasy about our year in Provence in a beautiful house to get me out of my old life."

Neither of us points out the obvious—that, stunning as the house is, what we ended up with was an expensive walk-in freezer that was nearly impossible to keep warm, a space for her so dark it was like a dungeon and down a set of stairs so steep that trying to climb them did her other knee in. Not to mention the essential problem, which was that it was a house filled with the tension of three generations who never should have tried to live together.

But now she's a happy woman. As we're driving along the crest of a hill overlooking the bay, she tells me once again how much she loves San Francisco and how she can't believe her good fortune in having landed in such a wonderful city. She also tells me about a friendship that's blossoming, with a woman who is a New York transplant. I sense that the two women are growing close, and I couldn't be more pleased. "Maybe I'll be the Grandma Moses of life. I'll really start to get it when I'm eighty," she says. Since my mother's abrupt departure from San Diego, she has become her own version of intrepid. She's now parallel parking all the time, sometimes just for fun, and she's a public-transit champion. In less than a year, she's gone from frightened shut-in to urban thrill-seeker. What's next? Will she be leading tours of Alcatraz?

Geriatricians speak of a life-space "diary," which defines the geographic distance an elderly person will travel. Early on, retirees go on adventures, taking cruises and traveling to places they haven't seen. The world is their oyster. Later, travel is domestic—first the country, then the region. Eventually, trips out of the city become rare, and sequentially the neighborhood, house, bedroom, and bed become their life space. My mother, a born anomaly, appears to be doing this in reverse order.

Her vitality is certainly inspiring. Once she was away from Norm, my mother was ready to have her life back. Apparently this often happens after a woman is widowed, especially for a woman my mother's age, a relative spring chicken. "You've done something pretty incredible, making a new life for yourself," I tell her. And I mean it. I'm genuinely impressed with what she has done and wonder if I would be capable of starting over at her age.

Once we get home, she crunches a few numbers, incorporating the amount she'll be paying for rent in the new apartment. She figures that at the rate she's spending her money, she'll have just enough to get her to eighty-eight. "I'm spending it down," she says. She seems to think not only that eighty-eight is far into the future but that she might not make it that far. I, on the other hand, am thinking, if this is the Grandma Moses of life, she's only getting started, and in ten years she'll have burned through all her savings, every last cent. Then what?

A WEEK LATER, MY mother finds me downstairs in the laundry room, and within seconds she's hovering. "That's probably dry already," she says, pointing to a shirt I've left out to line-dry.

She's doing her swaying. Is she regretting her intrusiveness? Having second thoughts about the move? No, as I'm about to discover, she's thinking how to break her big news to me. Then she comes out with it.

"The mover inspected the new place and decided the Steinway would be too difficult to carry up five flights of stairs," she says. "So I've decided to sell it."

She sees the surprise on my face. "Katie, you don't want that piano," she says, having decided for me what it is I want. Then she launches into a list of grievances against the instrument. It's too big. It's too loud. Even the tuner recently referred to it as "a beast."

"But I *like* that piano."

I know I haven't been playing and that on the rare occasions when I do play I don't play at all well, but that's not the point. I want the piano because it is her piano and because I am her child and thus, I presume, one of her heirs. I want the piano so that it can someday go to Zoë, who has genuine musical talent.

"I'm selling it," she says, obviously having made up her mind. It's the value of the piano—some $40,000—that she's focused on. From a financial perspective it makes perfect sense for her to liquidate the asset and put the proceeds toward her final years. But because the Steinway is the one valuable tangible object that I asked her for and that she promised to leave to me, I've grown invested in having her fulfill this singular request. A codicil to a will is an unambiguous promise. And I want the piano because this is a promise my mother can still make good on.

She has nothing more to say, and at this awkward and painful moment, neither do I. I take my shirt off the line, fold it over my arm, and go upstairs. The issue might be resolved in my mother's mind but not in mine. For the next few weeks, it follows me around. I'll be in the middle of doing something, and the conflict over the piano will bubble into my consciousness and enter its recursive loop. To my mother, the piano is merely a thing. But to me, it has ceased being a musical instrument and become something far more—a pure distillate, a centrifuged pellet comprising all our struggles.

Part Four

Spring

26.

Home Sick

the thing I came for:
the wreck and not the story of the wreck
the thing itself and not the myth

—Adrienne Rich, "Diving into the Wreck"

As vivid as the memories of my mother's negligence are, I can also recall with some clarity times during my childhood when she was sober and she did take care of me. So completely was she mine during a flu that I occasionally feigned illness, wrapping my hand around the glass thermometer in hopes of making the mercury rise and eliciting more of the tender devotion I longed for. When I broke my leg, part of me was happy, because my mother spent hours near my bed and bought me comic books by the dozen. This is the kind of mother she always had the capacity to be but rarely was.

Now my stomach is roiling. It could be that I ate too much Mongolian beef at the neighborhood Chinese place where Zoë and I went for dinner earlier tonight. As I lie in bed reading, I feel the first shudder of nausea. I shrug it off but notice I've just read the same sentence five or six times and I'm still not sure what it said. Within a few minutes, the internal convulsions are impossible to ignore and I dash for the bathroom.

My retching is so violent that Zoë hears it from behind her closed door down the hall. "Mommy, are you all right?" I look up to see her standing in the open doorway of the bathroom.

She surveys the scene. I'm lying on the cool tile, trembling from the sheer force of the purge.

She looks worried. "Do you need to go to the hospital?" I pull myself together enough to say, "I must just have a stomach flu."

Zoë is visibly relieved to hear that I'm in no immediate danger of dying, her first thought whenever I complain about something as minor as a headache. Then her concern turns to disappointment. Moms aren't supposed to get sick. At all times, they should be up and doing for their children. Even sleeping late signals a shirking of one's duty, which is why kids like to get up in the morning and find their parents already up and cooking pancakes, ever at their service. I sense all of these emotions churning in Zoë as she looks at me.

"Well, I'll leave you to your stomach flu," she says, and goes back to bed.

I know I'm in for a bad night. I fall into a deep sleep, only to be awakened by the second wave. My gastrointestinal tract is now a thing unto itself, the rest of my body incidental. And so it goes, hour after hour, well after I have given the toilet all I have to offer.

By dawn, the worst of the emetic crisis seems to have passed. I feel so depleted that I'm a blank slate, ready for life to begin anew. But the entire episode has left me too weak to sit up. I lie in bed and wait for the rest of the house to stir. At 7:00 A.M. Zoë pokes her head into my room to ascertain that I survived the night, then leaves for school. I send a text to my friend Carolyn, a primary-care doctor, who calls in a prescription for an antinausea medication. She offers to make a house call, but I warn her away. "This thing is evil."

Besides, I don't want Carolyn. And I don't want Bob. I want my mother.

I keep waiting, and by 8:00 A.M. I finally detect sounds of her downstairs. I hear her walk across the kitchen floor, turn on the burner under the teakettle, put a few stray dishes away, and open the dishwasher, preparing to empty it. I pick up my cellphone and call her separate home line. I hear her walk to the phone in the front hallway.

My voice is so weak it alarms her, and she comes straight up to see me, bad knee be damned. She feels my forehead (a mother's instinct) and goes to the pharmacy to fill the prescription that Carolyn had called in. She returns with not only the prescription but ice cubes and ginger ale. I'm dehydrated but also weak, and I suck on the ice cubes while slowly sipping the ginger ale.

My mother becomes my Florence Nightingale. She rushes home from her continuing education class to minister to me, hover at my bedside, replenish the Canada Dry once it's gone, and give me another antinausea pill. Can I eat anything? Oh, God, no. By the late afternoon, I'm sitting up in bed, quickly regaining strength. My gratitude to my mother is immense.

By the next day, I have recovered enough to go with my mother to a session with Lia, whom we've been seeing roughly every other week since October. Each visit has become a trial. Now that we have launched the plan to live apart, we are no longer working on the practical issues that had brought us into therapy in the first place. But since that session early on, when I broke down and talked about the prelude to my mother's loss of custody, instead of closing the door on those memories again I've wanted to wedge it open just a bit more. Now, in the safe haven of Lia's office, I am trying to get my mother to hear a little more about what happened during those periods in our past that are a complete blank to her.

Somehow we get onto the topic of money—who paid for what when Sarah and I were children. Once the subject is introduced, my mother sees an opening to what might have been at the top of her agenda for this session all along.

She turns directly to me and says, "I feel like the only reason you asked me to come to San Francisco was for my money."

I'm flabbergasted, but before I have a chance to collect my thoughts, Lia jumps in. "You're sure about this?" she asks.

"Oh, yes. I know exactly; I can call every shot. I've been holding it in for the last six and a half months." Her voice has taken on a small childlike quality, with a lisp.

"You've done something huge just now, Helen," Lia says. "You were able to come in and say something, open up, to give yourself permission to say it."

While my mother sits quietly, taking in the "attagirl" for her courageous comment, I'm thinking that if ever there was a wrong time for "good for you for expressing your feelings" therapy blabber, this is it.

I sit in stony silence, my mind racing. Her money? Assuming she'll live well into her eighties, she has barely enough to last until then. Had I wanted her money, I never would have suggested she move to one of the most expensive cities in the world. In fact, I'd never have allowed her to leave San Diego and *Norm's* money. I'd have told her to strap the poor demented man to a chair, not let him out of her sight, and get a restraining order on his daughter. And the *Playboys*? Who knows? Maybe they were worth something. Maybe the Marilyn Monroe issue was in that stack.

Now Lia is asking me to respond. But my mother's accusation feels so egregiously beyond the pale that I'm stunned into speechlessness. I don't know how to take the charge in, much less respond to it.

Instead of saying what the impact of my mother's words has been, instead of expressing my outrage, perhaps because the emotion is so intense—and so frightening—I do my best to strike a measured tone. "I'm not sure where you're getting this," I say, my voice quiet but steely. "Maybe you sense that I feel a need for compensation." In case there's any doubt about what I mean by needing compensation, I remind them that I had been left to myself as a child, and had largely worked my way through college.

Money is a subject that has come up with Lia before, but never in such an explosive way. Over the past months Lia has warned us that every adult child with an elderly parent runs into it, often in the context of a tiff over a family heirloom. Now, trying to take the tension down a few notches, she explains that while family fights may seem to be over money, the subtext is almost always about power and control. Elderly people, in particular, she says, often feel that they are losing control and can become very—and she chooses her next word carefully—

"sensitive," in place of the word I am sure she means, which is "paranoid."

My mother's accusation about my motive for bringing her to San Francisco is preposterous, but it's also a symptom—of dashed hopes. Both of us had held on to a belief that everything would be just fine once she got to San Francisco, partly because of our "best friends" fantasy, which was built on wishful thinking and mythology. Now I see that we needed physical distance for our fantasy of closeness to work. Once the relationship was put to the test of reality, it was doomed to failure.

Our time is nearly up, but Lia isn't about to let us walk out the door with all these emotionally charged particulates floating freely in the air. She takes a stab at closure, giving voice to the idea that my mother and I are both stuck in our respective childhoods, replaying old hurts and grudges that torment us still. Nice try, but Lia's diplomacy strikes me as ludicrous in the face of my mother's all-bets-are-off statement of ten minutes earlier. And my mother doesn't have much use for it either.

"I'm sure I did terrible damage to my children," she responds instantly, "but all that is almost half a century ago, and I can't go back and hear the horror stories. I carry my own stories, but I don't want to go into those stories either."

"Well, ideally, if you were able to really open up about your own bad story—"

My mother cuts her off. "I know my bad story, and there's not a damned thing I can do to change it."

With that tip of her hat to the Serenity Prayer, my mother is out of her chair and through the door. The session is over. I look at Lia and she looks at me. I follow after my mother and drive her home, where we retreat to our separate quarters.

The next day, I'm still livid but I try to be polite, as does my mother, who goes on as if nothing had happened in Lia's office. Perhaps now that she's said her piece, she's feeling unburdened and ready to move on. That afternoon she asks if I'd like to take a walk down to the grocery store. We begin by making small talk, but halfway into our ten-minute journey, she says, "More than love me, I want you to like me."

At this moment, she is asking too much. Do I like this woman, the one who just accused me of wanting her in my life for nothing more than her money? Do I find likable this person who has misread my motives so profoundly that she is causing me pain that feels almost physical? I feel that I owe her my love and my sympathy—she's my mother, after all. But do I like her? I stay silent.

27.

Ikea

Real love is a pilgrimage. It happens when there is no strategy, but it is very rare because most people are strategists.

—Anita Brookner, in an interview

THE SURPRISE PARTY FOR BOB'S FATHER IS AT THE COUNTRY CLUB in Boca West, a 1,400-acre subdivision of Boca Raton. It's the quintessential well-to-do Jewish retiree community, Long Island shifted 1,200 miles south, complete with palm trees, fake waterfalls, four golf courses, three dozen tennis courts, and bountiful flower beds. It's the land of the early-bird special, a place where people begin plotting their next meal before they've finished their last. Bob, of course, reminds me that on *Seinfeld,* Jerry's parents lived in an ersatz Boca West, called "Del Boca Vista."

The country club is sprawling and opulent. The preparations for the party have been elaborate, and Bernice, Bob's mother, has managed to keep everything a well-guarded secret. When we get there, an hour before the couple is supposed to show up for "lunch at the club," guests are already mingling. Many have flown in from far-flung places to celebrate with these people whom they love so much.

At the club, a crowd of nearly a hundred friends gathers, and when

Bob's father, Murray, enters the room, only to see people from all eras of his long life standing there, his brief moment of shock turns to delight and then to what Bob tells me later is a typical Murray reaction. His eyes settle on his wife, with a "how did you pull this off?" look, then he says to her, "Who's paying for this?"

To get the entertainment part of the celebration started, Bob sings the song he wrote—Murray's life set to the tune of "If I Were a Rich Man" from *Fiddler on the Roof*. Each of Bob's sisters, Andrea and Lori, speaks, and Lori shows a video montage she put together, with footage from family movies going back many decades: Murray and Bernice in the Catskills with their parents, Ida, Jack, Adele, and Julius; Bernice glowing while very pregnant with Bob; Murray horsing around with his young children and doing his best imitation of Wild Bill Hickok, twirling a fake revolver; Brandy the collie pulling three-year-old Bob on a tricycle; and finally Murray and Bernice with their five grandchildren.

By the end, guests are wiping tears from their eyes. I met Bernice and Murray an hour ago, and I'm crying too. Bob has told me how untroubled his childhood was, but it isn't until I'm here, taking all of this in, that I truly understand what he means. It's the generational continuity that gets to me—the a priori assumption that, as your own parents did for you, your most important role in life is to make a world for your children, that you are the weight-bearing pillar for these young lives.

I know better than to get too starry-eyed. Even in this family there have been resentments over time, conflict and subterfuge. One of Murray's brothers, for example, isn't here—they haven't spoken for years. And Bernice's relationship with her sister is strained. But it's a family as cohesive as any I've encountered, a Jewish version of Matt's. I'm already pleased to have come, and I know the entire trip has been worth it when I see Murray dancing with his youngest grandchild, fourteen-year-old Amanda. In a private moment I happen to catch, she looks up at her beaming grandfather and mouths the words "I love you."

Family friends lavish attention on Bob, the Big Successful Doctor. As much as Bob enjoys the adoration, which keeps him busy conversing with his parents' friends, I also sense a protective eye on Zoë and me. He must be keeping us in his peripheral vision, because he knows where to find us at all times: Every ten minutes or so he appears at my side and places an arm around my shoulder.

Given what has just happened back in San Francisco, I find myself thinking about Bob's family and how *they* are about money. I can tell that they like having it. In Bob's parents' circle—upwardly mobile second-generation Jewish immigrants from the New York area—the signs of success in life are your wealth and your kids' accomplishments. Murray did well in the women's clothing ("schmatta" to insiders) business in New York, and Bob has told me that his father talks about money constantly but has never taken it very seriously and certainly never used it as a bludgeon. Bob grew up assuming that there would always be enough money to go around and that his parents used it as a means to an end, which was the happiness of the people they loved.

At one point during the festivities, Zoë turns to me and asks, "Mom, what do you think Grandma Helen would do in a situation like this?" My daughter may be a stranger to all of this, but what she sees is a loving, connected family that radiates warmth and humor. What my mother would see is a collection of well-to-do Florida Jews who are nothing like the well-to-do Florida Jews who spawned the likes of her father, the famous physicist. Many of the guests have been in the same circle for fifty-five years, and many were the first generation to attend college, or even high school. Bernice and Murray have one semester of college between them. These are self-made people who live for their families, enjoy their lives, complain about their ailments, and eat their meals at the country club. "Sweetie," I say to Zoë, "I have no idea."

WHEN WE RETURN FROM Florida, my mother is in the throes of preparing for the move to her new apartment. She has scheduled it for the end of March, and Cheryl the downsizer is flying up from San Diego to help with both ends of the move.

The Steinway is a hulking presence in the living room, untouched and unmentioned.

My mother and I need a break from the tension that has poisoned the air between us ever since our session at Lia's. And since boxes from

Amazon have been arriving at an unprecedented clip—two or three a day, filled with coffee mugs and canisters, dishes and a dish drainer, and numerous other kitchen items for her new apartment—I hit on the idea of driving across the bay to Ikea. The store contains everything she could possibly need, most of it far less expensive than anything she will find on Amazon. It also seems like the perfect field trip, one we will both enjoy. I suggest the outing, and my mother's face lights up.

What should we do for lunch? Lunch at Ikea is always fun, I tell her, as we pull in to the parking lot. My mother loves the idea of an Ikea meal and says she'll treat me to lunch. Once we're inside the cavernous store and eating our birdlike meals of salad and salmon, I can tell my mother is eager to start shopping, so we finish our lunch quickly and set off with our cart. She's delighted by the low prices. Around the first corner, she picks out three 99-cent cutlery trays.

She's just getting into the swing of being on a penny pincher's spending spree when Candace calls to say that her mother, Ramona, has taken a turn for the worse. While Candace was out of town for a few days, Ramona lost all the weight she had so painstakingly gained. She didn't shower or change her clothes. Candace has made an appointment for Ramona to have a memory assessment, but now Candace's sister wants to have a conversation with Ramona about helping her end her life. After I hang up, my mother, who has overheard snatches of the conversation, wants to know how Ramona is doing. I give her a brief rundown.

"Is she in the hospital?" my mother asks.

"I think she's headed for the hospital."

"I think she's headed for the grave, sadly."

Ramona has become a reference point of sorts for my mother, the yardstick against which she gauges her own deterioration. Hearing how badly Ramona is doing reminds my mother how well she is faring by comparison. But she also sees herself—sometime in the future—in Ramona. The physical effects of advanced old age, something she got a preview of in that anguished moment on the hill outside Carolyn's house when she discovered that she was unable to propel her body up the sidewalk, are undeniable. Since then my mother has often voiced her fear of falling (geriatricians call this "anticipatory anxiety"). What she really fears is a broken hip resulting from a fall and the downward spiral that often follows. She's aware of the frightening statistics: The chance of an elderly patient dying in the year following a hip fracture is one in five. My mother's anxiety is all part of the process of coming to terms with her limits and, ultimately, her mortality.

I tell her about the conversation Candace's sister has suggested having.

"I hope that's a conversation you'll have with me," she says. "I'm only going to bring this up once, but I want you to know I have a lot of Darvon."

I'm not entirely sure what Darvon is, but I know this is not something I want to discuss while pushing a cart through Ikea. "Mom? Can we not?"

I see she's already well distracted by a small butcher block on wheels, the perfect answer to a problem with her new apartment that has been nagging at her—kitchen counters that are too high. She hits on a salad spinner and dish towels, glasses and just the dirt-cheap stainless steel she's been looking for. She can't contain her delight.

"I'm like a kid in a candy store."

"That's what Ikea's all about."

At the checkout counter, my mother takes extra newsprint to protect her new glassware and triple-wraps each one-dollar item.

Driving back through San Francisco, we're waiting at a red light on a dicey stretch of Divisadero Street when we see a crazy guy in earmuffs riding an imaginary bike while conducting a phantom orchestra. Six months earlier, my mother would have locked the doors. Now, having gotten the hang of living in this city, she just laughs.

28.

Letters

What still stands between me and the person I would like to be is this illusion of perfect love between my mother and me. It is a lie I can no longer afford.

—Nancy Friday, MY MOTHER/MY SELF

SYLVIA PLATH, THE PURVEYOR OF FAMOUSLY DARK POETRY, RE-served some of her cruelest imagery for her dead father. But to the day of her suicide in 1963 at the age of thirty, she loved her mother with a devotion that permeates the piles of letters she wrote to her over the years. The fictionalized mother portrayed in *The Bell Jar* is a darker figure, to be sure, but in Plath's letters home, which rolled out of her typewriter at a steady clip, she confided in her mother endlessly. And for all we know, she did not regret doing so.

Epistolary evidence suggests that Karen Blixen, aka Isak Dinesen, also adored her mother. In 1921, Blixen wrote to her mother from Africa: "For me you are the most beautiful and wonderful person in the world," she gushed. "Merely the fact that you are alive makes the whole world different; where you are there is peace and harmony, shade and flowing springs, birds singing; to come to where you are is like entering 'heaven.' "

I've just stumbled upon a stack of letters to remind me of how deep inside a dream of unassailable mother–daughter love I once was.

Cheryl has already been here for a couple of days and has packed most of my mother's belongings for her. I come downstairs to find both of them already at work in the kitchen. Kieran the mover shows up at about 9:00 A.M. with three of his Irish helpers, and my mother starts supervising them. Kieran, who is also a friend, has been amused by our living experiment from the start. He calls himself the Voice of Reason. Having hauled my mother's possessions from San Diego to San Francisco only seven months ago, he is well aware that something must have gone wrong to warrant moving everything out again after such a short time. "It wouldn't be the first time three chicks moved in together and they all started in on a cat fight, y'know?" he says in his charming brogue.

My mother is amused by this remark. "Kieran probably just summed it up better than anything Lia could say."

The loading goes swiftly, and once the truck is filled, I'm amazed. The contents of her 2,500-square-foot house in San Diego have been pared down to what will fit into a sixteen-foot moving truck. My mother has taken her upright piano with her; the Steinway remains in the living room. For now.

After they've all taken off for my mother's new place, I go down to the lower level to survey what's left to be packed. Among my mother's things I see a large manila envelope marked KATIE LETTERS. Picking up the envelope, I see that it contains a few dozen letters I wrote to my mother on thin blue aerograms in 1977, the year I spent in Germany as a junior in college. I was nineteen years old.

I've taken the envelope and walked down to Starbucks to read the letters. The lightweight single sheets are all addressed to both my mother and Norm, by then two people breathing as one. The letters are filled with youthful angst, which is consistent with my memory of that year. They also contain a constant outpouring of love and warmth, along with dozens of requests—for soaps, shampoos, and assorted other practical items (I have no idea why I didn't just buy these things in Germany, and the letters don't explain it). By November, several months after Candace had entered my life, I was asking for care-package items for her too. And judging from my expressions of thanks, my mother must have filled every request. Soon Candace was also writing to her, even calling her "Mom," telling her she loved her and that she couldn't wait to meet her and Norm and accompany them to Bully's, their favorite prime rib restaurant.

My letters chronicled a pilgrimage I made to Prague to visit Kafka's old haunts and confided my ups and downs with a handful of men I met in Germany. I'm taken aback by how ardently I had expressed my dreamy, romanticized love for my mother. Many of the letters were signed "your little one." In one letter, I told her about one of my off-the-wall dreams, involving my sister and my father, and ended by saying, "If getting analytical, you might say I dreamt about everyone whose feelings I question or feel unsure about. Glad to know you weren't in it."

Candace's parents were going through a rough patch, and in one letter I wrote, "Candace . . . points out the difference between my going home and her going home. Were I to go home I'd have loving arms to cuddle up in, someone who understands. And she has nothing really to go home to." I find this one particularly puzzling, since I have no memory of having cuddled up with my mother as a young adult. Now that I've become aware of how much I have invested in a fantasy version of my relationship with my mother, as I read through the stack of letters, it occurs to me that the fantasy may have much older roots than I remember.

I was setting myself up for disaster. When I returned from Germany, I got sucker punched. My mother persuaded me to give up my cozy bungalow in downtown La Jolla and move in with Norm and her for my senior year at the University of California, San Diego. Of course, I should have known better than to consider living with her (and the irony in the fact that I would repeat the mistake three decades later has not escaped me), but she had made the suggestion while sober, and her entreaties had been wrapped in such warmth, filled with such hope and promise, I couldn't resist.

Being under one roof with her became a nightmarish déjà vu. My mother's drinking seemed worse than ever. Late one morning when I was home, I heard the jangle of keys, which put me on guard. She had run out of liquor and, visibly hammered, was on her way to buy more. I intercepted her on the staircase. I pleaded with her not to drive the car.

The only compromise we could reach was that I would do the driving. I was old enough to drive but too young to buy alcohol, so I remained in the car, shrunken with shame and embarrassment behind the wheel, and watched her stumble into the store to restock. Though I was unaware of it, my actions were those of a classic enabler. At the time it seemed like the best outcome I could hope for. I felt stuck, trapped. I guess I could have taken the keys, then refused to drive her, but I feared her wrath too much to do that. Norm checked her into a detox place to dry out, and I visited her. For the thirty minutes I was there, we spoke of everything but her drinking.

One day earlier that same year, 1978, Betty Ford's husband and children confronted her about her pill and alcohol addiction. Each family member was armed with a script and a list detailing specific instances of the former First Lady's behavior while drugged or drunk. President Ford spoke of times she had slurred her speech or fallen asleep in a chair. The Fords' son Steve told his mother of a painful incident that occurred when he cooked dinner for her while she sat in a daze in front of the TV, drinking. Mrs. Ford went in for treatment, and her public confessions—first to the pills, then to the alcohol—made headlines. I don't know how many families of alcoholics were spurred to action by Betty Ford's brave disclosure, but my guess is that the number was high. Yet who knows how many other people, like me, heard the news and didn't listen? When I could have been reciting to my mother a painful litany of incidents as a prelude to telling her that she needed real help—not the quick fix of a detox center—I stood at the foot of her bed, chitchatting about trivia and wanting nothing more than to get out of there.

I went to see a therapist at UC San Diego, a graduate student who was young but insightful. I had never been to a therapist before and sat in her office feeling self-pitying and tongue-tied. She helped bring me to the realization that I needed to move out of my mother and Norm's home, which I did.

Shortly thereafter, Candace came to visit from Berkeley, where she was now finishing college. And just as Candace had dreamed of doing, we went with my mother and Norm to Bully's, a dimly lit, red-upholstered throwback of a restaurant. My mother was into her third or fourth drink when the verbal bile started to pour out of her mouth. Somehow the conversation had turned to the custody hearing from eight years earlier, and my mother railed against the dirty tricks my father's lawyer had pulled.

I remember none of what happened next, but Candace does. According to Candace, my mother then directed her bitterness at me. Candace remembers not my mother's words but my reaction to those words. I melted into the blood-red leather booth, disappearing behind a curtain of long, dark hair. Norm, Candace recalls, sat quietly and said nothing. And neither did Candace. She still remembers feeling horrified and protective yet powerless. She remembers putting her arm around me, not knowing how to make the outburst stop. "It was the way you feel when you're watching a car crash and you can't do anything," she told me recently when we were recalling the visit. "Your mother was either unaware of the impact she was having or else she didn't care. You had given me this image of your mother as a loving, generous maternal figure. And I was dumbstruck by how this person you had been telling me about was now being so verbally abusive."

As I sit in Starbucks reading these letters, I'm overwhelmed by the memories they bring back. I'm struck by how much I longed for my mother's love. Candace had been writing from Germany to the mother I wished I had, a mother who didn't exist. And the fact that my mother saved all those letters could mean that she wished the same. When I get home, my mother and Cheryl still haven't returned from their trip to the new apartment. I place the manila envelope back where I found it.

29.

The Interview

They say that "Time assuages"—
Time never did assuage—
An actual suffering strengthens
As Sinews do, with Age—

—Emily Dickinson

MY MOTHER HAS BEEN IN HER NEW PLACE FOR JUST A FEW DAYS when Carolyn invites us to her Passover seder. The dish Carolyn assigns to me is tzimmes, a sweet vegetable casserole made of diced carrots and yams. While I'm cooking, my mother calls to say she's made up her mind; she won't be returning to see Lia.

"It takes me about a week to recover from one of these grueling sessions of feeling so guilty and not knowing what on God's earth I can do about it," she says. "If you want to keep lashing out at me about what happened fifty years ago, okay, but I'm opting not to know."

I, too, know that therapy isn't working for us. Every time we step into Lia's office, I feel as if we're entering Kafka's closet. It's an image from *The Trial*, Kafka's novel about an accused man in search of his crime. In the midst of his travail, Josef K. opens the door to a small storage room and sees a man poised to flay two others with a rod. Sometime later, he opens the same door and the three men are still there, in precisely the same position. Were anyone to open the door to Lia's office, there we'd be, week after week, in the same chairs, torturing each other. And getting nowhere.

My mother wants to slough off the past, not recall it. Lia and I have been trying to plumb a depth my mother has no desire to reach. For all these months, I've been acting on a perverse impulse to demand my pound of flesh. And Lia has considered it her role as mediator to help get at some kind of essential truth. But my mother has felt cornered, and that's just plain unfair to her—and, I now appreciate, unhelpful to both of us.

It dawns on me while we're talking that since the phone has been our most comfortable mode of communication in the past, perhaps it will allow me to ask her the questions that have long been simmering.

I start with a tiny matter-of-fact speech. "Mom, it didn't all happen fifty years ago, it was still happening well up into my twenties. And the reason I know this and you don't is that, when you're an alcoholic, there are a lot of things you don't remember."

As I say this, I realize we've made some progress after all, because my mother now freely acknowledges that her problem was alcoholism and doesn't protest when I refer to her as an alcoholic. I go on. "I'm glad we've gotten to the point you can tell me that you have chosen not to know. But maybe you can understand that there are things *I* want to know, that maybe you could help me understand."

I take her silence as tacit permission to proceed. I begin asking questions of her, as I might someone I'm interviewing for a story.

"I've never been all that clear on when you started to drink. Or why."

I'm hoping that perhaps this neutral, professional tone of voice will help dispel her reluctance to talk about the past. And it seems to work.

"I think I started around the time I got a divorce," she replies. "I don't remember going on benders before that. But I don't understand what was going on with me that I felt it was necessary to start drinking."

She falls silent. A rookie reporter would jump in with the next question, but I know better. I use the silence as I have hundreds of times in the past with interview subjects—to invite her to keep speaking. After a long pause, she continues.

"Part of it was that it was the early sixties and the cocktail culture. Everyone was drinking cocktails all the time. I was totally frazzled, and it led to the overdrinking. I couldn't wait to have a drink at five."

That's not true, I think. She wasn't the kind of drunk who got quietly plastered on martinis every night, then rose the next morning, living for the five o'clock bell in her head, when it was socially acceptable to start that evening's slow, numbing drip. That was not my mother. My mother drank herself senseless on those cocktails. There was no waiting until five and certainly no getting up the next morning.

She's read my mind. "But I was a binge drinker," she says.

"I know."

She goes on, and as she talks I hear profound regret in her voice—regret not over what she didn't get from life but over what she failed to give. "That was the most irresponsible time of my life. There I had children, and I was gone. I was out to lunch; I was a terrible mother. I felt so insignificant and so worthless, and just so . . ."

Now she brings up her childhood. As a twelve-year-old, she says, with servants taking care of her, she was happy. "We lived in apartments in New York City, and I think that's why I'm so happy in this apartment. It brings back a happy time of my life. When I was out at dance classes all the time, it was good. I was never in the house. And then we moved to Boston, and I was devastated. I had lost everything. And after that, I only remember being shouted at and screamed at by my mother."

Ricocheting among many different time periods in her life, she recounts that when she was in her fifties and being interviewed for the job she got at Digital Equipment Corporation, she needed a government security clearance, which required that she go through hearings about her drinking. She relived that experience recently, she tells me, when she and Cheryl were going through old files. "We shredded all those papers." The papers are gone now, but in the course of choosing what to shred, she must have come face-to-face with a lot of painful memories. My mother may not want to replay the wretched parts of her life in Lia's office, but it's now clear to me how much she has been confronting on her own time.

We've talked all the way through my preparation of the tzimmes, and it's nearly time for me to go pick her up for the trip across town to

Carolyn's. I'd hoped Zoë would join us, but since she knows my mother is coming, she opts to stay home and do schoolwork.

This time, I park just a few dozen feet from Carolyn's house. And it also helps that this time my mother is psychologically prepared for the hill. Knowing there will be at least two doctors present tonight—Carolyn and her husband—my mother jokes as she inches her way up the sidewalk: "Do these doctors do stretchers?"

When we walk in the door, people are already milling. My mother and I both latch on to a college kid who says he wants to be a computer programmer. Together, we find ourselves telling him that my mother had been one in the 1960s.

"She was the real deal in those days," I say proudly.

"What were computers like back then?" he wants to know.

"As big as refrigerators," my mother says. He had no clue about any of this, and his eyes grow round. He starts asking questions, and I can see my mother relishes the chance to tell of her adventures as a programmer, especially programming in machine language, which brings the coder so close to the machine.

The formal part of the seder is pleasant and brief, and at dinner I look over and see my mother laughing and enjoying herself. She's radiant, and just as on the evening of her birthday six months ago, when people clustered around her, I think, *Now, here's a woman who still knows how to light up a room.*

30.

A Sentimental Education

The crest of the mountain
Forever remains,
Forever remains,
Though rocks continually fall.

—Paiute song, recorded by John Wesley Powell

"SEE THAT CVS OVER THERE? IT USED TO BE A GROCERY STORE, and I used to shoplift there."

"Mom!" Zoë is shocked. "You shoplifted?!"

"I did. It wasn't good, I know. It was a gang of us in eighth grade. We did it all over town. And then one day another girl and I got caught and we all stopped."

Zoë and I are parked on a downtown street in Amherst, Massachusetts, doing the spring-break college tour around New England. One privilege I am determined to give my child is the college of her choice. When I was a teenager, my college plans barely qualified as an afterthought for the adults in my life. I drifted through high school, amassing good grades but no knowledge. I graduated at sixteen, a year early, for no particular reason. Ever the iconoclast—and tightwad—my father claimed to be opposed to college, despite the fact that he was a college dean. As it turned out, my father hadn't saved a dime for his girls' college education, and my grandparents weren't about to chip in. (They did once offer to pay for Sarah's college tuition if she agreed to cut off all relations with our father, but she refused.) "Live with me for four years," my father said to me, "and I'll teach you everything you need to know." Vivienne took no interest in my post-secondary education either.

My mother had little to say except that I should apply to the University of California at San Diego. Her reason had nothing to do with me and everything to do with her. It's true that UC San Diego had fine departments in science and math, and perhaps she thought I shared her love of those subjects. But I lacked both interest and aptitude in those areas, a fact that would have been lost on her, since by then she knew almost nothing about me. Nor did it occur to her to tell me that other UC campuses—UC Berkeley, for one—existed, with tuition as low as UC San Diego's and excellent departments in writing and journalism, the areas I did want to explore. So I followed my mother's suggestion and ended up at UC San Diego, where the modest in-state tuition was subsidized by an academic scholarship and earnings from an on-campus job.

Zoë's experience is to be different. I've worked hard to save for her college education, and I'm happy to indulge whatever desire she expresses about exploring schools.

Zoë is starting to show signs of wanting to spread her wings. She has signed up for a six-week summer trip to Brazil, and I can't imagine how I will cope for that long without her. If I can't face putting her on an airplane for a six-week trip, how will I handle a college drop-off? I've joked with her that after she says goodbye to me on freshman move-in day, she should check under the bed in her dorm room.

I've spent weeks planning an hour-by-hour itinerary for our trip, shuffling Post-its around on a road map of New England. Having recently gone through this process with his older son, Doug, Bob weighed in with a few practical considerations and rearranged my Post-its to help me maximize the number of schools we could visit in the allotted time. I'm nearly a caricature of the modern parent helping his or her kid do the college thing. Of course, my eagerness and industry are partly to compensate for my dread—I will become an empty nester in a blink, and I'm not looking forward to it.

For our week in the east, we have only one fixed date. My stepmother, who still lives in western Massachusetts, has a doctor's appointment on Thursday of the week that we're going to be back east. I've remained close to Vivienne through the years, in part because my default setting is loyalty, and in part because I know that although she didn't love me as her own, she took us in when she didn't have to and did her best by us—or at least by me. Had she refused, it's likely we'd have gone into foster homes or—perhaps worse—to my mother's parents. I also stayed close to my stepsiblings, especially my stepsister, Julie, who, as Sarah drifted further from my orbit, remained a steady presence. I'd like to take Vivienne to the appointment and offer my stepsiblings, none of whom live nearby, another set of eyes and ears. This also turns out to be very convenient, because the independent-living place where Vivienne now resides is in South Hadley, the town where Mount Holyoke is located. Had I been able to attend college in New England, I'd have put Mount Holyoke high on my list, and I tell Zoë she should really see the college. She shrugs indifferently and says, "Okay."

On our first night at our hotel in southern Connecticut, I check my email and find a cheerful note from my mother, who has been busy nesting in her new apartment. "Things are good," she reports. "Day is glorious."

The next day, we visit two campuses in Connecticut. The first calls to mind a collegiate version of Vintage Golden Gate, one of the senior communities my mother and I visited in February. Classes are in session, but we see only a handful of students. During the tour, Zoë sends me a text from five feet away: `h3LL@ d3pPr3$$!Ng`. She's also madly texting back and forth with her classmates. `ALL ASIAN` reads one text from a friend visiting Yale. `This is where fun goes to die,` reads a missive from Wellesley. `Too pretentious` is the report from Brown. We head next to Boston, and Tufts, where the group of prospective students and their parents is so large that as we follow our tour guide, it feels as if we are an advancing army, sending our backward-walking guide in retreat.

That afternoon, as we're driving to Amherst, which isn't far from Vivienne's place, Zoë says, "Mom, can we please not reminisce?" She has heard me talk about Amherst enough to warn me that she'd rather not hear it all again. She does allow me to show her two things: the McDonald's on Route 9 where I worked ("Really? You worked at McDonald's?"), and the parking lot next to the town common where I first laid eyes on her father ("That's pretty cool"). Then, once we're parked in the center of town, I spot a pharmacy that used to be Louis Foods and is now a CVS.

I've used up my reminiscing chits, but I know I can cheat because I've got a doozy for her, and I bring up the shoplifting. After my brief confession, I say nothing more about it, and neither does she. But as we're driving down South Pleasant Street to our B&B, my life of crime passes before my eyes. We pass the hippie clothing store, where I stole a pair of corduroy pants, and the former site of John's Mini-Mart, where Vicky White and I got caught after stuffing panty hose and candy bars under our jackets. John himself caught us and called Vicky's parents. Vicky was grounded for a month. Every day for weeks afterward, whenever the phone rang, I ran to pick it up, hoping to intercept Mr. White's dreaded call to my father and stepmother. Until then I had been nothing but the perfect child, the one with perfect grades who never rocked the boat. Had they found out that I was a little thief, who knows what would have happened? But for some reason Vicky's parents never called, and, while mystified, I was also infinitely grateful for being spared the wrath of my parents.

Had I lived in a stable home and not a dysfunctional one, I'd have known that whatever punishment I got was because my father and Vivienne loved me. But even then I knew that punishment doled out against the backdrop of my warring family, with its ceaseless conflicts around whose child was more "trouble," had nothing to do with the child in question and everything to do with the turf battles of the adults. Now I think that this may be why I had such anxiety over what seemed to me like Matt's bad-cop approach to parenting. Having grown up in an intact, happy family, he was simply more comfortable with imposing discipline than I was. Matt possessed the basic confidence that allowed him to see punishment as something that loving parents mete out to their children to guide them. That had not been my experience of punishment; erratic and irrational as it was in my own childhood, it only frightened me.

We drive to South Hadley to pick up Vivienne at her independent-living place, several miles from town in a very rural area. When she opens the door, she hugs me and holds on tightly. My stepmother is not a woman given to hugs, particularly lingering hugs, and I read a great deal into her reluctance to let go of me.

Vivienne has finally, at age eighty-four, stopped dyeing her hair blond and has let it turn not gray exactly but an odd straw color. She has applied her eye makeup but apparently with a trembling hand, as the lines she has drawn with her brow pencil are coarse and jagged. Her two-bedroom apartment is roomy, the bookshelves stacked with books she has kept with her through the decades. The kitchen is small but fully functional, a far cry from the sorry little food-preparation spaces my mother and I saw in San Francisco. And Vivienne has equipped it with dishes and cookware still familiar to me from our years in Amherst.

After a quick look around, I tell Vivienne we have to leave in order to get to her doctor's appointment on time. Pride prevents her from taking her cane, and we make our way slowly to the car, where Zoë is waiting. Zoë and Vivienne have always enjoyed each other's company. When Zoë was small, she called her Grand-Vivienne, and Vivienne, for her part, has always made a point of asking Zoë questions that will engage her. But I can see that the slow-moving, elderly Vivienne is making Zoë uncomfortable, and on the drive to Northampton, Zoë remains silent in the back while Vivienne talks about how isolated she feels living in the country, especially since a small stroke stripped her of her driving privileges and forced her to rely on the facility's shuttle vans. She's taking the driving ban very hard. She feels imprisoned, she says, especially on weekends.

Vivienne asks how my mother is getting on in San Francisco. I've already told my stepmother about our failed attempt at living together, which my mother so diplomatically refers to as our "transition period." Given Vivienne's lonely circumstances, I'm careful not to say too much about how well my mother has adapted to living there, but she can tell from even the little I say that my mother is thriving. "She's so fortunate to be in such a wonderful city and to have you so close by," she says, her voice tinged with envy.

Soon after we arrive at the clinic, we are shown to an examining room to wait for Vivienne's longtime physician, Henry Simkin. When Henry enters the room, he practically bows to my stepmother, as if greeting the Queen Mother. "It is a pleasure, Vivienne!" Henry, a tall and courteous man who was also my father's doctor, greets me just as enthusiastically.

Vivienne has an entire list of things she'd like to talk to Henry about. The most pressing item is her dissatisfaction with where she is living; her unhappiness ranges from the cost of the place to the limited transportation options. And she feels abandoned by her three children. Not only do they live in different states but they aren't especially attentive. Henry listens carefully, playing the role of therapist as well as doctor, something so few doctors are willing to take the time to do these days.

Vivienne is also eager to hear the results of a neuropsychological test she'd taken recently. "The bottom line is very gradual decline," Henry says. "You have what's called pseudodementia."

Vivienne hears "dementia" and reaches for my hand.

"It's not as bad as you think," Henry says, and explains that it's a scary term for "spotty cognitive problems." Pseudodementia, I learn later from Bob, is depression in the elderly that manifests itself with memory loss and is often mistaken for Alzheimer's disease.

Then Henry rolls his stool close to his patient and leans in, not five inches from Vivienne's anxious face. "You're not your usual vivacious self, the Vivienne Hafner I've known for twenty years, but you still have a lot of health left in you," he says. "But here's what I'm seeing: excellent blood pressure and a brighter countenance than the last time I saw you." *Wow,* I think, *she must have been pretty down before, if this is a brighter countenance.* I'm also impressed with Henry's use of the word "countenance," formal enough to appeal to Vivienne's British sensibilities. After the appointment, Zoë and I take Vivienne to lunch at a small café near Henry's office, then, pressed for time, we drive her back to her place so that we can race to South Hadley for the Mount Holyoke tour.

Two days and two more campuses later, we board the plane to head home to San Francisco. I open my computer and buy the in-flight Wi-Fi. An email drifts in from my mother. I assume it's her daily update, but the subject line puts me on guard: "The Steinway." The email is brief, and she informs me that she put the piano on Craigslist and "it is gone." The piano, my mother writes, became a nasty source of friction between us (no argument there), and she has done what she considers right "on many levels."

Zoë is immersed in a movie. I tap her on the shoulder to show her the email.

Her eyes widen. "Mom, aren't you furious?!" I'm not really sure what I'm feeling. I'm definitely impressed by my mother's cloak-and-dagger work. All week she's been sending me chatty check-ins without one mention of her plans, all while taking snapshots of the piano and uploading them onto Craigslist.

Seeing Zoë's reaction, I realize that she is holding not just her anger at my mother but my anger at my mother as well. "Mom," she says. "Grow a pair of tiny little testicles and send her an email right this minute."

I take a deep breath and compose an email to my mother. It takes all of sixty seconds to write:

> I'm not sure how to respond. Yes, it was a source of friction between us, mostly because it was my understanding that I would someday inherit it. I know you've said I don't play at all, but I've told you many times that I'd like to get back into playing, once my life calms down.
>
> I think you believe that I didn't want the piano, but the money, and that's not true. I wouldn't have sold it. I'd have passed it down to Zoë.
>
> It's true that the piano was yours to sell, and I guess there's nothing that can be done about it now. But I would be dishonest if I didn't say that I feel that this is a betrayal.

I hit "send."

Zoë has been watching over my shoulder while I type. "Good," she says, and turns back to her movie.

We get home and head straight into the living room. Where the piano once stood is a large empty space.

"Well, that does it," Zoë says. "I never want to see her or speak to her again."

When I tell Bob about the stealth sale, his reaction is typically laid back. "I'll miss that piano—it was awfully nice," he says. "But such is life." He'd invoke a relevant *Seinfeld* episode, he adds, but none comes to mind.

But I brood. I continue to puzzle through my mother's reasons for her unilateral action. No doubt her decision was wrapped up in the feeling that I had brought her to San Francisco only for her money. So the piano had to go. And in a maneuver executed while I was out of town, she took our negotiations about it off the table.

My email to her goes unanswered.

31.

Upon Second Reading

The important thing is not the camera but the eye.

—Alfred Eisenstaedt, in an interview

NOT LONG AFTER WE RETURN, ZOË GOES OUT ON A SATURDAY NIGHT with her friend Gwen, with plans for Gwen to spend the night.

Zoë is sufficiently sketchy with me about their agenda for the night that I conclude that whatever they do will involve drinking. The girls return at around midnight, and Zoë comes into my room to say good night. To my relief, she appears stone sober.

It's Gwen I should have worried about. Zoë might have been the model of abstemiousness, but Gwen made up for it. Thirty minutes after saying good night, Zoë bursts into my room to tell me that Gwen is throwing up, spreading the contents of her gut across Zoë's bedroom. While Zoë is telling me this, I hear Gwen, who has since managed to get to the bathroom, still retching. The house is beginning to feel like a regular vomitorium.

Zoë wants me to help clean up. Absolutely not, I tell her. I'm not going anywhere near that mess. She argues with me. "But Laurel Hackett's mom does that when drunk kids throw up at parties at their house," she says. "I've seen her do it." This is pretty unbelievable news on many levels, especially since the Hacketts are mega-millionaires and I can't imagine Sue Hackett cleaning up after someone else's child. I stand my ground. She and Gwen are to take responsibility for this, and they are to scrub the room until no trace of Gwen's debauchery remains.

I hear Zoë go downstairs for cleaning supplies. Then she's outside my door in the hallway, putting soiled objects into plastic bags. I hear her speak soothingly to her friend, who is in no position to help. Zoë tells her she thinks they should go sleep downstairs, because her bed is now unusable.

The next morning I see that Zoë has done a remarkably thorough cleanup of her room. Both girls are asleep in my mother's former quarters, in beds conveniently supplied by the real estate agent's stagers in anticipation of our planned move to a smaller place. I go downstairs and seat myself quietly at the edge of Gwen's bed. She wakes up and tells me she's feeling better. I know she isn't my daughter, but I can't resist the temptation to tell her that excessive drinking at any age is just a really bad idea. Then I raise the question of what I am going to say to her parents. At this, she looks stricken. "Oh, Katie, please don't. That will be the end of me." I know about her terrible home life in a blended family, and I'm fairly certain she's not exaggerating.

All of this leads me to remember my eternal gratitude to Vicky White's parents for not informing my father and Vivienne about my shoplifting. Their decision was a gift. Now the least I can do is pay that gift forward. I assure Gwen that I won't say a word.

As I sit there, I am silently rejoicing that it isn't Zoë who made herself sick drinking. I don't know what lies in store for my daughter at college, where the pressure to drink is still greater, where she will be without the tempering influence—and presence—of a mother to issue reminders of her family history of alcoholism. But for now she doesn't seem interested in drinking, even for the sake of experimentation, and is genuinely grossed out by last night's events.

ZOË AND I ARE now in our new apartment, and Candace comes over one morning to help me unpack. Bob has spent the night, and while I make breakfast he sits down and asks Candace how her mother is doing. "Not well," Candace answers. Ramona is losing more weight and is down to an alarming eighty-two pounds. From the questions Bob is asking, I can tell he has been following Ramona's case from the periphery. At a dinner we had with Candace and Ramona a couple of months earlier, he noticed her fragile condition, and his medical antennae must have gone up.

His next question: What were the results of the thoracentesis, the removal of the fluid abutting the lung, a test Candace had taken Ramona in for weeks earlier? Candace never got them, she tells him, and when she called to follow up, she was told they had been lost. When she says this, I'm horrified, but Bob, who has written extensively on the topic of medical errors, just rolls his eyes. Candace says she does have the results of a recent echocardiogram. Ramona's "ejection fraction," she tells him, is 15 percent. I see Bob's expression change.

Ever so subtly, Bob transforms from someone making polite conversation at a breakfast table to a caring, concerned doctor. And that doctor quietly steers the conversation to a place he must have navigated many times before: an end-of-life discussion. First he gives Candace an explanation of what is happening with Ramona's heart. The ejection fraction is the fraction of blood pumped out of ventricles with each heartbeat, he says, and at 15 percent Ramona's volume is far below the normal value of around 60 percent. Such diminished volume means that Ramona's weakened, fragile heart could stop at any moment.

As Candace absorbs what Bob has just told her, it's clear that Ramona's physicians have not taken the time to explain in much detail Ramona's condition and its implications. When Bob asks Candace whether Ramona has prepared an advance health directive, she says yes, and that it contains a Do Not Resuscitate order, which is in her medical file. Candace thinks that's fine, but Bob knows it isn't. Again, very gently, and via a cautionary tale of a former patient of his whose DNR order was in a file but nowhere near the person himself, Bob tells Candace that when the prognosis is so grim, the situation so unpredictable, copies of Ramona's DNR order should be everywhere: on her refrigerator, on a bracelet on her arm, in her purse.

Next he sounds Candace out to see if she has considered the possibility that her mother might eventually benefit from hospice care. She looks surprised but asks him to tell her more. Bob's doctorly manner, which I am witnessing for the first time, is as respectful as can be. Rather than starting every sentence with "You should," he talks about a common misunderstanding people have when it comes to the concept of hospice. He tells her it's something people tend to think of only in relation to advanced cancer and other diseases that can seem more obviously terminal. With advanced heart disease of the type Ramona has, people think it can be treated, that it doesn't necessarily imply a grim prognosis. But with the numbers Candace has just given him, he says, Ramona's prognosis is probably no better than that of a woman her age with an aggressive metastatic cancer, and he would be remiss if he didn't bring up the topic of palliative care. Most patients who end up in hospice, he tells her, do so for only the last week or so of their lives—which is too bad, since hospice has so much to offer dying patients and their families. But many people misunderstand what hospice is about, and the instinct to fight on or even to deny reality is very powerful.

Here's Candace, hearing for the first time that her mother's heart could fail without notice, that Ramona has, at best, a couple of years left. Candace is taking it all in and says she'll get right on that medical directive. Bob nods approvingly. Seeing these two people—one of whom I have loved for many years, the other I'm just coming to love—talk through an issue this difficult moves me deeply.

As I look at Bob now, I'm beginning to unlock a riddle about our relationship—and why my mother is so very wrong about him. When Bob talks to Candace about her mom, he is the very essence of the sober, compassionate physician. His academic accomplishments are remarkable, and his professional side means a lot to him. Yet it's the other facet of Bob's personality that I've come to appreciate still more. As Bob turns to his French toast, maple syrup dripping during each brief trip from plate to mouth, I recall a story in which his ex-wife remarked that she could always predict what he would order off a breakfast menu by asking herself, "What would a six-year-old choose?"

That's not far off, for Bob is constitutionally incapable of taking life—or himself—too seriously. He has the gift of teasing out the lighter side of nearly everyone he meets. He certainly does that with me, but it isn't all he does. He supports and loves who I am without needing to be any of that. (Once, when I told him I'd like to send him poems, he responded, "Okay, but not too often.") And, amazingly, he reads my moods like no man I've ever been with. We warp and woof our way through the days, and there's something about that oddball synergy that just works.

A friend of mine who knows Bob sent me an email recently about another man we're both acquainted with, a brilliant writer who loves language and languages, loves to read, loves poetry, is passionate and deep, and would *get* my Kafka obsession. His intensity is a wellspring for all that exquisite writing. In her note, my friend said that she saw this writer, or someone like him, as the more likely match for me. I wrote back to her and said that there was a time when I would have agreed. But I now think the opposite is true. If I were with a man like our writer friend, I'd be dragged down by the deepness. What I need is not someone whose darker sensibilities mirror my own but someone who lightens that load for me.

ONCE BOB LEAVES, CANDACE and I start putting some loose papers into a tall, bulky wooden file cabinet with sticky drawers. It's an object that belonged to Matt, and I complained about it constantly when he was alive. But he loved it, and now I refuse to part with it. I'm going through a box of papers when I stumble upon the old papers from the custody hearing forty years ago, the documents I took from my father's house after he died. There's something about the lure of primary sources I can't resist, and before long I'm engrossed. Candace sees me and gets curious. I hand her some papers to look at too. She knows all about that time in my life, and she starts to read through them.

I see her lingering on one, then focusing on it intensely.

"Katie," she says, "your mother got screwed."

She hands me a few of the papers. One is a legal pleading my father wrote to the court two weeks in advance of the hearing for my mother's lawsuit demanding custody and back alimony. The eleven-page document makes for fascinating reading. In it, my father described his unhappy marriage to my mother, the "conspicuous" attention my attractive young mother received from men during their eleven-year marriage, and the pitiful condition Sarah and I were in when we arrived in Rochester in the spring of 1968. In his pleading, my father sought not just custody of Sarah and me but "release from all contractual obligations" to my mother, including all payments he might owe her in arrears, as well as any future alimony.

Candace has pulled out the same jovial lawyer-to-lawyer letter I read more than ten years ago while sitting in my father's house after the plane crash. After commenting on the theatrical potential of their day in court, Brooks Potter, my mother's lawyer, told my father's counsel, "I am convinced that Judge Cook was patently wrong in his decision to . . . suspend future alimony, and because of that, I find it necessary to appeal from that part of the decree."

I had gotten it all wrong. It was true that my mother had no plans to appeal the custody decision. But a decade earlier, when I saw that letter for the first time, I had managed to misunderstand what it was my mother was actually asking for, thinking she was trying to get him to pay child support after we were no longer living with her—which was what my father and Vivienne had told us at the time. My mother's lawyer was not contesting the discontinuation of child support but the alimony.

"She got completely screwed out of money she was entitled to," Candace says. She walks me through the documents. On the day in 1968 that Sarah and I arrived in Rochester from San Diego, my father had stopped all payments—not just child support but alimony too. So for the two years we were with my father and Vivienne, my father hadn't paid my mother a penny in alimony, and she had taken him to court for that money. During their marriage, my mother had hurt my father repeatedly, but to discover that he had been so niggardly about paying back alimony that he legally owed her disappoints me.

In the blurry aftermath of the plane crash, I had read those documents too quickly, come away with only a fragmentary understanding, then taken them home and never glanced at them again.

As he should have, the judge ordered my father to pay the back alimony. The question of continued alimony was something else entirely. In his statement to the court, my father argued that because my mother was perfectly capable of working, she wasn't entitled to future alimony. Since the court order isn't among my father's papers, the reason for the judge's decision to deny my mother any further alimony—a decision that reversed the financial terms of their divorce agreement, under which my father's legal obligation had been quite unambiguous—can't be known with certainty. Perhaps the judge agreed with my father's argument. Or perhaps this New England puritan had concluded that my mother's unfitness as a parent and a wife made her unworthy of support. The judge seemed determined to make an impression on this wanton young woman, cutting off all financial help—as if losing two children weren't punishment enough. My mother never told me about the revocation of the alimony agreement, or, if she did, she must have done so during one of her liquor-soaked rants, when I often found a way to block out her words.

I now understand more clearly than ever why money is such a charged topic for my mother. Given her experience, of course she has reason to distrust my motives for bringing her to San Francisco. As for the piano, while I might have viewed her selling it as reneging on a straightforward promise, when it comes to my mother and issues involving anything of monetary value, nothing is straightforward. It's time for me to let go of my resentment about the piano once and for all.

THAT NIGHT, UNABLE TO sleep, I go back to the file cabinet, pull out the custody folder, and spread its contents across the dining table. I see a letter dated July 20, 1972, from a Hampshire County social worker to my father's lawyer, and from the lawyer to my father, the sheets held together with a rusted staple. Sixteen-year-old Sarah—fresh from her ill-conceived move into the Amherst College fraternity house—was at the foster home, and both the social worker and the lawyer were having trouble reaching my father. Mrs. Eleanor Bolotin, the social worker, had written to Mr. Paul Rogers, an attorney in Amherst, to tell him that Sarah had two requests of her father. The first was for some money for clothing and other items. These are "expenses normally incurred by parents of any teenager," she wrote. The second was Sarah's request for "some form of psychotherapy." The lawyer sent a letter to my father the day after receiving the social worker's note. "I have tried several times to reach you via telephone and have been unsuccessful," he wrote. What could my father have been so busy doing that this wasn't a priority for him?

A full month passed before my father finally wrote back to Mrs. Bolotin. He did not say that he would do all he could to support his daughter. Instead, he had questions of his own. "I think we must clarify the nature of her current sources of support," he wrote. "Sarah was able to afford an expensive new bicycle, without as far as I know selling her old one. I hesitate to put forth extra allowances in a situation where she is clearly obtaining money from others." Someone—my mother, my grandparents?—was giving Sarah money, and that's what my father chose to focus on. Of Mrs. Bolotin's question about the psychotherapy, he said nothing at all. It was still about the money. My father wanted to know who paid for her bicycle. I had spent my life picking and choosing the parts of my father I adored and turning a blind eye to all else. But now, perhaps for the first time, I see that he, too, was a charter member of the bad-parent cabal that had upended Sarah's life.

AS THE DAYS GO by, with each of us in our separate apartments, my mother and I are growing closer. Mother's Day is approaching, and I tell her I'd like to take her out to dinner. She loves the idea, and when I ask her to choose the place, she names one of the few nice restaurants she's been to in San Francisco, which has become her favorite.

I start to look for Mother's Day cards, and at the local card store I flip through a few and read the messages inside:

Mom—you've always been there.

and

Here's to all the happy memories.

Hmmmm . . . I eliminate those candidates, then finally buy one with a neutral message and augment it with my own. I say that I know it hasn't been our best year but that I love and respect and admire her. I hope this will pass muster with her, that she won't feel any implied criticism.

On Mother's Day, Zoë suggests we go downtown for a shopping spree—for me, not for her. Her unhappiness with my dressing habits of late has made her determined to preside over a makeover. I've taken to wearing a pair of cotton pants I would describe as loose-fitting and Zoë says are "like scrubs but worse." On my feet I usually wear my trusty Asics running shoes with a hole in the top of the left shoe.

"Mom, you can still be comfortable and look nice," she says. "You're beautiful. Take advantage of your beauty before it deserts you." Once again Zoë's uncannily adult tone takes me by surprise.

At the mall, Zoë takes me into a store she knows that sells "age-appropriate" form-fitting dresses. We both pick out a few that might suit me, and I try them all on. Zoë is in high spirits, having just received prom invitations from two different boys, and one of her Mother's Day gifts to me is a moratorium on her usual impatience. She sits happily outside my dressing room and waits for me to model each of the dresses. I settle on one, and Zoë is thrilled to see how good I look in it. So am I.

Over lunch at the food court, Zoë tells me she can't stop thinking about the incident with Gwen, which made her lose respect for her friend. "I don't think drinking is cool," she says. "I don't like the taste and I don't see what people are trying to prove to each other, just by showing how much they can drink. People are ugly when they're drunk. And knowing the effect it has on your body, it's disgusting. Did you know alcohol crosses the blood–brain barrier?" More intent than ever on becoming a doctor, Zoë has been accompanying Bob on rounds at the hospital lately. Tagging along with him and the teams of young residents he works with hasn't merely reinforced her desire to be a physician; it has made her determined to become a hospitalist, like Bob. As for me, I don't know what the blood–brain barrier is or why the traversing of same would be a bad thing, but I nod anyway, surprised and impressed by the mix of clinical detachment and passion with which she delivers her speech. Although I wish there had been a less unpleasant way to underscore the point, I'm also relieved by Zoë's revulsion for heavy drinking.

I say nothing to Zoë about joining my mother and me for Mother's Day dinner, she doesn't ask for an invitation, and my mother has also been mum on the subject. For this I am grateful. I'm no longer trying to yoke these disparate elements together, and I guess they're as relieved as I am. Just before going to pick up my mother for dinner, I drop off a miniature rosebush with the card at the restaurant and ask the maître d' to put them at our table.

Once we get to the restaurant, and my mother sees the plant waiting for her at the table, I can tell she is touched. When she opens the card, she seems almost overwhelmed and begins to cry. I order a glass of wine, a delicious red from Portugal that I select whenever I go to this restaurant. My mother and I start to chat and I notice right away that we seem to have found a new ease with each other, perhaps a consequence of our no longer living together, or maybe it's the fact that we've finally put the issue of the piano behind us. We talk about how much we both love our new apartments. My mother tells me about a new organization called San Francisco Village, which helps seniors figure out ways to stay in their homes as they age. The idea of building networks of friends, family, and service professionals to help people "age in place" is catching on, and San Francisco Village is one of a dozen or so such communities sprouting up around the country. My mother is apparently so happy in her new apartment, so intent on remaining there for as long as possible, that she recently even paid a $600 annual fee to join San Francisco Village.

My wine arrives and I savor every sip. I tell her I just watched *Up in the Air*, the George Clooney movie about a hatchet man who flies around the country laying people off, and I didn't like it much. My mother says she not only stopped watching the film less than halfway through but had to take it out of her DVD player and return it to Netflix immediately because all she could think about was my own layoff from the *Times*.

I tell her about the incident with Gwen and Zoë's reaction to it. She listens carefully, and even a topic that could have turned heavy doesn't. The vomiting from too much alcohol, yes, she says, she knows about that. "That's a problem I never had," she adds. Her drinking is now something we can talk about, in general terms, and treat like an unwelcome visitor from the past that we're well rid of.

Every topic we touch feels as light as air—with one exception. She tells me that she now talks to Sarah three or four times a day, which is to say that Sarah calls three or four times a day and my mother picks up the phone every single time she sees it's Sarah calling, whether she feels like it or not. This, she tells me, is the way she can finally give something to

Sarah, who seems to need her so much. I'm listening to this, nodding, and wondering how long this dance between Sarah and my mother can go on before the collapse. But that's probably beside the point, for I also sense that for now, at least, this is a good thing for both of them. My mother clearly believes that she is helping Sarah, and it's equally clear to me that she is helping herself. These phone calls are a balm for her guilt.

She tells me that during these conversations, Sarah does nearly all the talking. Mostly, Sarah talks about her favorite TV shows, movies, books, handbags, and skin products. Not only does she recommend that my mother try this lotion or that cream, but she sends bottles and tubes of whatever she is championing at the moment. Sarah also sends some framed pieces of her own striking artwork. I'm moved by my sister's generosity, even if it comes wrapped in a guilt trip, as Sarah often goes out of her way to remind my mother that the object in question was "expensive."

"You know," my mother says between bites, "I've learned not to even utter your name to Sarah."

I say nothing, and she continues. "A few weeks ago, I told Sarah I was going to a concert with you, and she blew up. She said, 'You *do* love Katie more than me,' and she hung up."

For years, Sarah has resented what she perceived as my closeness to our mother. Here I am, coming to understand that my bond with my mother was unhealthy for both my mother and me. Yet how was Sarah to know this? A wave of compassion for Sarah sweeps over me. Even in times like this, when Sarah and I don't speak, I know we will always have each other and I will always be grateful for what she did for me during the worst of our childhood together. If what Sarah needs now in order to feel close to our mother is to fence me out, then it's what she should have.

"What did you do after she hung up?" I ask.

"I waited for a few hours, then I called her back."

I'm impressed by the steady calm with which my mother interacts with her volatile, fragile older daughter, and I say this to her. For years she wasn't there for Sarah, and now she is.

It's near the end of the meal, my wineglass is empty, and the waiter asks me if I'd like another. I ask if I can have half a glass.

"And I should have the other half?" my mother asks.

"Absolutely. It's delicious."

When our wine arrives, my mother takes a sip.

"It's divine," she says.

She takes two more sips, then leaves the rest. I knew she would do that, because she really is that rare alcoholic who can enjoy a sip or two without retriggering the horrible cycle. At this moment, in this restaurant, at this table I share with my mother, I am content.

While driving home, tired to the bone, I worry I'll fall asleep while Zoë and I watch *Desperate Housewives,* our weekly ritual. When I arrive, I find Zoë eager to model her entire prom outfit for me, complete with accessories. I'm honored to be invited for a preview a week before the event. When she emerges from her room wearing the pink strapless dress and gold heels she's picked out, she appears slightly bashful, as if she's uncomfortable with her emerging womanhood. The child is stunning—and not looking very much like a child. "Gorgeous," I tell her.

She changes back into her sweats and we settle on the couch for *Desperate Housewives*. The whole gang is in trouble. Bree is being blackmailed by a young weasel; Lynette is about to be strangled by a wacko who's been killing off women in the neighborhood all season; and Carlos finally confesses to Gaby that he's not so wild about her lasagna after all.

Zoë tucks herself close to my side, and I think of my mother safe in her own apartment, complete with a backup toilet. I manage to stay awake for the entire show. And later, when I do go to bed, happiness lays a warm paw on my chest, and I descend into a heavy, peaceful sleep.

32.

A Prayer for My Daughter

Considering that, all hatred driven hence,
The soul recovers radical innocence

—William Butler Yeats, "A Prayer for My Daughter"

ZOË AND I ARE PREPARING FOR HER TRIP TO BRAZIL. I'M WORRIED about how she will weather this absence from me. But as we race around getting the visa, buying the travel-sized toiletries, stocking up on sunscreen, and going to the doctor for the necessary typhoid, yellow fever, and influenza shots, I can see that Zoë is more concerned about how I'll do without her.

"Mom, maybe we should take a cab to the airport, because I'm worried about you driving back by yourself," she says one morning as her departure draws near. "I know you'll be pretty upset."

I'm touched by her concern. "Don't worry, sweetie. I'll be fine."

"Mom," she says, switching gears, "which do you think is worse for a kid—having parents who are divorced or having one of your parents die?"

"I don't know," I reply. "Both are bad, but in different ways. Why do you ask?"

"Because I have friends whose parents are divorced, and it looks so terrible."

"Really? Who?"

She rattles off a list of troubled households among her classmates, some of whom I know and others I don't. I'm aware of the tough circumstances in which Gwen lives, but I'm surprised to hear how intractable some of the other problems sound.

She must be thinking of this because at the moment we're headed to a store to buy Matt's birthday candle. The Matt birthday cycle, like so many other reminders of our loss, seems to be getting easier. When Zoë's prom night came and went without my anguishing over yet another important event in her life that her father wouldn't witness, I felt lighter. With time, I'm finding that Zoë and I can truly celebrate milestones that had once been overshadowed by her father's absence. As the day of Matt's birthday approached, I did not assault her with a drumroll of reminders, as I had always done in the past. Only when she got home from school on the actual day did I say anything. She looked crestfallen. She had forgotten. But I told her not to worry, that it didn't mean that she loved him any the less and that we'd honor the day as we always do.

Every year on Matt's birthday, we carry out the same ritual: We go to a small Parisian *perfumerie* in Union Square to find the perfect candle. It's just the kind of place my aesthetically minded late husband would have liked—a boutique devoted to nothing but expensive scented things. We're the only customers in the store this day, and the salesman indulges us as we make a production out of smelling each of the candles. He doesn't merely hold them up for us to sniff but pops them out of the glass with a whack at the bottom, for the full effect.

One of the candles is fig-scented. "Guys really like that one," says the salesman. It's settled, then. The cheerful salesman offers to gift wrap the candle. I look at Zoë and she says, "Sure." Zoë turns to me. "Let's just pretend he's alive," she whispers, an echo of what she confided over Christmas. "Isn't it fun?" I smile. Yes, for her, right now, it is. In some ways Zoë is dealing with the reality of her father's death, and in other ways she isn't. She needs to process it at her own pace.

We unwrap the candle at home and light it. Then we have a "what do you remember" conversation, and she tells me her strongest memory of her dad is his reading *Harry Potter* aloud to her. Matt read the books *con brio,* putting on an English accent and dramatizing the action with expert inflection. They made it through the first three volumes before he died. Zoë read the next four on her own, and at the height of her separation anxiety, one surefire method she had of calming herself down was to read *Harry Potter* or, better yet, listen to it on her iPod.

And with that, we've ushered in Matthew's fifty-fourth birthday.

ZOË'S QUESTION ABOUT DIVORCE and its effect on kids rouses my curiosity. A couple of days later I wander around Amazon.com and find a book titled *The Unexpected Legacy of Divorce,* written by psychologist Judith Wallerstein. I immediately recognize the name: She's the same woman who counseled me so well on the day Matt died, as she would do again in the pages of her book.

Reading the book is a revelation. I see myself everywhere in its pages. I recognize my lifelong fear of conflict and my inability, until Matt came back to me, to do much of anything except flee—anything to avoid reliving the turmoil I experienced as a child. In Wallerstein's vivid case studies, I see Sarah in the role of substitute parent she took on for her younger sister—a degree of caregiving that involved no small amount of sacrifice. Wallerstein also helps me to understand Sarah's clinging to my mother's side at the court hearing three decades ago as a mix of neediness and protectiveness. How could she abandon my mother, who had no one but us? Wallerstein describes the love and compassion that daughters of divorce—and I see both Sarah and myself on this page—feel for their mothers who are alone. "Negotiating separation becomes a heroic task."

Besides Matt's death, this is the most important challenge I have had to face. It finally came into focus for me in the months we spent living together, months of mounting disappointments, during which I learned I had to surrender my fantasy of my mother and me as best friends.

Thinking about all this sets me to thinking about the house in Rochester. The family home may be a symbol of continuity for children of intact families. But for children of divorce, Wallerstein emphasizes, it's a symbol of what has been lost.

When I read this, I flash on Sarah's quilts. In her thirties, Sarah started to make quilts covered with colorful houses, each structural element—the chimney, the walls, the windows, and the front door—cut by hand and stitched together into an individual panel. Depending on the size, one of Sarah's quilts could contain dozens of houses. For years, she made house quilts and only house quilts. When Zoë was born, Sarah made her a miniature house quilt with an extra touch: Onto the fabric she placed silk-screened photographs of assorted family members. Then she took a glow-in-the-dark pen, and in one corner she wrote, "I love you, Zoë." It was years before I noticed that message, late one night after I switched off the light in Zoë's room.

My mother calls to chat, and before I can stop myself, I'm saying to her, "There's a book I'd like you to read, about the effect of divorce on children." Since my mother vigorously swore off introspection about the past when she quit the Lia sessions, I immediately regret my words, but her response surprises me. While we're on the phone she goes to Amazon.com, finds the Wallerstein book, and buys it. In a few clicks, she's done something I wouldn't have dared suggest just a few months earlier. "I'll read it," she says. Her voice is steady and resolute.

That night, I take Wallerstein's book from my bedside table and reread something she mentioned only in passing: the ambivalence that many adult children of divorce feel about their obligation to their aging parents. So lasting are the effects of divorce, so disruptive to the bond between parent and child, that some of these children find that when the roles are reversed and it is their parents who now need them, they want to pay them back in kind. What they didn't get, they don't want to give. Yet even as I read this, I don't budge from what has become a personal mantra for me: *Our parents do the best they can with what they have to work with, and we owe them the same.*

I get out of bed, go to my computer, and send my mother an email. As I watch the words form on the screen, I know that what I am writing comes from a quiet, true place:

> I want you to know that I will do all in my power to make sure that as you get older, you are well taken care of (by me), and that you will not end up somewhere you don't want to be, that if you want to age in place, we will make it possible.

—

ON THE MORNING OF Zoë's flight to Brazil, I agree to stop at Starbucks on the way to the airport. I usually grouse about their overpriced drinks, then get angry with her when she takes just a few sips of her four-dollar mocha and leaves the rest. But on this morning, when my daughter is about to leave for South America for six weeks, had she wanted ten mochas and taken a small sip from each, that would have been just fine with me.

As I'm waiting for her, I notice we're parked close to the very spot where I happened to be when I was driving to work one morning two years earlier and got the call telling me I had been laid off from the *Times*. I have a choice: I can allow the anger to bubble back to the surface, or I can take a deep breath and take stock of my good fortune. And I realize how much good fortune I have had since then. I'm now freelancing occasionally for the *Times,* and I have the luxury of choosing my topics and setting my own schedule. I can devote time to Zoë without giving it a second thought. And, even more important, I have a daughter who is now doing just fine and a man whose company both Zoë and I enjoy more with each passing week. I am beginning to have a relationship with my mother that is set against a backdrop not of denial but truth. And both my mother and I are finding a way to implement the all-important boundaries Lia mentioned over and over, especially when it comes to inappropriate and gratuitous comments about Bob, which only crop up from time to time. When I speak of him to her, my tone is matter-of-fact, making it clear that I am not soliciting advice of any kind. There will be no magical moment of understanding between him and my mother, or between her and Zoë, certainly not anytime soon; this fact, too, I am coming to terms with. I can have relationships with all of the people I love without needing to connect the dots between the individuals. This is a liberating thought. Zoë returns to the car and hands me a bag containing a walnut scone. "I'm worried you won't eat," she says sweetly.

Zoë was correct in predicting that I'd be flustered. I miss the exit for the San Francisco airport—an airport I've driven to hundreds of times. When we arrive, I invite her to buy as many magazines as she wants.

Ditto the candy and gum. As the parent of a minor, I'm issued a special gate pass and we head for the gate. Zoë insists I stay put until the plane pushes back, and I dutifully station myself in a chair at the window. All I can see is the plane's nose and the two pilots holding their coffee cups. Zoë texts me from her seat to tell me she's already met someone in her program, also headed for Brazil. This, I decide, is a very good sign. I watch the plane back away from the gate.

When I return to the car and see Zoë's mocha in the cup holder, still three-quarters full, my heart lurches.

The next morning, Zoë sends me a text to say all is well and Rio is `soooooo amazing!!!` I find the scone from Starbucks still in my bag, slightly stale. I see that Zoë took a small bite out of it. I heat it up in the toaster oven and finish it off.

And then my mother calls.

"I've been reading the Wallerstein book," she says. "I was reading it sitting propped up in bed and shaking. She draws the picture so well of what these kids were going through. It was painful, but I have a better idea of what I did to you and Sarah. And I'm very glad that I read it."

I'm quiet.

"What I did to you two was immoral," she says.

"Immoral?" I respond. "Mom, it was tragic. And it was confusing and damaging to your two girls. But I don't think it was immoral."

I hope she's heard me, but she heads off on a slightly different tack. "The bearing witness you and Lia were talking about," my mother says. "This could be what you were aiming at."

"Yes," I say softly. "It could be."

"You have to understand that I was very young and very self-centered. I was very wild and a pain in the ass and I needed to grow up. But telling you I turned to jelly doesn't begin to describe the drive home from that custody hearing. I was wailing, and these terrible waves of grief and loss would come up. And then we got back to Belmont and my mother said to me, 'You have sinned.'"

Now I see how the notion of morality entered her head, not just this week but forty years ago. "Oh, Mom, she said that? I'm so sorry."

This conversation isn't only marking a change in my mother as she realizes what Sarah and I had endured—but in me. I see more clearly than ever that as terrible a mother as she was, as much as she deserved to lose custody of us, she also loved us deeply. She has already paid the price for her terrifically inept parenting, in ways that I'm only now beginning to appreciate.

My mother's reaction to the Wallerstein book has also got her thinking about Rochester and her marriage to my father. When she was considering leaving him, she tells me, she went to see a shrink. "I was worried that if I left, I'd fall apart, so I went to see the psychiatrist," she says. "And at the end, he concluded I wouldn't fall apart. But I did." I make a sympathetic noise, a tiny "hmmmm," just to let her know I'm listening. "I should have stayed," she says. "I should never have left. I should have stayed married to Everett. It would have been so much better for you and Sarah."

That could be true. But then there was the alcohol to consider. Somehow I doubt that staying with my father would have helped, for she was already drinking heavily when she was married to him, and there's no reason to think that staying in the marriage would have changed anything. But there's no need to point that out.

I'm grateful to her for reading the book and touched by the remorse she is expressing.

Gradually, our conversation transitions back to the present, and we move to my mother's current situation. She couldn't be happier in her new apartment. And she's pleased to have jettisoned so many of her possessions, as she has friends facing unexpected health crises who are still living in their cluttered houses and would like to pare back but are too overwhelmed by now to do so. This is one of the lessons she has learned during this year's journey, not through Provence, exactly, but through a more realistic representation of life.

And now she is being realistic about what lies in store. "When I really need care, it's not going to be San Francisco Village. It's going to be something more like Coventry Park," she says, referring to the second place we saw the day we were out with the senior-placement specialist. I shudder at the thought of my mother living out her final years there, and I remind her of my email from a few days earlier. She tells me how grateful she was to receive that email. "I can't ask any of my friends to come and babysit me," she says. "In the end, it's a family thing." Yes, indeed it is.

"All I ever wanted was for you to love me. And I love you so much." Her voice trails off, and I know she's waiting for me to say the same.

"I love you too," I reply. Without ambivalence. I feel a wave of tenderness for the woman on the other end of the line a mile away. This woman, my mother, isn't merely carving out a new life for herself; along the way she's finding she can look her past mistakes square in the eye and express contrition in a way that also makes her daughter feel something approaching unburdened love, even pride.

I once heard that the way we let in emotional pain is like the eye's response to light. When the brightness is too intense, the iris—the circular ring of muscle that surrounds the pupil—contracts to protect the eye. Then the iris muscle starts to relax, and as it does the pupil gradually opens, letting in a little more light at a time, until the iris stops constricting altogether. This is when we see our world for what it is.

Epilogue

DECEMBER 2010

A LITTLE AFTER 8:00 A.M. ON A SATURDAY, THE HOME PHONE RINGS. I see it's my mother calling. It's early in the day for her to call, but I'm eager to talk. I want to tell her about a TV series I've discovered and know she'll like. I want to hear about the play reading she just did with a group from San Francisco Village and about her most recent trip to the ballet with her friend Betty. Our conversations these days are filled with effortless good cheer—minus any hint of subtext. I pick up the phone and give her my standard greeting: "Hihowareyou?"

She's usually chirpy, but her tone is matter-of-fact.

"I just got off the phone with John. Sarah's in the hospital."

My sister's husband, John, told my mother that Sarah developed stomach pain so severe that in the middle of the night she was taken by ambulance to the small community hospital in Greenfield, Massachusetts, near their home. John has reported to my mother that Sarah has an abdominal blockage of some kind and she's in surgery. She might lose part of her intestine. It sounds as if Sarah could be headed for a colostomy, and John, my mother says, is very upset.

My mother has just told me the sum total of what she knows, which isn't much but feels like a lot to take in. It leaves both of us with plenty of room for speculation. We cover a range of possibilities. We agree that a colostomy, which we understand to be the worst-case scenario, would be a terrible thing for Sarah, for whom a mild cold occasions a week of bed rest.

I ask my mother to call me when she knows more and wait anxiously for Bob, who is coming over to take Zoë and me out to breakfast. When he arrives, I tell him.

As usual, Bob looks unfazed, even after I mention "intestinal blockage."

"Has she had prior abdominal surgery?"

"No."

"Then it's unlikely that she would have a bowel obstruction." I'm confused. How could Bob know this but John, who is there with Sarah, doesn't?

"So what do you think it is?"

He shrugs. "I have no idea."

Bob uses the news to teach Zoë about the causes of bowel obstruction, which irritates me. Once we get home, I call my mother again. She's just spoken with John, who told her they're now having trouble getting blood flow to Sarah's organs. My mother says she needs to get out of her apartment and go for a walk.

For the first time that morning, Bob has a frown of concern. Of course, he's been taking it in all along. He heard bad belly pain and emergency surgery. And now, when he hears low blood flow, he concludes that sepsis, perhaps overwhelming septic shock, has set in. He says he's guessing her intestine is perforated and there are bacteria in her bloodstream. His next words are "abdominal catastrophe." Unlike most medical jargon, this phrase's implication is exactly as it sounds.

Bob has seated himself at the dining room table and begins typing on my computer. He tells me he's emailing a colleague who works at the hospital's main branch in Springfield, to see if the friend might help expedite Sarah's transfer to the larger hospital, where the level of care might be better for someone this sick. He's taking control; I'm relieved and grateful.

"You should call the ICU," Bob says.

When I identify myself to Jean, the ICU nurse, there's a pause. I don't like it. Then she says haltingly, "Have you spoken with her husband?"

"No." I say. My heart is racing. I know exactly where I am. I am in the gulf of time—two seconds, maybe three—between the words I know are coming and the words themselves.

"Katie, your sister is dying."

Bob stands in the doorway between the kitchen and the dining room. I hand him the phone. I have no use for this phone.

I sink into a corner on the floor of the dining room and hug my knees to my chest. Bob is two feet from me, the phone to his ear, nodding. He isn't saying much. Or maybe he is, and I'm not hearing it. Bob and Zoë are both near me, and Bob is trying to wrap his arms around the awkward, sobbing bundle I've become on the floor.

I have to find my mother. I call her cellphone, and she answers right away.

"Mom, I'm coming to get you. Where are you?" I'm crying and wish I wasn't. If I'm crying, she'll worry.

"I'm out walking," she says. Her tone is unsteady. How much of this is she absorbing? "But I'll walk back to my building."

"I'll be there soon. I'm coming right now. Stay out front. I'm coming to get you."

I can't find my shoes. Or my handbag. Or my keys. My keys were right here, just a minute ago.

"We're coming with you," Zoë says, and Bob nods. Bob drives. We pass the very same buildings we pass every day, but now everything looks different. Why is that?

We find my mother pacing back and forth in front of her apartment building, her face obscured by her hat. She is waving her arms. At no one. We park across the street and I start to get out of the car.

"Do you want us to come with you?" Bob asks. Or maybe Zoë asks this.

"No."

I walk across the street to my mother. She looks up at me. "Have you heard something?" I put my arms around her. She seems smaller than usual. "She's dying," I say. "You're coming home with us."

When we get back to the apartment, my mother and I sit down on the couch and I call the same ICU nurse I had spoken with an hour earlier. "Kathy," she says. She gets my name wrong, which shouldn't faze me, but, bizarrely, it does. I want to correct her, but there's no time. "Kathy, I'm sorry, but your sister died a few minutes ago."

I look over at my mother, who is looking at me. She keeps opening her mouth but no words come out. Just small, pitiful sounds from the back of her throat.

I have only one question for Jean the nurse. "Was she in pain?"

No, she says, she never woke up. Even after they removed the anesthesia, she didn't regain consciousness. The last time she knew anything at all was just before they put her under for the surgery.

At some point, the nurse gives me the name and pager number of the surgeon who operated on Sarah.

Bob calls the surgeon's pager, and within thirty minutes the surgeon calls back. Bob introduces himself as an internist in San Francisco, and my husband. I appreciate the white lie he offers in the name of securing his spot among Sarah's kin. Bob places the handset on the coffee table and puts it on speaker. The man whose voice was probably the last my frightened sister heard now lets out a long, low whistle. Unaware that three other people are listening, he says to Bob, "Can you believe that?"

Bob asks him to describe what he found, and within seconds they're talking doc to doc, in staccato shorthand. When Sarah ("a healthy fifty-five-year-old woman with no previous history") came in, she had severe pain, with AMS (altered mental status), leukocytosis (raised white-blood-cell count), and an acutely tender abdomen. The "films" showed distended loops of bowel, so when he "went in," he'd expected to find a bowel obstruction. Instead, he saw that the bowel was a dusky blue, evidence of widespread ischemia (low blood supply), with no apparent cause. While I can't comprehend the words I'm hearing, I can make out the gist of the clinical scenario. But one doesn't have to be a doctor to hear the tone of the surgeon's voice: I can tell he's mystified and still rattled. And so is Bob.

During the surgery, Sarah's blood pressure dropped so low that the surgeon decided to close her up and get her to the ICU to be stabilized. Her abdomen, the surgeon tells Bob, was so swollen he couldn't close her entirely—when she reached the ICU, her loops of bowel were extruding through her gaping abdominal incision. It's a gruesome image.

"I saw calcification in her pancreas, indicating chronic pancreatitis," the surgeon says.

"Yes, she had an EtOH history," Bob says. He tells me later that this is code for "alcoholic." Doctors use the euphemism—drawn from the chemical formula for alcohol—routinely, especially in the presence of patients and their family members. Bob hangs up, explains how rare this scenario—a dead bowel with no obvious underlying cause like a blood clot or severe heart failure—is, and also says that the surgeon sounded competent. "I don't think he missed anything," he says, by way of reassuring us.

There is nothing more to do. I stay close to my mother, and Zoë stays close to both of us. Now my daughter has another sudden death to come to grips with. For years, sudden death has been pacing in ever-smaller circles around us, inching its way toward the nucleus of our family. She tells me later that she feels as if it is closing in on the two of us, stalking us with a menacing patience.

Over the next fog-filled hour, my mother and I leave messages for John. We call my mother's sister, and Bob's colleague from Springfield calls. Bob thanks him but says it's too late, no transfer is needed after all. John finally calls my mother's cellphone. She asks him about an autopsy, and I gather from what I'm hearing that he doesn't want one. I understand what he's feeling. How could he ever forgive himself if he discovered she might have lived if he had gotten her to the hospital a few hours sooner? Bob tells us he doubts it would have made a difference. By the time Sarah was in acute pain, her bowel was already dying, and so was she.

My mother wants to go for a walk. I jump up from the couch to go with her. Zoë says she wants to come too. Wanting to give us space, Bob remains behind. While the three of us walk around my block and through the small park in front of Grace Cathedral, we say very little.

When we come home, my mother says she wants to get something to eat. I doubt she's hungry, but I can tell she'd rather do anything besides sit still. Zoë wants to come as well. The three of us drive to a little pasta restaurant my mother has never been to. She says how happy she is to discover a new place to eat. She isn't ready to talk about anything else. We focus on the food. We've all ordered minestrone, and Zoë says she likes my minestrone soup better. Zoë is solicitous of my mother and asks her if she's eaten enough. After we eat, my mother wants to go home. She insists she'll be fine by herself.

After dropping her off, all I can think about is what John must have felt when he returned home from the hospital. Their four cats. The bed left behind in a cloud of panic and pain. The kitchen with dinner dishes still in the sink. The movie they were watching still in the DVD player. I can imagine every detail of what he faced when he walked in that front door.

I call my mother to see how she's doing. She's subdued. She tells me she's having trouble believing it.

"It's the first time you've lost someone you really love," I say.

"That's true," she says. There is no talk of dogs. She knows this is different. Sarah was her child. My mother is clear-eyed about this. She has spent months on the other end of a phone line, letting Sarah know she would never again desert her, until the day she died. And now she is the one left behind.

JOHN DECIDES TO WAIT until the spring for a memorial service. My mother sees no reason to travel east until there's a formal service, and my friend Carolyn suggests that my mother and I hold our own small West Coast shiva service. Michael Lezak, the gentle rabbi from our reform synagogue who presided over Zoë's bat mitzvah four years ago, will come to our home.

I turn the apartment into a forest of framed photographs: Sarah at age eight at the Cape house, cross-legged and folding origami; a series of photos with Sarah and me in matching sunsuits, my arms wrapped around her; another two or three years later, and I'm still looking up at her with all the adoration of a younger sister while she stares straight at the camera; the two sisters as adults, walking down a street in Manhattan, Sarah's arm around my shoulder; a joyous Sarah at her wedding to John; and old black-and-white photos of my glamorous mother posing with her two small children.

On the night of the service, Carolyn and two other friends show up early with platters laden with food. Half a dozen or so of my mother's new San Francisco friends come—all of them lovely people, most at least eighty years old.

Rabbi Lezak starts the service. Zoë is seated next to him. After leading a few prayers, the rabbi asks people who knew Sarah to speak up and tell stories. There's silence. Many of my friends know one another, but none has ever met my sister, who seldom left her little New England town. Candace is the only exception, but she's eight thousand miles away, on a business trip to Qatar.

I speak. I talk about how much I adored Sarah when we were little. Although we grew apart, I always felt her there. I tell one funny story that doesn't strike me as particularly symbolic until I'm halfway through it: One summer, when we were sixteen and eighteen, we took a Greyhound bus across the country from Amherst to San Diego to visit our mother. We were pretty worldly in some ways but naïve in others. Without knowing what we were doing, we boarded a local bus. On what should have been a three-day cross-country trip, we took four days just to reach Chicago, at which point we finally figured out that we needed to catch an *express* bus. People chuckle. Then I talk about Sarah's quilts covered with fanciful houses. I had looked for Zoë's baby quilt to show the group but wasn't able to find it. So I describe that quilt—one of dozens Sarah sewed over the years, adding up to hundreds and hundreds of nothing but houses, cut and stitched together.

My mother speaks next. If Sarah were here, "she would have been making faces" during the prayers and "I would have been telling her to behave." This is what a mother would say to a small child, as though Sarah is fixed in her mind at age ten. Our mother missed so much of our growing up.

I'm surprised when Zoë speaks. She delivers a touching little speech about the boxes Sarah had sent the previous year and the eccentric collection of items they contained: the remainder-table books, the hair clips, a kimono. But the five seasons of *Weeds* were the best, Zoë says. She would always be grateful to her aunt Sarah for introducing her to the television show.

Afterward, people mingle and eat. Bob leaves to catch a plane for a work trip. One of my mother's friends stands fixated before a photograph of my mother when she was young and married to my father. In it, she's holding her two small daughters on her lap. The friend takes me aside to express her awe at my mother's beauty, and I'm delighted that someone noticed. My mother was stunning at age twenty-five and remains beautiful to this day. I wish Sarah could be here with me, be at my side, see what I see.

SARAH'S DEATH MAKES ME redouble my commitment to our mother, on my sister's behalf as well as my own. In the days following, I call her at least twice a day to check in. A week after Sarah's death, my mother takes me out for a late birthday dinner—to the same fancy Italian restaurant I had taken her for Mother's Day. This time, Zoë comes along. "I'm so glad we found a favorite restaurant," Zoë says during dinner, "for when the three of us want to go somewhere special." The next day, my mother calls to tell me how happy she was to hear Zoë say that—"the three of us." I'm happy, too, but I've learned not to expect too much, too soon.

That morning, my mother also wants to talk about Bob, not to harp but to recant. On the day Sarah died, Bob rose so admirably to the occasion, she observes. And my mother has seen that when it comes to Bob's clinical manner, he's consistent.

"He doesn't effuse about anything," she says. "He doesn't treat you any differently than he treats me. And with Zoë, he's just the same."

"Yes, that's right," I say. "That's Bob."

It takes me several weeks to remove all the photographs of Sarah. Late one night before going to bed, I do a sweep of the apartment, removing the framed photographs. But there's one I don't put away, because it has always lived on my hall table. It's a large black-and-white print of Sarah and me on our trikes, in front of the Rochester house, at ages five and three. Sarah the free spirit is barefoot, and I'm in a pair of well-worn but sturdy saddle shoes. Sarah is wearing a white blouse and full skirt; I'm in a plain plaid dress with short sleeves, stiff white cuffs, and a white collar that suggests a future in the clergy. But it's Sarah who looks the more angelic. She directs a tentative, vulnerable smile at my father's camera, while my own expression is noncommittal and earnest, Platonic in its blankness—like I'm taking it all in, already learning to observe, not engage. Sarah is looking straight at the camera, but she's also whispering something to me, something intimate and promising.

I've passed that photo several times a day for years, but until this moment I haven't bothered to look at the background. We two sisters are on the long driveway; there's a carefully trimmed hedge behind us, and two young trees. I take the photograph and put it next to my computer on the dining room table. I type the address—122 Chelmsford Road—into Google Maps. Up pops the house. I zoom in on the photo. There's the big stucco house, set back from the street. And there's the long driveway, as long as I remember, and the very same hedge, now unkempt, and the trees, now matured. Those two little girls on their tricycles have long since been plucked out of the picture. No doubt there have been many other kids, in strollers and wagons and on trikes and pogo sticks, bicycles and skateboards, then hand-me-down cars, traveling that driveway in the forty-seven years since Sarah and I left the scene. I look at the photograph again. We're going somewhere on those trikes of ours, we just don't know where.

ACKNOWLEDGMENTS

THE IDEA FOR THIS BOOK OCCURRED TO ME IN NOVEMBER 2009, NEARLY three months after my mother and I began our experiment in multigenerational living. I started out with no clue as to what might happen in the next week, let alone the next year. Nonetheless, Jim Levine, my agent, thought that whatever happened, it was bound to be interesting. Susan Kamil and Beth Rashbaum, my editors at Random House, agreed—and they never wavered, even as the story took unexpected turns. For that, and much more, all three have my considerable gratitude.

For friendship, hospitality, editorial input, and unalloyed honesty, I am grateful to Susan Alexander, Sam Barondes, Josh Benditt, Tony Bianco, Mara Brazer, Louann Brizendine, Teresa Carpenter, Julie Beckett Crutcher, Bill Davidow, Dan Farber, Sheila Fifer, Laura Fisher, Tina Frank, Joe Freda, Danielle Gasbarro, Sarah Glazer, Denise Grady, Anisse Gross, Alison Gwinn, Bobbie Head, Michele and Steve Heller, Brigitte Hesch, Mollie Katzen, Paulette Kessler, Carolyn Klebanoff, Dan Kornstein, Rosanne Leipzig, Anita Lester, Steven Levy, Denny Lyon, Nancy Miller, Carol Pogash, Diana Raimi, Jessica Raimi, Adele Riepe, Richard Rockefeller, Robert Saar, Marlene Saritzky, Tiffany Shlain, Amy Slater, Blair Stone, Candace Thille, Deborah and Brooke Unger, Abraham Verghese, Andrea Wachter, Bernice Wachter, Murray Wachter, Cathie Bennett Warner, Meredith White, Lori Wolfson, Amelia Zalcman, and Jeremy Zucker.

Many thanks to D'Vera Cohn at the Pew Research Center, Steven

Ruggles at the University of Minnesota, and Rebecca Plant at the University of California, San Diego, for their insights into multigenerational living. Chris Chorazewski and his colleagues at the London Library provided me with a quiet place to sit and work.

Beth Rashbaum and Susan Kamil, editors nonpareil, are every writer's dream. They pushed, prodded, suggested, commiserated, and inspired—all in the right mix and always at the right times. The manuscript also benefited from the keen and careful eyes of Kathleen Lord, Diana D'Abruzzo, Loren Noveck, and Benjamin Dreyer. Many thanks to Molly Turpin, who shepherded the book through its incarnation as a paperback. Many thanks, too, to Sam Nicholson, Susan's assistant. In addition to Jim Levine, thanks to Kerry Sparks, Beth Fisher, and the other skilled hands at the Levine Greenberg Literary Agency.

Judith Wallerstein, who died in 2012, greatly influenced my thinking on the lasting effects of divorce on families. I was so taken with her work that I went to visit her at her home in Marin County while I was writing this book. She was warm and welcoming, and we became friends. Were she alive, I would thank her deeply for her contributions to the study of the psychological effects of divorce and loss.

My thanks and love go to Bob Wachter, for claiming never to tire of reading the manuscript in its various stages of completion (the number of times he read it far exceeds his golf handicap), for demanding "more cowbell" at crucial points, and for being so wonderfully Bob throughout. Little did I know when I began this book that I'd be chronicling not only a relationship among three generations of women, but also one between me and an exceptional man, who also happens to be a damned fine writer and editor.

I have changed the names of several people, including that of my mother, the central character of this story, which describes not only the problems that cropped up between us during a critical time of transition, but her triumph in making a new life for herself in San Francisco. While she has been less than thrilled to be featured in her daughter's memoir, I hope that she will ultimately see this as an honest portrayal of a brilliant and complex woman whom I continue to love and who, I believe, did the best she could at a terrible time in her life. I know there is much in the story that she would rather not relive, but I hope she understands that in the process of my reliving it through this book I have come to admire her all the more.

It can't be easy for a teenager to see her life put out there for all to read. But Zoë Lyon, my infinitely wise and generous daughter, has been unreserved in her encouragement. She instructed me from the start to write the book as I saw it—and she didn't change her mind. Zoë, thank you not only for being my darling daughter, but also for reminding me every day of the memory of your father. I love you more than my arms could ever stretch.

BIBLIOGRAPHY

Bassoff, Evelyn. *Mothers and Daughters*. New York: New American Library, 1988.

Edelman, Hope. *Mother of My Mother*. New York: The Dial Press, 1999.

Friday, Nancy. *My Mother/My Self*. New York: Delta Trade Paperbacks, 1997.

Karr, Mary. *Lit*. New York: Harper Perennial, 2010.

Knapp, Caroline. *Drinking: A Love Story*. New York: The Dial Press, 2005.

Lessard, Suzannah. *The Architect of Desire*. New York: The Dial Press, 1996.

Levinson, Kate. *Emotional Currency*. New York: Celestial Arts, 2011.

Plant, Rebecca Jo. *Mom*. Chicago: University of Chicago Press, 2010.

Plath, Sylvia. *Letters Home*. New York: Harper Perennial, 1992.

Robertson, Nan. *Getting Better*. New York: William Morrow and Company, 1988.

Roth, Philip. *Patrimony*. New York: Vintage, 1996.

Ruggles, Steven. "The Decline of Intergenerational Coresidence in the United States, 1850 to 2000." *American Sociological Review* 72 (December 2007): 964–89.

Sexton, Anne, Linda Gray Sexton (ed.), and Lois Ames (ed.). *A Self-Portrait in Letters*. New York: Mariner Books, 1992.

Silkworth, William, Bob Smith, and Bill Wilson. *Alcoholics Anonymous (the Big Book)*. New York: Alcoholics Anonymous World Services, Inc., 1939.

Wallerstein, Judith S., Julia M. Lewis, and Sandra Blakeslee. *The Unexpected Legacy of Divorce*. New York: Hyperion, 2001.

PERMISSIONS

Grateful acknowledgment is made to the following for permission to reprint previously published material:

Dell, an imprint of The Random House Publishing Group, a division of Random House, Inc.: Excerpt from *My Mother/My Self* by Nancy Friday, copyright © 1977, 1987 by Nancy Friday. Any third party use of this material, outside of this publication, is prohibited. Reprinted by permission of Dell, an imprint of The Random House Publishing Group, a division of Random House, Inc.

Grove/Atlantic, Inc.: Excerpt from *Practicalities* by Marguerite Duras, copyright © 1987 by P.O.L. Editeur, translation copyright © 1990 by William Collins. Any third party use of this material, outside of this publication, is prohibited. Reprinted by permission of Grove/Atlantic, Inc.

Latin American Literary Review Press: One line from "Ode to Life" by Pablo Neruda. Reprinted by permission of Latin American Literary Review Press.

The CS Lewis Company Ltd: Brief excerpt from *A Grief Observed* by CS Lewis, copyright © 1961 by CS Lewis Pte Ltd. Reprinted by permission of The CS Lewis Company Ltd.

W. W. Norton & Company, Inc.: Three lines from "Diving into the Wreck" from *The Fact of a Doorframe: Selected Poems 1950–2001* by Adrienne Rich, copyright © 2002 by Adrienne Rich, copyright © 1973 by W. W. Norton & Company, Inc. Reprinted by permission of W. W. Norton & Company, Inc.

Oxford University Press: Thirty-nine words from a letter dated March 1, 1921 from Katherine Mansfield to Dorothy Brett from *The Collected Letters of Katherine Mansfield, Vol. IV*, edited by Vincent O'Sullivan & Margaret Scott (1996), letters copyright © 1996 by The Estate of Katherine Mansfield. Reprinted by permission of Oxford University Press.

Persea Books: Excerpts from *The Unquiet Grave* by Cyril Connolly, copyright © 1981 by Deirdre Levi. Reprinted by permission of Persea Books. All rights reserved.

Princeton University Press: Brief excerpt from *C. G. Jung Letters, Vol. 2*, edited by Gerhard Adler, translated by Jeffrey Hulen, copyright © 1953, 1955, 1961, 1963, 1968, 1971, 1972, 1974, 1975 by Princeton University Press. Reprinted by permission of Princeton University Press.

Random House, an imprint of The Random House Publishing Group, a division of Random House, Inc.: Excerpt from "The Revenant" from *The Trouble with Poetry* by Billy Collins, copyright © 2005 by Billy Collins. Any third party use of this material, outside of this publication, is prohibited. Reprinted by permission of Random House, an imprint of The Random House Publishing Group, a division of Random House, Inc.

Charlotte Sheedy Literary Agency: Brief quote from *Her Mother's Daughter* by Marilyn French, copyright © 1987 by Belles-Lettres, Inc. Reprinted by permission of Charlotte Sheedy Literary Agency.

The Wylie Agency, LLC: Excerpt from *Midnight's Children* by Salman Rushdie, copyright © 1981 by Salman Rushdie. Reprinted by permission of The Wylie Agency, LLC.

Mother Daughter Me

Katie Hafner

A Reader's Guide

Recommended Reading from Katie Hafner

I am a greedy reader. That is, I gravitate toward books that help me articulate my own life experience, or help my own writing. When I read, I am on the lookout for inventive turns of phrase, for risks with language, for unlikely pairings of nouns and adjectives, verbs and adverbs. My self-centered reading habits are reflected in this list, as eclectic as it is inspiring.

Growing Up by Russell Baker

Russell Baker, the famous columnist, published his memoir in 1982. It was the first memoir I can remember reading, and it has stuck with me to this day. It's easily one of the very best of the genre—a classic that all aspiring memoirists should read. Baker's father died when he was five, and he was raised by his mother during the Depression. There isn't an ounce of flab to his prose, nor a hint of self-pity. He's matter-of-fact and funny.

The Architect of Desire: Beauty and Danger in the Stanford White Family by Suzannah Lessard

I was far less interested in the tawdry aspects of the infidelity and murder of the Gilded Age architect Stanford White than in Lessard's beautifully rendered portrait of her famous family (she is White's great-granddaughter) and its legacy of troubled relationships. My favorite quote from the book draws an analogy between family history and architecture: "Like architecture, it is quiet. It encompasses, but does not necessarily demand attention. Like architecture, too, family history can suddenly loom into consciousness. One can go about one's life with no thought of the past, and then, as if waking from a dream, be astonished to see that you are living within its enclosure."

Lit by Mary Karr

Mary Karr is a national treasure, and this book is, in my opinion, her very best. I thoroughly enjoyed watching her roll up her sleeves and practice her craft of great, tight, image-filled writing peppered with her trademark acerbic, right-on wit. The scenes in which she is too blotto even to care for her own child are so raw and frank they made me wince.

Diaries: 1910-1923 by Franz Kafka

Kafka is my lifelong hero, and his diaries, which span the years 1910 to 1923 (he started keeping a diary at age twenty-seven), offer a fascinating insight into the life of a man who sees the world through scenes, scenes that can turn on a dime, from reality to pure invention. I know of no better primer for writers than these observations of daily life, mixed with ideas, fears, dreams, and story snippets.

Autobiography of a Face by Lucy Grealy

Speaking of writing that's void of self-pity, Lucy Grealy's memoir about her disfigured face is just that. At age nine, Grealy was diagnosed with a serious cancer. When she returned to school with a third of her jaw removed, her classmates taunted her cruelly. She spent the rest of her short life undergoing an endless string of surgeries just so her face could resemble something approaching normal. Her writing sings: "Unlike some stroke victims, who are physically unable to name the person in the mirror as themselves, my trick of the eye was the result of my lifelong refusal to learn how to name the person in the mirror. My face had been changing for so long that I had never had time to become acquainted with it." And there's this: "I spent five years of my life being treated for cancer, but since then I've spent fifteen years being treated for nothing other than looking different from everyone else. It was the pain from that, from feeling ugly, that I always viewed as the great tragedy of my life. The fact that I had cancer seemed minor in comparison."

Drinking: A Love Story by Caroline Knapp

I love this book because of its raw honesty and Knapp's no-holds-barred approach to her own story. I read very few memoirs while working on *Mother Daughter Me*. But I did read this one, partly to absorb her total honesty, and partly to learn about the mechanism of alcoholism—something I had never really understood—from someone who had experienced it.

Patrimony by Philip Roth

I don't love each and every one of Roth's novels, but I do love each and every word of his memoir about his father's decline and death. Not only is the writing just plain excellent, but the themes he touches on—watching a parent's decline, role reversals, the symbolic importance of objects—were all themes I addressed in *Mother Daughter Me*. And in the middle of so much upset and chaos, Roth finds humor. Now, that's the sign of a great memoir.

I Capture the Castle by Dodie Smith

I can't resist tossing my most cherished novel into the mix. I love it partly for sentimental reasons. It was my sister's favorite, and for as long as I can remember, she always had at least three copies scattered around her house. It's a romance, it's funny, its setting—yes, in a castle—is at once exotic and accessible, and it's suspenseful. I first read it when I was a teenager and, as with any great book, there are certain lines that just never leave me. Here's one of the most memorable, from Cassandra, the book's heroine: "I have been hungry ever since; which is ridiculous as I had a good tea egg not six hours ago." When I read that, I remember thinking, *That must have been one big egg.*

Questions for Discussion

1. Do you find Hafner's mother to be a sympathetic character? Why or why not? Do you think the author herself is a sympathetic character? Why or why not?
2. Hafner often finds herself in the middle of arguments between her mother and her daughter. Do you think it was possible for her to effectively mediate, while also working out her own difficulties with her mother?
3. Money plays a significant role in the book. Discuss why money can be such a flashpoint for families. Why do you think it was a point of contention in *Mother Daughter Me*?
4. Objects, such as the piano, also held great emotional significance throughout. Did the piano and other gifts carry different meanings for Hafner and her mother? How did their different understandings of the symbolism of those tangible objects lead to conflict?
5. Hafner is a longtime journalist who turned to memoir writing. How do you see her skills as a journalist employed in the writing of *Mother Daughter Me*?
6. Memory—and the presentation of memories—can be tricky when writing memoirs. Many of Hafner's childhood memories emerge during sessions with the therapist Lia. Others surface when she finds letters and other documents from the past. How

do you think Hafner handles the reliability of her own memories, especially from her early childhood? How do you think she handles the issue of memory when her recollections differ from her mother's?

7. In its piece on *Mother Daughter Me*, the *San Francisco Chronicle* wrote of children of parents who drink, "While their parents black out and forget, they remember, and their memories, their stories, matter. More than assigning blame, this is Hafner's point—and her memoir is a brave manifestation of it." Do you agree with the writer? Do you think Hafner steers clear of assigning blame? To what extent do you think it is necessary make a parent confront the details of a difficult past?
8. After Hafner's husband, Matt, dies suddenly, Hafner tells the reader, she quickly does everything wrong. Instead of waiting to make any big changes, she acts hastily and, as she admits, inappropriately. What is your opinion of Hafner's hasty decision to make large life changes? Are you sympathetic?
9. Bob, the man Hafner starts to date during the year chronicled in the book, is an anchor of sanity and stability throughout the book. How do you think Hafner was able to let another person into her life in during this year of such chaos and tumult? What role did you see Bob playing as he entered the family?
10. Hafner discusses the difficulty that subsequent generations often have in not repeating the mistakes of their parents, especially when it comes to inflicting trauma on one's children. Do you think Hafner succeeds in breaking the cycle of intergenerational trauma that her own mother was unable to break?
11. Hafner discusses the long-term effects of divorce on children, citing Judith Wallerstein's book *The Legacy of Divorce*. Why do you think she chooses to discuss divorce at such length, when alcohol might seem to be the bigger problem?

12. Hafner's father comes off as a complex, much-loved, but muted character in the book. Why do you think Hafner chose to keep him in the background of the narrative?
13. Do you think Hafner has created a balanced view of herself and her mother? Was she even in a position to do so? Are there examples of why or why not?
14. Why do you think the author's sister had a life that was so deeply troubled, while Hafner herself, despite coming from the same background, was able to make different, healthier choices earlier in life?
15. Despite being in many ways a typical, occasionally difficult teenager, Zoë also shows herself to be surprisingly adult and insightful at times. What role do you think she plays in the choices that Hafner makes once Zoë's grandmother comes to live with them?
16. Hafner describes in detail her relationship with her daughter, and the fierce attachment between the two. What do you think drew them so close? Does their bond add to the challenges they faced that year?
17. The mother-daughter relationship is inherently complicated, which Hafner makes very clear in the book. What are your thoughts on what makes the mother-daughter bond so complex, and often so fraught?
18. Toward the end of the book, Hafner states that instead of feeling the need to act as the constant pleaser and appeaser, she can finally "have relationships with all of the people that I love without having to connect the dots between them." Does this insight seem like a good life lesson? Is there a contradiction in loving two people while knowing they may never reconcile? How does Hafner confront this question?

PHOTO: © JESSICA RAIMI

KATIE HAFNER is a frequent contributor to *The New York Times,* covering healthcare and technology. She has also been on staff at *Newsweek* and *BusinessWeek*. Her work has appeared in *The New York Times Magazine, Esquire, Wired, The Huffington Post, The New Republic,* and *O: The Oprah Magazine.* She lives in San Francisco. This is her sixth book.

ABOUT THE TYPE

This book is set in Fournier, a typeface named for Pierre Simon Fournier, the youngest son of a French printing family. Pierre Simon first studied watercolor painting, but became involved in type design through work that he did for his eldest brother. Starting with engraving woodblocks and large capitals, he later moved on to fonts of type. In 1736 he began his own foundry, and published the first version of his point system the following year.